If you are viewing this book for free, please visit

www.Owlinkmedia.com

or

www.WildernessAwareness.org

and make a donation to support great educational tools such as this, reaching as many people around the world as possible. Thank you!

Kamana Student Services are now Online!

Connect with a **community of thousands** of Kamana students worldwide — or in your backyard!
Receive **personal feedback** from Kamana instructors to enhance and guide your journey.
Receive Kamana **video, audio and other resources** — not available elsewhere!
Participate in **monthly roundtable phone discussions** with the Kamana community…

How do we make Kamana more accessible and more effective?
We listened to Kamana student feedback, and with **Kamana Online** we lowered the price of student services significantly to make it more accessible for everyone. At the same time, we designed Kamana Online to be the ultimate resource for those engaged in naturalist training!

We know; we've been there. There are many distractions in our lives that can make it challenging to keep up with any ongoing course. In the world of martial arts, music and naturalists, there are countless beginners and very few "black belts". With Kamana Online, you have a human-powered resource — available 24/7/365 — to continue to inspire, connect and help you to navigate any bumps in the trail ahead.

We've been mentoring students in the Kamana Naturalist Training Program for over 15 years, and Kamana Online takes all that we've learned and offers it to you at a **lower cost and lower risk** than ever before. We've made available to you tools that were not possible to deliver without an online medium, and we are excited about how much more this will add to your experience!

Is Kamana Online easy to try?
Absolutely. Go to www.Kamana.org and click on "Join Now". Add the information needed for the subscription — and you're in! Each month you will be automatically charged $9.95. This is a significant savings over the previous student services pricing, all while bringing more effective tools to your naturalist journey. You receive even greater savings when you sign up for a year!

What if I decide it's not for me?
Cancel anytime before the end of the month, and you owe nothing more. You can always renew your subscription in the future when you are ready.

Free Student Resources at www.Kamana.org
Even if you aren't sure right now about signing up for a student services subscription, please visit Kamana.org and enjoy for free the many Kamana student resources you'll find there.

We look forward to seeing you at Kamana.org, and out on the trail…

WELCOME!

We'd like to start by welcoming you to *Kamana One*. We hope it will be rewarding experience for you.

Here's what you do...

Acquire these resources (needed for Part Three):

1. *Seeing Through Native Eyes: A Journey of Connection*, with Jon Young. **8 cd set.**
2. *Reader's Digest: North American Wildlife.*

These resources are available from Wilderness Awareness School at www.WildernessAwareness.org

1. Read Part One. Then, pick a day to begin Part Two. When you start Part Two, try to keep on track every day for two weeks.

2. Read and complete all exercises in Part Two, *Nature Awareness Trailhead*. Ideally, this will take every day for two weeks. <u>You can complete this section WITHOUT having the above mentioned resources.</u>

3. Read and complete all exercises in Part Three, *Resource Trailhead*. **You can do this at the same time as Part Two**. We recommend doing both at the same time, if you can afford more than an hour each day. If you do them at the same time, the book will take you two to three weeks to finish. If you do Parts Two and Three separately, it may take you four to six weeks.

4. If you choose to get certified for your work by Wilderness Awareness School, **see the** "Kamana One Field Pack" **form toward the end of this book for a detailed list of what to mail in.** This is now a **free** service. If this form is missing, you may download it at www.kamana.org.

If this is a library book or it belongs to someone else, you may want to write your responses on your own paper.

If you want to continue to the next level, *Kamana Two*, send in the registration form, the page at the end of this book, and we'll get you started right away. Additional forms are available at www.kamana.org. You can also order it today at www.WildernessAwareness.org.

If you need help with *Kamana One*, join our on-line student community at www.kamana.org.

Please write NEATLY in INK (Blue or Black)

KAMANA
NATURALIST TRAINING PROGRAM
www.kamana.org

Exploring Natural Mystery

Kamana One

written by Jon Young

© Copyright 2001 Jon Young

Kamana One: Exploring Natural Mystery
Written by Jon Young, with Paul Houghtaling and Matt Wild

Production/Layouts by John Gallagher

Artwork by Walker Korby

© 2001-2007 Jon Young. All rights reserved.

Kamana Naturalist Training Program
Author: Jon Young
Design consultant: Ingwe
Design Editor & Program Director: John Gallagher
Writers and Editors: Paul Houghtaling, Matt Wild, Alex Callen, Ellen Haas, Linda Cunio, Dan Gardoqui, Jeff Lambe, Jonathan Talbott, Doniga Murdoch, Cara Burrow, Kelly Ann Moore, Jessica Perkins
Artist: Walker Korby

Kamana One: Exploring Natural Mystery, First printing: July 2001
© 2001 Jonathan R. Young
ISBN 1-57994-008-0

Kamana Naturalist Training Program and Derivative Works © 1996 by Jonathan R. Young
Jon Young's Kamana Certification Program and Derivative Works © 1995 by Jonathan R. Young
Shikari Tracker Training Program and Derivative Works © 1998 by Jonathan R. Young

No part of this publication may be reproduced, stored in a retrieval system, or transmitted, in any form or by any means, electronic, mechanical, photocopying, recording, or otherwise, without the prior written permission of the copyright owner. Making copies of any part of this book for any purpose other than your own personal use is a violation of United States copyright laws.

This book is part of the *Kamana Naturalist Training Program*, which is published by Owlink Media. The *Kamana Naturalist Training Program* logo is a registered trademark. The Owlink Media logo is a registered trademark..

Owlink Media formed to help Our World Learn (OWL) through all forms of media, broadcasting and publishing utilizing succesful techniques gained from the art of mentoring. If you are interested in finding out more about Owlink Media, please visit at www.OwlinkMedia.com.

Wilderness Awareness School is a division of The Awareness Society, a Nonprofit Corporation, recognized as a Federal Tax Exempt organization under I.R.S. code section 501(c)(3). The Wilderness Awareness School logo is a registered trademark.

Wilderness Awareness School does not discriminate on the basis of race, color, creed, national or ethnic origin, or sexual orientation.

Information about the *Kamana Naturalist Training Program* and all Wilderness Awareness School programs may be obtained at www.WildernessAwareness.org or www.Kamana.org

Printed in the United States of America
10 9 8 7 6

DEDICATION

Without hesitation, the first and foremost to whom this work and this school are dedicated are the children of today, their children, and the future children for the next seven generations to come on this Earth...

WILDERNESS AWARENESS SCHOOL

As Design Editor and Program Director of the *Kamana Naturalist Training Program*, I would like to welcome you into Wilderness Awareness School. You'll hear all you need to hear about this course later on, so I'll just skip to the "special thanks."

I would like to honor program creator Jon Young (who put two decades of work into this even before he laid his hands on the keyboard!); curriculum co-creator and elder Ingwe (who shared with us wisdom, stories and teachings that gave our school a foundation and a mission); Consulting Editor Tom Brown, Jr. for all his contributions; Jake Swamp; writers and editors Alex Callen, Ellen Haas, Linda Cunio, Matt Wild, Dan Gardoqui, Jeff Lambe, Cara Burrow, Jessica Perkins, Kelly Ann Moore, and Paul Houghtaling (special thanks to Paul for his dedication and the challenging work of re-designing the Resource Trail); artist Walker Korby; original Kamana team member Kirstin Young; Former and present CFPA members Diane Marie, Walt Hoesel and Warren Moon; former school director Debbie Winters; the *many* Student Service instructors over the years including Aidan Young, Tyler Hartford, Jenn Jacobson, Barbara English, and Greg Sommer. And last, because he deserves the attention, Jonathan Talbott. Not only was Jonathan the first graduate and a contributing writer and artist, but he was also the very first student services instructor who helped many navigate their way through Kamana.

Finally, thank you to all of our students, community, past and present Board of Trustee members, all those who will contribute to Kamana in the future, and anyone whom I may have forgotten.

Once again, welcome to Wilderness Awareness School's Independent Studies. May your Kamana journey be a rewarding experience.

John Manus Gallagher
Design Editor & Program Director, Kamana Naturalist Training Program

Contents

Ohen:ton Karihwatehkwen; The "Words Before All Else" i

Part One: The Kamana Songline iii
    Chapter One: Introducing Wilderness Awareness School 1
    Chapter Two: Introducing Your Instructors 7
    Chapter Three: An Old Story 21
    Chapter Four: Strategy for Taking This Kind of Course 28

Part Two: Nature Awareness Trailhead 30
    Day 1 38
    Day 2 44
    Day 3 50
    Day 4 56
    Day 5 60
    Day 6 66
    Day 7 72
    Day 8 78
    Day 9 84
    Day 10 90
    Day 11 94
    Day 12 98
    Day 13 101
    Day 14 104

Part Three: Resource Trailhead 116
    Chapter One: Welcome to Resources 118
    Chapter Two: A Little Bit of Knowledge 122
    Chapter Three: Adventures In The Back Yard 136
    Chapter Four: A Way To See 148
    Chapter Five: The Movable Feast 164
    Chapter Six: Step Back And Take A Closer Look 182
    Chapter Seven: The History of Your Landscape 196
    Chapter Eight: Learning To See The Forest And The Trees 206
    Chapter Nine: A Universal Language 224
    Chapter Ten: Wrapping the Bundle 240

Appendix A: The Tourist Test 246
Appendix B: Invitation to Continue with Kamana .272

OHEN:TON KARIHWATEHKWEN; THE "WORDS BEFORE ALL ELSE"
—from the Thanksgiving Address, Iroquois tradition

"The first thing that's done is you give thanks to everything. You thank the waters beneath the Earth, the stones, the soil, all the way up to the stars. It's just a reminder of where we are. We should never forget that.."
—Kahionhes John Fadden, Turtle Clan of the Mohawk Nation.

"If all of the children of the world were to be a part of this kind of Thanksgiving each day, I believe that the problems of the world would start to go the other way."
—Mohawk Sub-Chief Tekaronieneken Jake Swamp

Today we have gathered and have come from many different places. We have all arrived safely at this place to share with each other our gifts from the Creator. So we bring our minds together as one in Thanksgiving and Greetings to one another.

We send greetings and thanksgiving to our Mother the Earth who, like our own mother, continues to give for our well-being. She continues to care for us and has not forgotten her instructions from the beginning of time. We now bring our minds together in Thanksgiving for the Earth.

Now, as one mind, we turn our thoughts to the Waters of the Earth, that continue to flow beneath the ground, in little streams and in rivers, in lakes and wetlands, and in the great seas. They quench our thirst and help us to keep clean. We now bring our minds together in Thanksgiving to all the Waters of the Earth.

With one mind, we send our Thanksgiving and Greetings to all the Beings that dwell in the Water which provide for us in many ways.

Now we direct our thoughts to the many kinds of plants that live low upon the Earth—the mosses, the grasses, the herbs, the food plants and the flowers, for they too have not forgotten their Original Instructions. There are many members of this Nation who sustain those who walk upon this Earth and take away the sicknesses of the human family. With one mind we send our thoughts and Thanksgiving to the Plant Nations.

We now gather our minds together and send Greetings and Thanksgiving to all the Animal Life in the world, for they continue to instruct and teach us even today. We are happy that many still walk us with although their natural world has been changed and life has become very difficult for them at times. Sometimes we may see a fox or a deer eye to eye and we are reminded of that feeling of kinship we get when we see the animals. With one mind we send our Thanksgiving to all the Animal Life in the world.

With one mind we now think of the Trees. According to their Original Instructions the Trees still give us shelter, warmth and food, and keep the air clean. When we see the trees we are reminded of the beauty and power of the natural world. With one mind we send our Thanksgiving to all the members of the Tree Nation.

Most of humanity throughout history has said prayers to the powers of surrounding nature, which they have recognized as their source of life. Surely it is not too late to recover this ancestral wisdom.

– Richard K. Nelson

We now bring our minds together to send our Greetings of Thanksgiving to the Birds. At the beginning of time the Birds were given a very special duty to perform. They were instructed to help lift the minds of the Human Family. Many times during the day our minds are lifted by their songs. With one mind we send our Thanksgiving to all the Birds of the world.

We are thankful to the Four Winds who continue to blow and cleanse the air in accordance with their Original Instructions. When we listen to the Winds it is as if we are hearing the Creator's breath, clearing our minds as it blows through the Trees. With one mind we send our Thanksgiving to the Four Winds.

Now we turn our attention to the Thunderbeings. They welcome the springtime with their loud voices. Along with the lightning, they carry the waters of Spring on their backs. With one mind we send our Thanksgiving and Greetings to the Thunderbeings.

Our minds are one as we send our thoughts to our oldest brother the Sun. Each day the Sun continues according to his original instructions, bringing the light of the day, the energy source of all life on Earth. With one mind we send our Thanksgiving and Greetings to our oldest brother the Sun.

We now gather our minds together and give Thanks to our oldest Grandmother, the Moon who holds hands with all of the women of the world, binding all of the cycles and rhythms of the Waters. With one mind we send our Thanksgiving and Greetings to our Grandmother the Moon.

With one mind we send our thoughts to the Star Nations who continue to light our way during times of darkness to guide us home, and who hold the secrets of many forgotten stories. With one mind we send our Thanksgiving and Greetings to the Star Nations.

With our minds as one mind we think of the Four Spirit Beings who live in the Four Directions. We know that they are helping us when we are moving through life and a feeling tells us not to go a certain way, or that we are on the right path. And now we gather our minds together as one and send our special Thanksgiving Greetings to the Four Spirit Beings.

Now we have arrived in a very special place where dwells the Great Spirit that moves through all things. As one mind we turn our thoughts to the Creator with Thanksgiving and Greetings.

We have now become like one being, with one body, one heart, one mind. We send our Prayers and special Thanksgiving Greetings to all the unborn Children of all the Future Generations. We send our thoughts to the many different Beings we may have missed during our Thanksgiving. With one mind we send our Thanksgiving and Greetings to all of the Nations of the World.

Now our minds are one.

Part I
The Kamana Songline

Chapter One

Introducing Wilderness Awareness School

Welcome to Our Kamana Program

Wilderness Awareness School has been a dream come true for those of us who have fallen in love with the natural world and want to share our knowledge and skills with others. We are delighted that you have chosen to sign up for our introductory course in naturalist studies. We name this course Kamana after a word from the Akamba people, natives of Kenya known for their tracking skills, that means "apprentice." The exercises here are designed to be simple and fun. They will initiate you into a way of seeing into natural mystery, a way of recognizing patterns that will entice you to follow them up into greater mastery. We hope you will get a glimpse of the mystery that unfolds as you follow the tracks that start in your own backyard.

Exploring Natural Mystery

This school has a story — we call it a "songline" — a body of lore that gives us a map of where we came from and where we're going. It began with an Apache Scout living at the end of the American Frontier. In his old age he found himself passing down his wisdom to a pair of twelve-year-old suburban boys off their back porches in the Pine Barrens of New Jersey. One of those boys grew up to be Tom Brown Jr., well known author of *The Tracker* and founder of The Tracker School. In Tom's book, he describes how his wise mentor initiated him into the mysteries of nature.

"Stalking Wolf gave us the questions that would lead us to our answers, but he never told us an answer. He taught me to see and to hear, to walk and to remain silent; he taught me how to be patient and resourceful, how to know and how to understand. He taught me to see invisible things from the trail that all action leaves around itself.

He taught me how to teach myself the mystery of the track...I could not see the bird, but I could see the actions of the bird in the traces he left and in the disturbance made by his actions. I could see what was out of place since he had come and gone, the seeds where they did not grow, the tracks in the snow, the snow itself dusted down where it would not have been naturally. I could see the bird go through his routine almost as surely as if I had stood there watching him.

The first track is the end of a string. At the far end, a being is moving; a mystery, dropping a hint about itself every so many feet, telling you more about itself until you can almost see it, even before you come to it. The mystery reveals itself slowly, track by track, giving its genealogy early to coax you in. Further on it will tell you the intimate details of its life and work, until you know the maker of the track like a lifelong friend."

Jon Young's Story

When he was twenty-one, Tom Brown Jr. found himself, in turn, training another scrawny twelve-year-old kid in the outback of the same New Jersey neighborhood. Like Tom, Jon Young was driven by a passionate desire to follow tracks deeper and deeper into the wilderness. So, young Jon Young inherited a legacy that led him to create Wilderness Awareness School. Jon learned "invisibly" from Tom throughout his teenage years, without realizing he was being trained in a native tradition, to be a consummate naturalist. He followed up his apprenticeship by earning a BA in Environmental Science from Cook College, Rutgers University, in a combined study of Anthropology and Classical Natural History. Needing a way to pass on the incredible knowledge he had been given, he began mentoring High School kids as their science teacher.

Wilderness Awareness School evolved from a test Jon gave his students. He went out with a camera and a tape recorder to record some common sights and sounds from the wild places around their area. The slides included such shots as a chipmunk's eye peering out from a wild rose bush, wildflowers in winter and other common sights. When he administered the first version of this test to 125 high school freshmen and sophomores, the results were mind-boggling. The test was simple identification, with 100 questions made up of slides and sound tracks. When he collected the test papers, the pages were almost entirely blank. It was as if his students were "aliens" in their own back yards!

Teaching Native Awareness

Jon knew that children of Native people living close to the land know, by the time they are in their teens, how to read the ground as we would read a newspaper; they know the calls of the birds and local animals and even understand the significance of the various calls, songs and tones that the birds and animals are using; they know how and where to find drinking water, how to find food, what wood to burn and why. By the time they are adults, their knowledge of the world around them is so vast and intricate that they could teach college with several doctorate degrees. Jon knew he had to find a way to teach this depth of "native" knowledge in his school. So it was that a test made a school.

Wilderness Awareness School has administered the Alien (also Tourist) Test to thousands of people around the world. After failing it, almost everyone expresses a great desire to be able to pass such a test in the future. The answers to the questions, the lore about plants, tracks, bird language and animals are fascinating, and people long to recover this knowledge.

The most commonly expressed frustration is that people do not know where to begin. They look at the Wall of Green out there and throw up their hands. Students see the overwhelming array of available books and field guides and have no idea which way to turn or which ones to begin with. They can't see the forest for the trees!

Jon's Wilderness Awareness School's unique approach to environmental education responds to the need this test reveals. Since 1983 we have learned to assist people to penetrate the Wall of Green. Our mission is to foster native awareness by teaching people how to see the forest *through* the trees. We pull you outdoors and get you to quiet down. We show you how to alert your senses – five and more of them. We use tracking to teach you to pay attention to the little disturbances whose trails tell stories. We show you how to use the field guides so that they can act like living mentors as you wander through your studies. We focus your eyes and widen them to mystery at the same time.

The Mission of Wilderness Awareness School

Wilderness Awareness School is dedicated to caring for the earth and our children by fostering understanding and appreciation of nature, community and self. Through dynamic programs that combine ancient and modern ecological wisdom, we empower people to become stewards, mentors and leaders.

Founded in 1983, Wilderness Awareness School is a national non-profit environmental education organization based in Duvall, Washington. Over the past two decades, we have grown from a small group of visionary individuals to a leading national organization impacting the course of nature education and inspiring many schools and individuals across the country and the world to share our teachings and curriculum.

By climbing up into his head and shutting out every voice but his own, "Civilized Man" has gone deaf. He can't hear the wolf calling him brother; he can't hear the earth calling him child.

—*Ursula LeGuin*

For more information on Wilderness Awareness School, visit www.WildernessAwareness.org. *Songline*, the first section of *Kamana Two* is available as a free download.

The Kamana Path

Kamana One: Exploring Natural Mystery, is the introductory course to our four level *Kamana Naturalist Training Program*. All levels are designed to take you down a path that will prepare you to be a skillful and fierce naturalist.

The Kamana Path has two trails, and each trail has many tracks. The Kamana trails intertwine as they expand and deepen awareness in the field, and sharpen it through journaling and sketching work with bioregional field guides and other resources.

We cover the whole field of Natural Science and Ecology from the points of view of both the modern scientist and the traditional scout. We encourage you to do one Kamana level after the other and keep up your momentum because the very essence of nature and scout awareness is that everything is hitched to everything. You can't reduce it or immobilize it; you have to go with its flow.

Indeed, this is a lot—and it will probably take awhile. And then you discover that the *Kamana Naturalist Training Program* is only the beginning of a lifetime of discovery! We aim to instill a sense of confidence in your abilities and a sense of direction in your interests as a naturalist.

The Nature Awareness Trail

This trail focuses on developing your awareness in an expansive way. It is about using your eyes and ears and other senses in ways not often challenged in academic training. *Kamana One* through *Kamana Four* contain **Field Exercises** to practice. If you work on them every day, the result will be new patterns in your awareness, an increase in your "mind's eye" ability to visualize things, a strengthening of your gut feelings, and an ability to be in the right place at the right time. In short, this trail invites you to explore natural mystery.

The Resource Trail

The second trail guides you into research to develop background skills using resources. Though this may sometimes seem like an academic exercise, trust us, it is not. There are elements of poetry, spirit, and power in the observational experience inherent in this exercise series. The goals on this trail are manifold. Most important, we want you to increase in your ability to use your "mind's eye" as a tool for field observation—while providing your mind's eye with a set of "mental file cards" to work in concert with your newly developed observation skills.

To do so, we'll guide you toward an overall sense of the patterns that define the various families and groups of plants and animals in your area. Through investigating all six tracks on this trail, you will gain an appreciation of the language of science, and you will develop self-sufficiency in research. You will learn to sort through nature's overwhelming diversity to focus in on key species. With each Kamana level, you will go deeper with your investigations until you have finally completed your apprenticeship with a sense of mastery.

See Appendix C at the end of this book for a detailed description of the Kamana Resource Trail; Kamana Two, Three, and Four; and a Registration Form to sign up for Kamana Two.

Chapter Two

Introducing Your Instructors

Scientists are storytellers. Scientists live and die by their ability to depart from the tribe and go out into an unknown domain and bring back, like a carcass newly speared, some discovery or new fact or theoretical insight and lay it in front of the tribe; and then they all gather and dance around it. Symposia are held in the National

A WORD FROM MATT WILD

Greetings.

Please allow me to start by telling you a bit about myself since we are going to be working together for the next couple of weeks; maybe even a couple of years.

Wandering the stone walls

I grew up in rural Rhode Island. Well, at least it used to be rural—like too many places on the East Coast, development is sneaking in and taking over the farmlands and woods I used to wander as a child. I've always had a passion for the outdoors, loved to listen to the birds, and spent hours looking under rocks and in the rivers. With encouragement and guidance from my parents and great-grandmother, a huge nature enthusiast, I used to wander the woods endlessly and find my way home by the old and forgotten stone walls that connected property lines in southern New England.

As it was for most of us, I soon turned into a "regular old kid," playing sports, music, and hanging out with friends. I soon came to neglect my time in the woods, but when I did, something was always missing. I always thought of the woods and dreamed of being able to wander around without the need to carry water, food or a sleeping bag. I have never forgotten that dream and can still hear the voice of my great-grandmother reminding me of the peace and freedom to be found in the wilderness.

I used to love to look at the ground and find the tracks of an animal. I would sit down and just stare at them, wondering what the heck could have made them. But, I never, ever thought that I would meet someone who knew the answers.

All of that changed for me in September of 1992 after I left Rhode Island to attend college in southern New Hampshire. A fellow freshman who lived across the hall from me and I quickly befriended one another. Soon we found ourselves wandering the 800 acre campus together, looking at trees, tracks, plants and listening to the birds and winds. First, he taught me how to walk quietly so I didn't disturb "the flow of the woods," as he called it. Then he showed me a brand new way to use my eyes and ears to see more in nature than I ever knew was there. After just a few months he had shown me how to track, identify some of the common trees and plants, how to interpret the language of the birds—even how to build a fire without any matches!

Academy of Sciences and prizes are given.

There is fundamentally no difference from a Paleolithic campsite celebration. The scientists tell the story, and the natural history writer's one great function is to translate it into the rhythms and the idioms of storytelling.

And why do we need that? For unknown thousands of years the brain was expanding by genetic evolution, in part because of the palaver and increasingly extended and complex storytelling that was told around the fire.

So, the factual information that we get and the new metaphors created out of science somehow have to be translated into the language of the storyteller—by film, by speech, by literature, by any means that will make it meaningful and powerful for the human mind.

- David Rains Wallace, The Klamath Knot

I couldn't believe he actually knew these things. I had been wishing for this since I was a little boy. Where did he come from? I had images of him being from some farm in the western United States. Maybe even raised by Natives somewhere, wandering and hunting during the fair weather months and hunkering down in a big village for the winter. The truth was hard to believe…he was from New Jersey.

Encountering Jon Young

He told me he had been mentored by a man named Jon Young who was more at home in the woods than he was inside his own house. Could this really be true? I called Jon on the phone that same day and asked what I could do to become a Master Tracker and Naturalist. What he told me on the phone is what we are about to share with you in this program.

I started following his instructions right away and just couldn't seem to learn fast enough. Within a couple of months, I had moved in with Jon and his family in New Jersey. He started mentoring me and sharing the ways of the wilderness right away. Eventually, Jon employed me as a youth programs instructor to work with inner city youth in New Brunswick, New Jersey. After a couple of years of that, I helped him work with high school and college students. He took me under his wing and I've been flying there ever since.

Over the course of the years Jon has, patiently, brought me to a place to teach and share with people of all ages. I still work for Jon and the Wilderness Awareness School as an instructor for the *Kamana Naturalist Training Program*, as well as our Shikari Tracker Training Program. I also help out with local programs, teaching tracking and awareness, and love to go on our expeditions around the country!

It's always tons of fun to hang out with Jon and go tracking or birding with him. He takes full advantage of every single opportunity to teach someone something. Jon's style of mentoring is always just fun somehow, and never feels like a learning process. It wasn't until I started reading Tom Brown, Jr.'s books and understood some of Jon's background that I began to see how very lucky I was. Jon likes to call it "invisible learning" and you've just signed up for it!

Still, Jon continues to invest in his students in a way I have never seen anyone else do. Despite the demands of thousands of students calling him on the phone, he still makes the time to take us out into the woods and go tracking. No matter where we might be, Jon is always asking questions, challenging our awareness—always poking and prodding us further down the trail. I have never witnessed anyone with his level of skills of mentoring and awareness.

So, I am deeply honored to join him in preparing the Nature Awarenesss Trail of this *Kamana One* course in Exploring Natural Mystery for you. I hope you enjoy your exploration as much as I have enjoyed collaborating with Jon in guiding it.

Matt Wild, Kamana Instructor,
White Pine Programs, New Hampshire

A WORD FROM DAN CORCORAN

Some folks come from a long lineage of farmers or hunters, or other types of people that are connected to nature. I grew up in the suburbs playing lots of video games.

I remember my first camping trip at a local county park in Northern Indiana. We went shopping and got lots of essentials – you know, hard-plastic egg containers, metal s'mores sticks, a cast iron skillet, and a dozen other items. I love my family, but we just weren't outdoor people. My biggest activity outside was playing sports: basketball, soccer, football, Frisbee, cross-country.

Sometime in college, that all changed. I started hiking, and then backpacking. Two friends and I went on a road trip to the Southwest and Rocky Mountains to visit several National Parks. Our big adventure was to descend the Grand Canyon and backpack at the Colorado river. We grossly underestimated how treacherous the terrain and weather would be.

It was scalding hot with virtually no shade. The descent was 12 miles long. Packing took longer than anticipated, and we started hiking at 11am – just in time for the peak heat of the day. We were 19 years old and invincible. Until we weren't. I became severely dehydrated and had some degree of heat exhaustion. We made it to the bottom, but I was in bad shape. I felt nauseous, and couldn't eat or drink. My dinner that night was a peanut. We made it out the next day, but it took all that I had. Somewhere during my recovery I thought that there had to be a better way. I didn't just want to walk through nature at a breakneck speed. I wanted to connect with my surroundings at a different pace.

My brother Tim was on a similar path, and introduced me to Kamana. I started doing some nature-connection routines, and it opened my eyes to parts of the natural world that stunned me. How had I lived my life without ever really listening to the birds? How had I missed the power of paying attention to all of my senses? The answer to those questions didn't matter. What did matter was that I realized the value of these practices and did something about it.

In 2002, I went on to attend the Anake Outdoor School, a year-long immersion in the study of nature, community and self. During that year I finished Kamana Two and Three. I continued on as an Apprentice and, during the process, finished Kamana Four. After two years of study, I wasn't done. I knew this was the path I wanted to walk in life. Fortunately, I was hired on as a Kamana responder and then as a Youth Program instructor. Over time, I took the reins from John Gallagher as Kamana Director.

I want to thank you for making this a priority in your life. There are many things competing for your time and energy. I know from experience that you will gain so much from following what is in this book. This journey is not easy or quick, but it is unique and powerful. Remember that there is a whole team of people at Wilderness Awareness School that are here to support you.

All the best,

Dan Corcoran

A WORD FROM JOSH LANE

A bit later in this course you'll be introduced to a core routine called the sit spot. I can still remember the first time I was introduced to this practice, over fifteen years ago, when I was a teenager attending a week-long wilderness skills class in New York state. The instructors had asked me what I wanted to learn about that week, and my answer was - just having read a bunch of Tom Brown's tracking books - "awareness stuff" (a vague but exciting-sounding reply that was the best I could formulate at the time).

To my surprise, I was asked to find a tree to sit under. The instructors promptly disappeared, saying only that they would return later, and, in the meantime, to sit there and use my senses. As I sat there, patiently I thought, attempting to observe my surroundings, a little voice in my head appeared, saying, "What is this? What a rip off! They left me to sit here in the woods by myself! What kind of a program is this. . ." Little then did I understand what a powerful and transformative tool I had just been introduced to. Looking back, I get a good laugh from that moment.

Years later, after many sit spots, I began to get a glimpse of understanding as to the depth of connection that occurs through this simple practice. I share this story because the core routines that you'll explore in Kamana can be like that – simple seeming, and easy to overlook. But through establishing quality connections in a repeated way over time, a profound level of transformation and deep connection occurs.

I'll always remember those timeless sit spot moments, forever etched as part of my being, with all the power of their full-sensory impressions:

The splendor of the first rays of sunrise hitting my body after a bone-chilling New England pre-dawn sit, when I could really understand in my body the visceral joy in the morning bird chorus, as the cold winter night ended...

The spring nights with a low curtain of fog over the meadow, draped thick as pea soup above the ground, with a sea of stars shining more brightly overhead than I'd ever seen, and the sharp howls of a coyote just yards away in the fog...

These are the types of experiences that reach beyond philosophical concepts, into a deep understanding that spans the body, emotion, and the mind. It is a direct experience - and nothing less - that we are after here.

Those memories are part of me now, just as that place became part of me, and now those connections are with me for a lifetime. I hope and wish good adventures for you, too, on your journey of deep nature connection.

A WORD FROM PAUL HOUGHTALING
Professional Tracking

I've heard Jon say that in all of his years of mentoring hundreds of people to become trackers, he had never had anybody say this to him "I want to be a professional tracker." That surprised me. After all, in my mind, who wouldn't want to be a professional tracker?

What is a tracker? Since finding Wilderness Awareness School, I've learned that tracking is much more than it is often perceived to be: studying footprints. In many ways, footprints are limiting, for there is so much more than just the ground on which the tracks are made. Certainly, whoever left their tracks was doing much more than putting feet on the ground . It was going somewhere, with a purpose in mind. With a few tools and the right questions, studying tracks can become a doorway to see through the eyes of the animal or person that made the tracks. The basic tools to enhance your ability to understand those things are what I am honored to share with you here in this course.

I suppose my first passion is mysteries. I can't stand a loose end. I feel a compulsive need to see it tied up. Perhaps this passion has arisen out of tracking. A track can be the beginning of a fantastic mystery that all starts with a simple question about the track that I can't answer. My drive to know the answer to that hanging question will push me to research, experiment, and observe until I've found the answer. Perhaps that is what tracking is to me—the art of asking questions that pull me further along until the mystery is solved.

Questions are around me at all times. In the place that I am living now and writing, I am surrounded by a community of people who study nature and tracking. We are constantly asking questions of each other to see if we have been paying attention to what is happening around us. "What was that bird that just flew by?" someone might ask. "What was the color of that car that just passed us on the highway?" One afternoon, several of us gathered in a Mexican restaurant. We spent nearly the entire time with our eyes closed asking each other questions about what was where in the room, what color the benches were, how many people were behind the counter and what they were wearing. Sounds a little corny, doesn't it? You can bet, though, that by the time we left that place we each were more aware of what had been happening around us. In many respects, a simple game like this helps to build skill as a tracker, too, for tracking involves knowing what is happening around you as well as being able to read footprints. This Kamana program is filled with exercises like this one that are fun but that also stretch your awareness of your surroundings. I'd recommend that you try these games by yourself or with friends.

I haven't always tracked or played games. It wasn't until I was almost in college that I even considered tracking as something that was possible as a profession. Once I heard about it, though, I spent a lot of time trying it on my own. When I first tried to track, I found that I was having a very difficult time. I spent almost two years on my own, crawling around on my hands and knees studying the tracks of animals. Through all of that time, I felt that my skills and abilities were not growing or getting me anywhere. The tracks were still just tracks, and their stories were still a secret to me. I didn't have the right tools and understanding of how to approach tracking.

Where to Begin?

Looking back on that time now, I realize that I did not know where to begin—I did not know how to ask that first question that would pull me into the mystery. I also didn't know where to find the answers to my questions as they came up. It was Double Jeopardy and I didn't even realize it. I feel fortunate that I met up with Jon Young and the Wilderness Awareness School, for the approach to tracking that I've learned since then has opened up a whole new world to me, and it has improved more than just my ability to track. The wealth of learning that Wilderness Awareness School offers inspired me to receive my Bachelor of Science degree from The Evergreen State College. My degree couples tracking and natural history with natural resource management under the title "Field Ecology emphasizing Tracking."

To date, I've had the opportunity to apply my tracking skills by mapping wildlife activity for the Washington State Department of Natural Resources as well as by coordinating a project tracking wolves in central Idaho. In my mind, tracking is the most common-sense approach to studying and mapping wildlife activity, and, in fact, it is my long-term desire to see these principles of tracking applied to the realm of land and wildlife management.

It was this desire to see more trackers in the world, too, that drove me to work with Jon to create the *Shikari Tracker Training Program*, which is Wilderness Awareness School's other naturalist training program that focuses on the Art of Tracking. Through Shikari I hope to shorten the learning curve for those who have the same desire that I had during those years on my hands and knees.

As you may surmise, I feel a great deal of gratitude toward Wilderness Awareness School and Jon Young for the wealth of knowledge, confidence, and skill they have shared with me. They have truly enriched my life beyond measure. Though it may sound somehow strange, my entire perspective on the world has improved, including my relationship with my family, friends, the world around me, and myself.

The basics of what I have learned since being at Wilderness Awareness School are in turn contained for you here in this course. This book is just one piece of the greater whole. Have fun with it. I know that over the years this information has helped me a great deal. In fact, the way that you will be guided through the world of the animals, plants, trees, and birds in this book has become as natural to me as breathing. Enjoy it, and take it one

PART ONE: THE KAMANA SONGLINE

breath at a time.

Ideally, now that I've had a chance to explain to you some of who I am and where I am coming from, I'd enjoy the chance to hear your story, and find out why you are taking this course. I've no doubt that it is an interesting story and one that will continue to lead you to new and exciting places. Perhaps some day we'll get the chance to meet.

Paul Houghtaling
Tracking Instructor, Wilderness Awareness School

A WORD FROM JON YOUNG

In the year 1978, when I was eighteen years old, I discovered something about myself that I had until that point not realized. Allow me to share a story with you about my youth that might help you understand what this journey might contain for you.

Invisible Learning

Much of my time growing up was spent in Tom Brown Jr.'s companionship. We wandered the forests and fields of Holmdel, New Jersey (which today are mostly gone), the Pine Barrens (which thankfully are largely still intact), and the wildlife sanctuaries along the coast. Tom and I both have a great fondness for the coastal environments and could often be found exploring jetties, crawling down in and among the rocks to watch fish or sandpipers, or to just be with the waves. We would examine tide pools for hours and wander the dunes of the wilder stretches of land studying the nightly wanderings of toads, fox, rabbit, shrew and mouse.

I was not formally tutored, in the Western sense. Rather, Tom used Stalking Wolf's method of coyote mentoring, which was completely invisible to me at the time. As far as I knew, Tom and I were just hanging out. This method of teaching created passion enough for me to spend nights and rainy days voraciously devouring information from field guides, magazines, and direct observation of skins, specimens, bones, fish tanks, pools and terraria with wild, native species of fish, reptiles and amphibians. I had my own nature museum (greatly enhanced by Tom's encouragement and gentle questioning).

If you snuck up on my parents' house during the seventies on a weekday after school you might have found me in the basement with the stereo up really loud. But, if you peered through the windows, you might have wondered about my doings. I would have been lost in a dream world, moving about in slow and deliberate fashion fully living in my mind as if I were the fox I was imitating. Or, I was the snapping turtle, the heron, or the weasel. Through role modeling and his willingness to be observed in his private exploration of imitative body movement, and martial arts, Tom had somehow passed on his passion for experiencing the animals.

Being a somewhat normal teenager with all of the angst that I see in my own son and other teens I have worked with over the past fifteen years, I didn't really perceive that my upbringing had taught me anything out of the ordinary. What I hadn't yet realized was just how much I knew, even though I felt (and still do) that I didn't know anything.

From the outside, I looked like your average white American suburban kid, but from the inside, I might as well have been living five hundred years ago. If it weren't for Tom, I would not have had anyone to talk to about my feelings, my grief and my experiences that were wildly spiritual at times and very different from those of my peers at the time. I know this, because when I tried to share my experiences with my peers, I met with a great deal of demoralizing verbal abuse and even shunning behavior that left me feeling quite alone and out of sorts.

So, I guess in my desire to *not* be different, to *not* stick out, I convinced myself that there was nothing special going on and that I was just like everyone else. I had so thoroughly convinced myself of this that I had no idea what I had learned about tracking. I actually consciously tried to rebel against tracking! After all, Tom, who was not famous, who had not written any books during my time with him, was just a guy up the street who liked to hang out in the woods. We were so much in each other's lives that, in many ways, I took him for granted. Yes, I even rebelled against him as a father figure!

Then, in 1978, Tom's book *The Tracker*, was picked up by *Reader's Digest* magazine as a condensed reprint. Tom found himself suddenly and surprisingly very, very busy. People were coming from all over America to seek out the possibility of learning from Tom. The Tracker School was born.

When he opened the new Tracker School with its unfamiliar and scary workshop format, Tom asked me to help instruct.

"Instruct? Instruct what? Survival? Tracking? What the heck do I know about any of that, Tom?"

"A lot more than you think, Jon."

"What am I supposed to say or do?" I asked sheepishly.

"Jon," Tom went on in a calm and deliberate tone that I knew very well. It made me feel very peaceful inside when he got that wise and older brother energy going. "Just think about the situation you are going to teach about, and ask yourself 'What would the animals be doing in this same situation?' and you will find that you have no end of knowledge."

Inside, I knew he was right. When I began to help teach I really began to see what I had been given by Tom's mentoring. The power of our internal blueprint sneaks up on us in such a manner that it feels like the most natural thing in the world, as natural as breathing

Reviving the Blueprint

You might think sometimes that what we suggest in this course feels like nothing or feels stupid or unnecessarily mundane. Guess what? That is often how it is when instructors and mentors are doing a good job. Exploring natural mystery with our help can feel like time-consuming nothingness. Let it be. It is not nothing; it is everything to your ancient memories. The Kamana program will help unfold your natural blueprint. It won't feel so much like learning something new as remembering something old.

In my years growing up with Tom, I spent uncountable hours, days, overnights, and later on, weeks, by myself in the natural world. The majority of my experience and time was spent in a couple of places only. One of them was a rich mixed forest and field area within walking distance of Tom's and my home. Within the couple of thousand acres that we explored and wandered, there was a core "territory" of a few hundred acres that I knew like the back of my hand. There was within that core area, a place of a few hundred feet in diameter that I knew so well as to still be able to travel there in my mind and visit with the trees and shrubs I grew to know by first name.

Literally, I came to know the one place near my home so well that I am now convinced that this part of the land had become me and I had become that part of the land. There are no two ways about it. My mind's perceptual abilities were created there. My identity is drawn from this place. To this day, I feel rooted there, even though, today, that place is only in my memory. The land moving machines, bulldozers and grating machines so changed the landscape and topography as to make it wholly unrecognizable.

Today, there are hundreds of homes in my core area. The people drive up to their houses in tinted window cars, automatically open garage doors, and pull into their space station without ever stopping to go outside. The garage port closes behind them and I never even have so much as an opportunity to talk to them. They do not know that place where they live. They have no recollection of the blueprint of their soul or knowledge of their place in Nature.

Ingwe, a tracker, trained in Kenya, who helped start this school, always says: "Find yourself in the wilderness of Mother Earth and you will always belong there in Nature. Even when you return to the city, your longing will be able to rest, for you know that all you have to do is return to your Mother Earth and she will welcome you back." What I have come to realize is that once we reactivate the ancient blueprint born into us, by patterning our senses and the focus of our mind's eye, we will never in our lifetime lose it, and we will be at home anywhere we travel.

Dirt Time

What Ingwe doesn't say is that regaining our connection with Mother Earth is a process. The process takes time, energy and *your* commitment to see it through. Reading a book or a thousand books on nature and native people *cannot* take the place of *real sensory experience* in nature. The books can help the mind's eye focus and increase the power of the experience, but that is ungrounded without the dirt time. Lots of dirt time. It's important that you not expect an instant miracle or a magic pill.

Taking five thousand workshops will inspire you but also confuse you with details to the point of not knowing where to begin or what to focus on. The inspiration will be *vitally* helpful as long as *you* go out and *practice* sitting in the forest alone for several minutes to hours at a time, through all times of day, through all seasons, through all weather conditions and through many years. There is *no substitution* for that. Most people find the experience of this routine to be the biggest challenge of all.

The river of modern life is large and powerful. The currents are pulling in the opposite direction, while you, a humble, common human being, seek to re-establish yourself with Mother Earth and your original instructions, or blueprint. There are and will be one million reasons not to go to your place in the forest. There will always be one billion responsibilities that take you from your path. This you must know in advance if you are to succeed. You must be committed. You must be determined, even downright stubborn about guarding your time in nature.

Help for Success

You must be efficient about it as well. We are all very busy these days, and you need to set yourself up for success. The *Nature Awareness*, and the *Resource* trails of Kamana One are designed to help you succeed.

There are many, many fine wilderness experience schools and many accomplished trackers and writers who are all there to help you. The Tracker School, Tom Brown, Jr., his writings and his instructors are there to re-inspire you and to instruct you with as much detail and skills as a person could ever digest in ten lifetimes! The Wilderness Awareness School programs, expeditions, products and services are all there to help you.

You just need to focus, make the commitment and go! *Kamana One* is a great introduction to the kinds of things you will experience—as study and routine—should you want to make a commitment to this journey on a more intense level.

So, I wish you well on your journey. It is my deepest hope that you will make a strong commitment. Each time another human being reclaims their natural instructions, the Earth and all of her inhabitants (including me, my family and loved ones) grow that much stronger, more healthy and hopeful. It is therefore *vital* to me and my staff that you succeed.

What you experience in the next few weeks or months will give a really good taste of what would lie ahead should you wish to go beyond the basics. Please explore and enjoy Mother Earth with my best wishes for your health and happiness and that of your family and friends and those you love.

With sincere hope for the Future Generations,

Jon Young

Jon Young, Founder of Wilderness Awareness School

Chapter Three

≈

An Old Old Story

"I would ask you to remember only this one thing," said Badger. "The stories people tell have a way of taking care of them. If stories come to you, care for them. And learn to give them away where they are needed. Sometimes a person needs a story more than food to stay alive. That is why we put these stories in each other's memories. This is how people care for themselves."

Barry Lopez, Crow and Weasel

Gather round the fire

A long time ago, somewhere in America, or Canada, Argentina, New Zealand, Tahiti, India or Japan, our grandparents, or their grandparents, may have sat on well-worn chairs, finely crafted by their own hands, or warmed themselves before a fire roaring in a hearth built of stone they had quarried. Or perhaps they sat on the warm, dry earth around the cook fire at the center of a circle of grass, enjoying a meal of wild roots.

In these long-ago days, the time of our grandparents' grandparents, the first words of the storyteller were greeted with much anticipation, for they were the magical doorway to other lands, to faraway places our forefathers could only dream of visiting, and to times much too old to be personally remembered.

With these words, storytellers the world over transport their listeners to exotic places, where wondrous beasts challenge heroes and heroines to do battle against impossible odds, where tales of great love and great sacrifice touch the heart and cause the gray heads around the fire to nod in a knowing way.

In the time of our ancestors, the accomplished storyteller was one of the most valued members of the community. This chronicler of events, this recounter of heroic deeds, this preserver of myth and legend, was at once historian, entertainer, keeper of records, guardian of culture, and teacher. Stories were true recollections of events, embroidered with a rich tapestry of imagery and sound, enhancing the telling—or they were symbolic representations of universal themes as old as human history.

In traditional native stories from the Pacific Northwest, animals were really people in animal form, exemplifying all their strengths and weaknesses. In the traditional Irish tales, "little people" and "fairy folk" were understood to be quite real. Their inescapable presence in traditional stories gave rise to the term "fairy tale," which took on the connotation of myth or legend. But in traditional societies of long ago, no distinction was made between "true" stories and "fairy tales." All were given equal credibility, for all served the same purpose—to preserve the traditions and cultural memories and to perpetuate the values of society. It was left up to the listener to decide whether a story was more "truth" or more "tale."

Come then, settle yourself by the fire while we throw on another piece of wood. Snug your blanket up around your shoulders. As the wood explodes in a shower of sparks, rising to join a million stars in the clear night sky, breathe deep the perfume of wood smoke, and allow your thinking mind to doze, warm and comfortable, like the dog at your feet. Let the music of crickets and frogs or the calls of the owl and jackal carry you to another time, another place, while I tell you a story. It is a true story—and it is a tale. It is about no one in particular, and it is the story of each one of us, at one time or another.

Martin and Sean

Martin and Sean lived in the same town, in the same neighborhood—in fact, they went to the same high school, and even walked the same path to get there, yet they hardly knew each other. They may as well have been living in two different worlds.

In Sean's world the alarm clock went off at a quarter after seven. Then the day would start again at 7:25, and at 7:35, or until his mom nagged him out of bed. Actually, the day didn't really begin for Sean until after he took his shower. Even then he would have just enough time to eat his pop tart while he rushed down the path, across the bridge, through the woods, and finally on to school. Most mornings he barely made it to class on time.

Down the block from Fox Acres where Sean lived, there was an old run-down farmhouse. The little patch of woods in the back was all that was left of the beautiful large farm that once contained apple orchards, cattle, sheep and acres of fields. This was where Martin lived with his Native American grandmother, whom he simply called "Grandmother."

In Martin's world there was no alarm clock to jar him from sleep. In the morning, so early that there was not even a hint of silver in the east, Martin would hear a soft voice, "Come on grandson, up." No matter how tired he was, he knew never to go back to sleep after Grandmother had called him. Grandmother had told him many stories about when she was young and how her father always got up with no alarm. So before the first light, Martin would begin his day.

As his grandfather had done before him, Martin would jump out of bed and go outside in his bare feet to greet the day. He would hear Grandmother singing in her language, and sometimes his mind would wander to the baseball game or a test he had that day.

When the first pale light appeared in the East, Grandmother would say, "Now listen—the Great Horned Owls will be flying off to sleep. Can you hear?" And she pointed them out. "You hear that sound? That's the mockingbird greeting the dawn. Soon you will know the voices of all the birds that have sung their song since the beginning of time."

She always told him things like that.

"Never just walk right into the woods; instead you stand on the edge and watch. And when you feel it is proper to go in, then you enter the woods, but always with respect, because you are walking among your elders when you are there among the trees."

When he crossed over the creek on the same little bridge that Sean used, Martin stopped to say a special thank you to the waters as his grandmother had been taught when she was a young girl. Martin took his time walking through this special place on his way to school. He knew where the red fox made its den, where the old great horned owl hunted by night, and which tree at the edge of the park it roosted in by day. Every morning, he ate a few dandelion leaves because Grandmother had taught him that they were good for his blood, and sometimes on the way home from school he stopped to gather medicinal plants for her.

Otters are Impossible!

One day, in Environmental Science class, Mr. Smith showed a film on river otters. After class Martin went over to his teacher and said quietly, "I know where a river otter is living. I pass her tracks every morning, and I've seen her playing in the creek."

Sean overheard him and laughed. "That's impossible. There aren't any river otters around here. I walk through those crummy woods every day and the only things in there are some squirrels, sparrows, and garbage tossed all over. The only animal in the river is maybe a river rat."

"I think you saw the muskrat that lives there—but there's more. There are all kinds of things, like the otter and a fox and owls and…"

All this talk from Martin, trying to make those woods seem like a real forest, was getting on Sean's nerves. "Oh sure, and I suppose there's bears, mountain lions, and an Indian tribe living there, too!"

"Be careful what you say," Martin warned him.

"And what are you going to do about it?" Sean retorted.

"Gentlemen!" Mr. Smith interrupted. "Good scientists don't fight—they experiment and observe. The way to settle this is with careful observation and agreement on your results. I want you two to work out the problem and let me know what you learn."

Martin got a funny look on his face. "All right, meet me tomorrow at dawn on the wooden bridge."

That next morning in the darkness Grandmother woke Martin up a half hour early. As he dressed, his heart was beating a little faster than usual. "Finally there is someone to share my woods with," he thought.

He slipped out the door and walked softly to the little creek, listening for the first bird songs and for Sean's footsteps coming through the forest. But Martin didn't hear anything except the owls, and he thought, "Sean must be here already, and he's hiding somewhere waiting to scare me. I'm ashamed of myself for letting him get here ahead of me!" Martin got down on his hands and knees and looked around. He couldn't see Sean, but he found a little thicket of spice bush to hide underneath and settled in to wait. "Well, I got past him anyway. When the light comes, I'll find him."

As the eastern sky turned silver, the horned owls quieted their calls and the stars faded into a morning so brisk Martin could see his breath. One bright star still shone in the east and the brightness of false dawn came, bringing the birds and their morning chorus. Still no sign of Sean.

Chattering robins alerted him in time to his old friend the red fox as it moved across the hill and disappeared into a thicket. A crow called out a warning as a large shadow passed overhead. It was the old horned owl flying toward the far end of the park where people never walked. Martin once followed the bird and discovered that by day it sat up in the tall Norway spruce just beyond the old farmstead. Still, there was no Sean.

At that moment, Sean's alarm went off. Sitting up in bed he remembered he had to meet Martin. "I've got just enough time. The sun's not up yet."

He jumped into his clothes, not even taking his wake-up shower. He threw on his boots, ran down the sidewalk and tramped into the woods.

Still sitting in his secret spot, Martin heard the robins' alarm calls as they flew toward him. Then he saw the grackles and blackbirds all flying from the same direction. "Must be Sean," he thought. Four minutes later he heard heavy footfalls come down the trail and across the bridge.

"Hey, where are you going?" Martin asked from under his spice bush. Sean almost jumped out of his skin. He looked around but couldn't see anyone.

"What the heck are you hiding for? Where are you?" Sean scoffed.

"I'm in here. Shh…with the racket you're making you probably scared everything away. Come on down here anyway."

"I don't want to get under there. There's ticks, and I don't have a hat on; besides, it's dirty."

"Don't worry, I come here every day. It's fine."

Sean reluctantly joined Martin in the thicket. "So where's the otter? I don't see any otter. I came through the woods…there's no otters here!"

Martin motioned to Sean to be quiet. Then he told Sean everything that had happened there that morning—about the owls, the fox and the robins.

"You're crazy!" Sean laughed.

"I don't think you're going to see anything, thinking like that," Martin said.

Suddenly there was an explosion of rasping bird calls at the edge of the woods. Silhouetted against the newly risen sun was a red-tailed hawk being ganged by crows. Its breast was shining white in the dawn light, its wings outspread against the wind. This hawk was an old friend. Martin knew this bird, as well as his mate, by sight, and could tell their war cries apart. He knew where they nested and that they liked to hunt mice and voles in the field behind his old barn. He had even given the hawk a name.

Sean's eyes almost exploded from his head. "It's an eagle! It's an eagle!"

Martin just looked at him, surprised, and shook his head. He didn't quite know what to make of this guy. One minute he was dead certain there could never be an otter here, the next he was jumping out of his skin over a common hawk. Martin was a little puzzled, but he was pleased that Sean was excited.

Darkness Before Dawn

"Why don't you come here again tomorrow, but this time come at dawn."

"I thought this was dawn."

"No, dawn is when the darkness ends and the light just begins."

"Are you crazy? I am not getting up that early."

"Do you want to see the otter?"

After a week of trying, Sean finally got there in the darkness before dawn. He heard the owl for the first time as it silently lifted off its hunting perch and headed home to the white pine at the edge of the old farmstead.

Martin introduced Sean to the hawk and his mate, and Sean learned the difference between a red-tailed hawk and the only other large raptor he had ever seen, the stuffed golden eagle at the museum. One day Sean tumbled out of their secret hiding spot under the spice bush because he saw a fox. He jumped up and down, tugging on Martin's sleeve, "Up on the hill, up on the hill!"

Martin had to calm him down. "It's the red fox that dens up over on the other side of that hill."

One morning about three weeks later, after Sean had learned to relax with all his new experiences, the boys heard the startled calls of the wren in the thicket. They caught a glimpse of something shiny and bejeweled in the golden light of dawn. The light hit just right, making the wet fur glow as if lit from within. Something sleek and brown crossed a mossy log from the banks of the spring and investigated its way into the thicket. Sean only saw the movement of the brush as the thick, dark, tapered tail disappeared.

On hands and knees, the boys crept carefully up to the spring.

"Look! A gift," Martin exclaimed.

There, in the wet sand was a perfect set of tracks. Martin pointed out how crisp the prints were, the shape and size of each foot, and showed Sean how there were signs of webbing between the toes. Sean carefully sketched the tracks and together they ran back to Martin's house. Breathless, they tore open the field guides and found the section on tracks. Sean was speechless as he realized he had glimpsed his first otter, right in his own back yard.

Now, when Martin goes into the woods early in the morning, he often finds Sean already there, motionless, under the spice bush. Sean no longer jumps up yelling and screaming at the sight of the red fox, and he has even learned to tell the large female owl's call from that of her mate.

Sean has started to learn the lessons of Nature. Of course some of the lessons, like the ones that the poison ivy and yellow jackets teach, are uncomfortable, but Martin is there to show him how jewelweed and plantain can remedy these and many other problems. Sean is also learning the ways of the Earth, of plants, mammals, and birds from Martin's Grandmother. In fact, he spends so much time with her and with Martin that she has begun calling Sean "Grandson."

Reclaiming Our Natural Heritage

So that's the story of Martin and Sean. It's one of our favorites. What do you think of it? Do you think you have more in common with Martin or with Sean?

As you continue on your journey through life, you may find yourself growing close to a place on the Earth. You may find yourself uttering kind words to an old mossy rock. The great tree over your favorite sitting place has become a good friend. Your heart is full.

The words you use when you feel connected to a place are like the words of Grandmother—they are the words of the ancestors. These are the archetypal words of wisdom and love that come from your heart and fill your soul to overflowing.

This story is a composite sketch of many people I have known and worked with over the years. The character of Martin represents not only a connection to the past, when people lived close to the land, but it also represents those people who have reconnected to the land in the native way. It doesn't matter if you didn't know this chief or that wild person from the jungles of Borneo, this elder, or that shaman! What is important is the process a person encounters when they connect their senses and become rooted in and bonded with the land again.

The character of Sean is an extreme, but it is a common one. There are many people who are literally humming with the distractions and commotion of the modern world. They have never been shown how to slow down and connect with the natural world. This book is all about the many ways to do this.

Martin and Sean represent two extremes of experience. It is easy for us to become so involved in the "flow" of the so-called "real world" with all its demands, that we forget our natural, native roots. We can, at any time, be either the busy person who speeds past everything, barely touching the ground as we go, or the ancient native one who bonds deeply with a place. There is a calling inside many people these days to be rooted in Nature again, to find their place and to know how they fit, as living beings, into the natural world. Many people feel a strong calling to know the natural world, the magical world of wild places, and to deepen that connection, one spirit to another. With this course, you have begun the journey to reclaim your natural heritage as a native of this Earth. Welcome to the family!

Chapter Four
Strategy For Taking This Course

Now you know our Songline – the tale of our school, the legends of your instructors, and the basic story of exploring natural mystery the native way. It's time to begin "the course." We've suggested *Kamana One* is about "invisible" learning, yet we call this a "course." What's the deal? We want this experience to be pure fun for you, but we believe you have more fun when there's strategy to the game.

Become Like a Child

Common to all Wilderness Awareness School programs is our approach to learning, which is really what this course is about. Kamana One's *Nature Awareness Trailhead* is a basic introduction to seeing with native eyes. For those of you who have years, or even a lifetime, of experience in the woods and wilderness, the approach here may seem elementary. That's because it is! This is done intentionally. By no means is this program meaning to start you back at the beginning. Instead, what we are doing is ensuring that all of us—beginners and advanced students alike—are on the same track, because the complexity of what you may choose to study in future levels of Kamana will grow exponentially.

If you are an advanced student, we ask that you "empty your cup" and look at this experience anew. It is our hope that within all of these exercises, routines, and studies a new, or, at the very least, a *brightened* sense of natural mystery will benefit a student of any age or experience level. So please, go into this experience as a child would, and allow your curiosity to explore afresh the exciting trails of nature's mystery.

Although subtle, this is very, very important. Approach these activities with the mind of a child, as if they were all games. They are all games. Don't fall into the trap of thinking of them as assignments. Adults do assignments for other people with deadlines. Children play. Be a child. These exercises are simply fun ways to spend your time while capitalizing on every opportunity to make yourself more aware of your surroundings.

The Course

- **Part Two, the <u>Nature Awareness</u> readings and exercises are designed to be done on a consistent basis every day for two weeks.**
- **Part Three, the <u>Resource</u> exercises have no particular schedule, but understanding and memory builds up best if exercises are done on a fairly consistent basis.**

Should I do Both Trails at Once?

We encourage you to do both *Part Two: The Nature Awareness Trailhead* and *Part Three: The Resource Trailhead* at the same time. If you can make the time, we recommend doing them together, because students report that the intensive cross-focus enhances their learning. However, The Awareness Trail asks you to be alert all day long and to read and write a little every morning and evening, and the *Resource Trail* asks you to listen to a set of six audio tapes, do some reading, and a fair bit of exploring in field guides as well as writing and sketching. So, if you do both at the same time, you'll need to commit yourself wholesale to an intensive "immersion" for two weeks.

If you can't manage both at the same time, please begin by concentrating on the *Nature Awareness Trailhead* daily. Your experience with this trail is likely to fire you up with energy and curiosity. On those days when you do have a little extra time, get started on the *Resource Trail*. Read the Introduction and listen to the first of *Seeing Through Native Eyes Tapes*. Get hold of the *Reader's Digest Guide* and some sharp pencils or good ink pens and do some of the first sketches. Then, if you get overwhelmed, hang on tight to the daily schedule of the Awareness Trail, but give yourself a good extra month to complete the tapes and chapters of the *Resource Trail*.

Please write NEATLY in INK (Blue or Black)

How Much Time is Ideal?
Our experience is that people who do the whole course in two to six weeks get the most out of it.

How Do I Obtain Certification?
Find the pages at the end of this book. These pages explain how to copy, pack, and mail all your work to our offices. For a $10.00 administration fee, we'll send you a certificate of completion.

***If this is a library book or it belongs to someone else, you may want to write your responses on your own paper.

What If I want to Go On To Kamana Two?

Of course we hope *Kamana One* will be only the beginning. If that's so, please check out the end of this book.

The Appendix describes the next Kamana levels and provides details about our full spectrum curriculum.

The second to last page is a registration form. Just send in your registration along with your *Kamana One* Field Pack, and we'll move you on into *Kamana Two* instantly!

Part Two
Nature Awareness Trailhead

Getting Down To Play
〜

THE DAILY ROUTINE

Ready to go? I'd better tell you what we're going to be doing.

The Nature Awareness Exercises

You'll practice some exercises throughout your entire day. We've chosen ones that are easy to fit into any schedule and work place so that you don't have to take any time off from your other commitments for the day.

There will be two different kinds of exercises. The first type are Awareness Games that you can play absolutely anywhere. In the car, at work, making dinner, in a meeting, walking in the woods, waiting for the bus…*anywhere.*

The other type of exercise is still very much a game, but it will require that you sit down and focus on it without distractions. You can do it at night and combine it with your nightly writing, or you can make the time during your day.

The Writing

For each of the 12 days, you'll be taking time every morning to do some reading. The reading will explain everything you need to know for that day and will get you inspired to do it. At night you'll take about 30 minutes to do a little something we suggest and write *briefly* about it. "Brief" is the important word here. We are not looking for literature, only asking you focus your memory and insight.

Every time we ask you to write anything down, we have provided space to do so in this workbook. Please take advantage of it. We tried to make it just the right amount of space so, unless you write with very large writing, try not to go over. If you should happen to need more space, make sure you put your additional paper in this book so you can keep it all together.

If you'd rather type your thoughts, go ahead, but be sure to label where they would have gone in the book.

The Trigger

I want to begin by showing you a trick that will help you to remember to play the games during your busy day. It's very simple: "adopt" a little something that you already do or see many times a day, then use it's alarm call to condition your brain. Whenever you do or see your "trigger" thing, try to wake up into *consciousness* of the game for the day and put your *senses on alert*. These little reminder "triggers," can be anything at all.

I have a few triggers that I like to use, depending on my day. My favorite ones are: a ringing phone, walking through a doorway, hearing or seeing a bird, and stoking the fire in my wood stove. When I am here at the Wilderness Awareness School office, I use the sound of the phone and walking through a doorway. Do you have any idea how many times this phone rings? The phone trigger helps me remember to play my awareness game for the day while not distracting me from my task. When I'm at home or in the woods, I use birds and fire. You can choose anything at all, as long as you know it will actually trigger you. Don't feel like you have to go out and get half a dozen—start with just one.

Whenever I share this idea with people I ask them to get back to me and tell me what their trigger is. I thought you might like to hear a few of them to give you an idea: hearing your name, seeing brake lights in front of your car, flipping a light switch, seeing a screen saver on a computer, hearing the sound of city buses, seeing an airplane. Get the picture? Anything will do as long as it happens to you more than 10 to 15 times a day.

POP QUIZ

1) Where does the water in your house come from and go to? When you turn on that faucet to see the water, where was that same water yesterday? Last week? Last month? When it goes down the drain, where does it go? Where does it go after that?

2) Draw a little arrow on this page that points true North from where you sit and tell me, briefly, the difference between magnetic North and true North and how that applies to you.

3) What plant grows closest to your front door?

4) Write what you remember of the last sentence on the previous page of this book.

5) Name two types of poisonous spiders in your area. What are key identification field marks for each?

6) Why are trees your best friends in a Wilderness survival situation? Name two common trees in your area.

7) Draw an arrow that points to the closest moving water outside your home.

8) Shade in the circle below to reflect the phase the moon is in today.

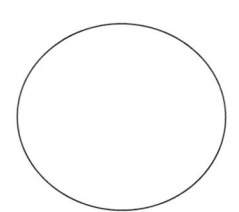

9) Name two birds that look like an American Robin. What are some key differences between them?

10) Name two mammals that look for food within 30 meters of your home.

OK, that's it. Take a deep breath. We'll talk about the quiz again later.

Set aside reading time in the morning and writing/reflecting time in the evening. Everything is self-explanatory. Just pick a place to sit down in the morning and have a pen handy. I'll see you then.

Good Morning!

Day 1

The Morning Session

Good morning and welcome to our first official day together. As you know, you'll be reading for a few minutes this morning to get a feel for what you'll be doing today.

The first thing to do is sit down somewhere nice and have a pen and paper handy. Take a couple of minutes to clear your mind.

Bookmark for Success

Think a bit about what "success" means to you in the context of this program. What do you want to get out of this course? Why are you doing this? How are you going to measure your success? And, most important, how will you *celebrate* it?

Pretend you are not studying Nature yourself, but teaching a friend. Your friend has come to you and said, "I want to learn about birds. I see them at my feeder but I can never see or hear them anywhere else." You're excited by the this opportunity to turn someone on to the beauty and joy of Nature through birding. They've actually requested it! Of course, you gladly accept and start teaching them what you know about how to see and hear birds. Just think of how this can enrich their life! You're invested, right?

After a little while, they come to you very discouraged. You're concerned and think maybe you didn't teach well enough.

"What's the matter? You're still not hearing any birds?"

"Well, yes, I can hear them."

"Great!"

"No, it's not great. I still can't tell what any of them are. Forget it. I'm no good at this."

You didn't foresee this. What do you say to them? How do you encourage them? It's easy to honor other people's achievements, isn't it? It's easy to see how wonderful their progress is while simultaneously looking forward to more growth. It's easy to be patient with a loved one. To enjoy this program and become a better naturalist and tracker, you must show yourself the same patience and support!

One of the best things you can do for yourself during this program is to honor and celebrate your achievements. Congratulate yourself just as you would congratulate your friend for hearing the bird song. Sure, there will always be more to learn. That's what makes it so much fun!. *Do not* measure your success against the naturalist you want to be *in 30 years*. Use those goals to inspire yourself, but measure your success against what you knew and how aware you were 24 hours ago.

Go get an interesting piece of paper somewhere in your house, maybe a card with a picture that's sitting around, or a bit of an old map, or something with unusual texture. Write down the supportive things you would say to your discouraged birding friend on it… Just a couple of phrases that capture how you want them to feel.

Do that now, before you read any more.

This piece of paper will play an important role in this program. Use it as a bookmark to keep your page in this booklet from now on. *Every time you open this book, read what you've written.*

Now, I'm going to give you two things to think about.

Trigger

First, I want you to try to come up with a "trigger" that will work for you for these two weeks. Focus on it. You have a couple of days to figure out a trigger that really works, so just try out a few. Notice *one* thing that happens to you a lot see if it's a good trigger. Does it happen ten or fifteen times a day? Do you notice it? The first step is seeing if your trigger actually triggers you! Pick one or two for today.

Attractions

The second thing is this: Take time to look around you all day today. Pay special attention to things that "capture your attention." They may be big or they may be small. They be natural or not. Some will be "landmarks," the obvious focal points that you use to steer your way through your day. Some may be more private special attractions – things that you always seem to notice as you go through your day. Just try to notice them. When you are "triggered" today, ask yourself "What is *attracting* my attention right now?" or "What am I *paying* attention to?"

THE EVENING SESSION

Were you able to find a trigger that works for you?

Mapping

Now it's time for your "focused reflection" on what you observed today. On the next page, draw a little map. In the center of the page put where you are right now and expand from there. Don't get too detailed on the map. We're only looking for the basics. Include the basic navigating landmarks that may have attracted your attention today—put in roads, stores, open spaces, whatever, but also include some of the little private things that captured your attention. Start pretty small, and keep expanding as far as you can. Don't worry about scale; instead, enjoy mapping the things natural and unnatural that strike you as worthy of including in your map.

As you expand, be aware of what you know and what you don't about the place where you live.

DAY 1 MAP

Name:
Date:

This icon means this is a page you'll be photocopying to send in if you desire a Certificate of Completion. More about this on the final Field Pack form.

Reflecting on Your Experience

Now it's time for you to do some writing. Briefly, in the space below

- Reflect on how the "trigger" exercise went for today. Write down what you decided to use today. Did it work?
- Also, write about how it felt to do the mapping. What things would you like to look for tomorrow?
- Next, write about how it feels to be enrolled in the program. Although it may not feel like you did much today, you did! Take some time to honor yourself and your commitment to this.

Thanksgiving: People

Now, on Day One, I'd like to introduce a practice that we call the "Thanksgiving Address." It's something we learned from Jake and Judy Swamp, members of the Mohawk Nation back East. You may have noticed, we've put the Thanksgiving Address in the beginning of this book because it is known as The Words Before All Else. The Thanksgiving Address is a way to stop, think about, and thank the things that support our life in this universe. The Iroquois People use the address to open every single community gathering and so do we at Wilderness Awareness School. It appears to be a subtle thing, but as time goes on, you will see that it can be a *major* factor in your development as a naturalist and a tracker.

The traditional Address includes language that addresses elements of nature as Beings and recognizes a Creator. This reflects the Iroquois beliefs. We use the Thanksgiving Address because we appreciate the power of gratefulness, and the flow of the sequence, but we have no intention of imposing personal Naming of natural forces on our students. So, please, in these exercises that refer to the Thanksgiving Address, use your own words, your own beliefs.

The address starts by gathering everyone's mind together to be thankful for the people of the world and the fact that we have all made it safely to where we are right now.

So, make a few notes that express your gratitude for **all of the people** in your life. Just take a couple of minutes to express your gratitude for people, on paper, in any way you wish.

After that, read your bookmark one more time and call it a day. I'll see you in the morning.

DAY 2
THE MORNING SESSION

Here's a little story to get you ready for the day...

New Brunswick Gray Fox
by Matt Wild

One of the most important things to remember when studying Nature is that wilderness is not just "out there." It's right here, right now. Even as you read this there are things happening around you, telling you what's happening. Whether it's regarding weather patterns, the neighbor's cat, the raccoon outside, or the sharp-shinned hawk flying overhead, your senses are already doing their job of noticing and recording these things. All we have to do is remember to monitor our senses to find out what they are perceiving. It's that simple.

Internalizing this idea will be an enormous part of your development as a naturalist and tracker. The power of the senses is not to be underestimated. In order to truly take this to heart, we must accept that wilderness is everywhere. I really mean *everywhere.* Studying nature will never be successful if you wait until you are away from people and noise and cars to practice it.

Of course, those places are beautiful and I always look forward to visiting them. However, if I waited until I got there to practice my awareness and internal quietness, I would spend my entire time there just trying to get back to where I left off last time. It took me a very long time to learn this lesson. I understood it and intellectually agreed with it, but it wasn't "inside" me. It took a real slap in the face before I vowed never to forget it.

I was living in New Brunswick, New Jersey, the heart of urbania. From my backyard I could see six other houses, hear two major roads and could always smell the foul city odors. I used to ride my bike several miles to a little organic farm and piece of woods where I would practice my skills. Needless to say, I never thought to look in my back yard for wilderness. After all, it was only 20 by 15 feet or so and was completely fenced in by a little three foot chain link fence.

For three months, I had been walking the same road to work and back home again. I tried to pay attention to what was happening around me, but it was all too easy to "tune out" what my senses were telling me about the people, cars and noise around me. I didn't want to see any of that. I wanted wilderness! I was so far removed from where I was, I would even spend my time walking, day dreaming about some of my favorite places in the woods and how aware I might be someday.

I used to have to be up for work before first light and one morning was delighted to see it had snowed about three inches. I love the snow. On my walk to work, just before sunrise, I saw a set of tracks in the snow. I recognized the pattern, but something didn't make sense. It looked like this:

The tracks were about the same size as a house cat, but this was no house cat. Look at that gait! I got down on my hands and knees and, taking advantage of the street light, could see four claws at the end of four toes. This could only be one thing, but I just couldn't accept it. A gray fox living in New Brunswick? Naw.... I'd been living here for six months and I'd never seen a gray fox. It must be some sort of weird cat, right? Back down on hands and knees. No. Those are definitely claws. And look at that heel pad! It was a gray fox all right! I still couldn't accept it and followed the trail for several hours. (Yes, I did lose my job, but that's not the point of the story.)

This fox wasn't just passing through. It lived in the city. It knew every hole in every fence, which street lights were out, and even where to cross the streets. This was a well used trail and the fox knew every inch of it. What was it eating? I was sure it had to be surviving on garbage, but as I followed, it seldom stopped to check garbage cans or dumpsters. Well, if it was not eating garbage, what was it doing for food? Hunting? No way. What was there to hunt around here?

I couldn't believe the beautiful places the fox trail brought me. An abandoned and boarded up house with rabbits under the porch, a hidden place along a little creek, compost piles and beautiful garden plots with tons of mice. Wow! I guess it was hunting for its food. After following the trail for a while, I came to a place that looked familiar, but I couldn't quite place it. The fox (with me trailing a few hours behind) circled a house on a busy street, ducked inside a familiar row of landscaped arbor vides, hopped a fence behind a garage and landed smack dab in—it's embarrassing to say—my backyard!

Needless to say, I couldn't believe it. I was dumbstruck. This fox had been cutting through my back yard for six months and I hadn't noticed because I was too busy looking for wilderness.

Don't let this happen to you.

Looking for Life

Do you ever find yourself looking high and low for wilderness while forgetting to see what lives under your porch? It's an easy rut to get into, but today we're going to break you of that habit.

The game for today is called "Looking for Life" and it's as simple as it sounds. It's a bit like yesterday's game, but today I want you to take it a step further. Use your trigger to remind you to Look for Life. Any kind of life: birds, trees, mammals, plants, insects, etc. No matter where you go today, really concentrate on finding something alive. Nature is everywhere. Have a good day and enjoy.

THE EVENING SESSION

Thanksgiving: Earth

This time, let's start with the Thanksgiving Address. It will help quiet your mind and put you in a good space for the session. Take a couple of deep breaths, and relax. Last night we thanked the people of the world. Bring your attention to the earth – the ground your gravity is settled on now. Remind yourself of what you know about the earth at your place – its geology, its slopes, and pits, and heights, and soils. How it affects your life. Find in your heart things about the earth that you are really grateful for. If you choose to, you can write as if you were writing the Earth a letter. Remember, you don't have to write too much, just enough to reflect.

Mapping On

Now let's move on to today's record-keeping. Did you find all sorts of new life? "Looking for Life" is a game that I play every single day. Somehow, it always has more to teach me. What did you find? Take 10 minutes (no more than that!) and turn to the map from yesterday and in a different color ink draw in symbols, words, or sketches that indicate the "life" you noticed today.

Oh, by the way, is North marked on the map? If not, go ahead and put it in. Is that magnetic North or true North?

Reflection

Just as you expected, it's time for you to do some writing about today.

- Did your trigger work? Are you happy with the one you chose? (If you want to improve on it, do so tomorrow.)
- Did you find/see signs of life that you had never noticed? I am always humbled to discover new things that have been "hiding" right under my nose.
- Did you find yourself moving more slowly today?

When you're done, read your bookmark one more time and close the book. Tomorrow, you'll need about an hour in the evening. Good night.

Day 3
The Morning Session

Hi there and good morning to you! Today, we're going to expand on our "Looking For Life" game by "looking for detail." But, first, another story:

The CIA Guy
by Matt Wild

When I think of noticing and retaining details there is one thing that comes to my mind before anything else. Strangely enough, it was a man I met at a bus/train station in Philadelphia. I don't know his name. In fact, I don't even know what he looks like. Maybe I should explain.

I spent three months living in Philadelphia, working at a bakery in 30th Street Station, the main mass transit terminal of the city. Essentially, I stood there for eight hours and poured coffee for impatient commuters. I served, literally, thousands of people a day. Very few people ever said "hello" or "thank you," let alone looked me in the eye as I gave them their change. I remembered the ones who did.

Four months after I left Philadelphia (and my spiritually and emotionally fulfilling job at the train station), I got a very, very strange call from my father who lives in Rhode Island. He's a very friendly guy and had gotten into a conversation with a perfect stranger in a restaurant. This stranger worked for the CIA and had just been working at 30th Street Station in Philly.

"Oh, no kidding. My son used to work there." My father loves to find common ground.

Now, hang on to your hat. You're going to have a hard time believing this, but it's the truth. The CIA agent looks at my father for a couple of seconds and says, "Of course! I can't believe I didn't see that. He looks just like you! Congratulations, he's a nice kid."

I'm sure you can imagine my father's astonishment. My dad, however, is a very sharp man with a real poker face when he wants to have it. He pressed this stranger and asked all sorts of questions about me. The man knew my first name, height, eye color, hair color and remembered the little space I have between my front teeth. Now keep in mind, I sold him coffee three times and he hadn't even seen me for four months! He noticed, and *remembered* noticing, that I wear moccasins and even the little scar on my ear that told him I used to wear an earring, but hadn't in a couple of years!

This is too much, isn't it? It gets better. My dad, like any good father, was concerned that a CIA agent knew so much about his son. After the man assured him that he didn't pay any more attention to me than any one else, my father started to play a little game.

My father started asking this gentlemen questions about the things and people behind him. The agent had only had an opportunity to see these things for two to three minutes as he walked in. He answered every single question correctly.

Paying Attention to Detail

A big part of expanding our awareness is in **attention to detail** We don't want to ignore the big picture, but the ability to notice and remember the details of an object can help a tracker in many ways.

Maybe the most obvious example is identifying plants, trees, birds and tracks. If we can remember key items about these things, we'll have a much easier time finding them in the field guide. But it goes far beyond that. Noticing details and things that don't seem significant at the time helps us to become better detectives. It also, somehow, stimulates parts of our brain that help with problem solving skills. We can practice these kinds of skills with anything, or anyone, we come in contact with.

Use your trigger today to practice looking for detail. I hope the story of the CIA guy helps to inspire you today. And, yes, you'll be asked to do some mapping and remembering later tonight. Keep working on that trigger and notice every little thing — and every little thing *about* every little thing that you can!

The Evening Session

Thanksgiving: Waters

As you may have guessed, it's time to add another level to the Thanksgiving Address. But, the first thing I'd like you to write about is how has it made you feel to write what you're thankful for. Are you enjoying doing it? Are you finding that you are feeling more thankful throughout the day?

Now, take some deep breaths and relax. Let's focus on the **waters of the world**. The oceans, lakes, rivers, streams, ponds, swamps, aqueducts, gutters —you name it. Consider, too, the less visible waters— underground, in the air, in the cracks and cells and veins of everything! What would we do without clean water in the world?

I encourage you to write a brief letter to the waters and let them (and the things that live in them and keep them clean) know how you feel and think about them. I'll stress again that this is *not* a religious experience. This is to develop your skills and connection to the world of Nature we are all a part of.

Details Game

After you write your Thanksgiving, we're going to do a little exercise. It will take about 30 minutes, so try to make sure you won't have too many distractions during that time.

What you're going to do, when you're done reading, is close your eyes. With your eyes closed, reach out around where you're sitting and grab six items at random. If your desk looks anything like mine, you never know what you'll get! Just grab them quickly and don't think about it. If you happen to get something that you are very familiar with, put it back. Place all of these items right in front of you. Open your eyes for a count of 10 (count like you're playing hide and seek and don't want to give the "hiders" too much time) and close them again. Push the items out of the way and make sure you can't see them when you open your eyes.

Get out your pen and start answering questions.
- What were the six things?
- Write down all of the colors.
- Which one was farthest away from you?
- Was there a long, skinny one? Which way was it pointing?
- How much do you think the smallest one weighed?
- What was the texture of each of them?

I don't need to go on, do I? Really challenge yourself with this. Keep asking questions—dig deeper and deeper. Make yourself remember.

Try it again with different items. Keep it up as long as you can and see how you feel. If it's at all possible, get a friend to help you with this. Have them pick items that you have never seen before. For obvious reasons, this will really enhance the experience for you. If there is no one else around, just be honest with yourself and really push your limits. If you have to, close your eyes and go to a different part of the room (be careful) and play the game that way. Have some fun.

Reflecting on Detail

Take the rest of the blank space provided to reflect on this exercise.

- Which kinds of details capture your attention?
- Which of your five senses remember detail the best?
- How long can you remember the detail you paid attention to?
- How does it make you feel to know that you aren't noticing all of the things you'd like to?
- Now: this is the big test: Without cheating, what page number is this?

To Look at Any Thing
- John Moffitt

To look at any thing,
If you would know that thing,
You must look at it long:
To look at this green and say
"I have seen spring in these
Woods," will not do — you must
Be the thing you see:
You must be the dark snakes of
Stems and ferny plumes of leaves,
You must enter in
To the small silences between
The leaves,
You must take your time
And touch the very peace
They issue from.

That's it for tonight. I hope you had fun and I'll look forward to tomorrow.

Day 4
The Morning Session

Top of the morning to you! I hope this new day finds you in good health and enjoying lots of happiness. Today's going to be a fun one.

Talbott's Game: Questioning Detail

Today's game is called "Talbott's Game" (Instructor Jonathan Talbott taught it to us) and is, by far, my favorite! I'm happy to share it with you. It's a bit of a combination of the game you played last night and the story of the CIA agent that my dad met. It's very simple...

Throughout your day today, use your trigger to remind you to quiz yourself about your surroundings. When you get triggered, ask yourself any and every question you can think of. Here are some examples to give you an idea:

- Which direction is the wind blowing from?
- What color is the seat you're sitting on?
- What was the eye color of the last person you talked to?
- What color was their shirt?
- Where is the nearest bird?
- What was the first thing you thought of this morning?
- What's the license plate of the car you parked next to?

I think you get the idea. Again, it can be more fun with another person. Playing by yourself will require more will power, but I know you have it in you. Be creative. Talk with you tonight.

Long live the weeds—
Theodore Roethke

Long live the weeds that overwhelm
My narrow vegetable realm!
The bitter rock, the barren soil
That force the son of man to toil;
All things unholy, marred by curse,
The ugly of the universe.
The rough, the wicked, and the wild
That keep the spirit undefiled.
With these I match my little wit
And earn the right to stand or sit
Hope, love, create, or drink and die;
These shape the creature that is I.

THE EVENING SESSION

Thanksgiving: Low Growing Plants

I hope by now you're comfortable with getting into the frame of mind for the Thanksgiving. Tonight, turn your attention to the low growing plants of your world. These include the grasses, mosses, ferns, herbs, so-called weeds, flowering plants in gardens and roadsides and rooftops, the forest understory, the tidal marshes, and all the low bushes everywhere. These are the plants that are accessible to hands and mouths of mammals such as we are, the plants that provide food and healing, cover and shelter for the little beings of the earth. Let's focus our attention on the **low growing plants** of the world: Write a letter to them to let them know why you're grateful for them.

Reflection on Questioning Detail

Well, what did you think about Talbott's Game? Humbled? Proud? Curious? I really hope you had fun with this one! Take a while to write about the experience and how you think you did. Try to answer some questions while you're at it:

What are your best questions?

How can noticing detail benefit a tracker? How can noticing detail benefit you in everyday life?

Is it possible to not see the "big picture" by paying too much attention to detail?

Jot down some notes about your thoughts. Enjoy your night!

Oh, I almost forgot...what color is the ink on the cover of this workbook? How long was Matt Wild's shift at the coffee shop in Philadelphia? Was it Philadelphia or Baltimore? How deep was the snow when he tracked the fox in New Brunswick that morning? How old was Jon Young when he met Tom Brown, Jr.? What year did Matt move to New Hampshire? Hmm...how are you doing?

DAY 5
THE MORNING SESSION

You've been learning to focus for the past couple of days. Now...we're going to start to make the transition from focus on details to a broader perspective. We're going to do that with a little bit of mapping, exploring your area, and a whole lot of fun. You are having fun, aren't you?

From where you are at this moment, which way is North? When you brush your teeth, which way are you facing? When you're at that stop sign down at the corner, which way are you facing? Which direction is the closest running water? Right now, point to the store where you buy your food. Don't just say, "Oh, I get it," and go on to the next paragraph. Stop, take a minute and actually do it. The true test isn't whether you got the answers right, but whether you asked yourself the questions and at least *tried* to figure them out.

For obvious reasons, when we're working on truly knowing where we live (or where we're visiting), these are very important questions to answer. Studying maps is one way to figure it out. Done in the right way, studying maps is not at all like studying algebra and memorizing features. It's more like playing "house" as a child. When I look at a map, I actually go there in my mind. I walk the hills, follow the streams and look for fox dens. I can spend hours sitting and staring at a map. In fact, my maps of my area show worn and dirty trails from my finger that correspond to the trails my feet walk in the woods.

Lost Valley

by Matt Wild

One summer, I was one of the instructors for a Wolf Tracking expedition in the backcountry of Idaho. There were five people in my group and we were out all day long for five days, searching, tracking and journaling. A tracker's dream! We were a long, long way from nowhere, and, for obvious reasons, I kept checking my compass. Because of our addiction to maps, the other instructors and I had been studying the local topographical maps for weeks. When I say studying, I mean *studying*. We didn't just look at them, we pored over them day and night. The maps were tattered and dog-eared in just two weeks from being folded and unfolded so many times. Coffee stains and holes from sparks of the campfire added a nice "broken in" look.

On the last day of our trip, my group decided to explore a hot lead to find a wolf trail we had been trying to locate for the whole week. It was the big missing link to help us find the wolf pack's winter den and hunting route. We had a good idea where it was, and there was just enough daylight to get there and back to base camp. As exciting as it was, there was a catch. A big one in fact—we were going to have to travel about 2.5 miles *off our map*. This would mean that we wouldn't know where to find water, roads, landmarks...anything. We had never been there before and we had no idea what we would encounter. We left shortly after breakfast. (Kids, don't try this!)

We were looking for a place called Lost Meadow. Lost Creek ran through it and it was smack dab in the middle of Lost Valley. Guess what? We got lost. No kidding.

I'm making jokes about it now, but believe me, I was *not* laughing then. This was serious business. I had five long faces looking at me, nine empty water bottles in my backpack and barely enough time to get back to camp before dark. Suddenly, all of my excitement turned to fear. I never told the people in my group, but I was already looking for places where we could build a couple of survival shelters to stay the night. I was, in fact, shaking in my moccasins!

There was only one chance of saving face. I decided we would leave the old logging road we had been traveling and "bushwhack" our way back. That was the shortest distance and, if we went the right way, we would be back to camp before dark and in time for dinner. I had my fingers crossed.

After we had traveled a ways, I left my group to sit and rest for a couple of minutes, then ran to the top of a small hill. I looked around and was delighted to see a hill I recognized! Because we had been paying attention to the directions as we traveled, we had already come back close enough to our "map area" that I could see a hill that was on our map.

Now, keep in mind, I had never been on that hill before. I only recognized it because I had traveled there in my mind. I knew the ridge ran North to South, with the highest point closest to the North. I knew it was a long narrow ridge with a tiny stream (probably from a spring) that ran down the Eastern slope. I knew there was a slightly larger hill just North-West of it. Everything matched up. I knew it had to be the one. I *knew* exactly where we were, and we were back in camp well before dark.

This was only possible because I had taken the time to study the maps. How well do you know your area? I am not asking you to go out and buy the USGS topo maps for your area and study them for weeks. It's a good idea, but honestly, if you don't like to do it, then it's going to be boring. If it's boring, you won't remember any of it anyway, and it's just a waste of time.

Mental Mapping

For today, whenever you're triggered, try to locate yourself in the territory using a "bird's eye view." Think about which way you are facing and what is facing you. Use Talbott's Game to ask yourself questions. For example,

- Where's the sun and what does that tell you about which direction you are facing?
- Where's the nearest hill or body of water? If you're in a city with streets, notice what street you're facing.
- Where is your home from where you are?
- If your car (or bike or bus) broke down, what would be the best route for you to take to walk home?

Just think about what's around you and how important it is to your orientation. Keep doing this all day today and I'll talk to you tonight. Don't forget to set aside a full hour for tonight.

THE EVENING SESSION

Thanksgiving: Animals

Ready to build on the Thanksgiving Address? The next thing we'll direct our attention to is the **animals** of the world: all of the walking, swimming, crawling, digging and slithering kin that we have on this Earth. Consider their variety of skills and tools that we humans learn from. Consider the gifts they give you. Remember particularly the animals whose paths you've crossed today. Write them a letter to tell them, and remind yourself, how thankful and humbled you are to think of them. Let them know that you remember them today and thank them for supporting your life.

Sketching the Mental Map

Tonight we're going to spend the "focus" time on some basic mapping skills. Go to the next page and map out everywhere you went today. Make it a "bird's eye view." Try to keep the map to scale this time and try to orient everything to North, South, East, and West, with North at the top. If you didn't go far today, be flexible and pick a day that you traveled at least a few miles. Make your house small on the map. Include nearby water, roads, farms, buildings; whatever is appropriate. Map out all the roads that you travel. Put the buildings on there, too. Once again, be creative. The more you challenge yourself, the more you'll get out of it. Pretend you are teaching mapping to someone else. Once you think you've put everything on there, ask yourself even more questions. Make it take a full half hour.

Day 5 Map

Date:

Reflecting on Everything

In the remaining time, reflect on your success in combining some "big picture" stuff with the details. We're stretching your mind now and this can get overwhelming. Remember not to get discouraged. "Concentration without elimination" (a great phrase from the poet T.S. Eliot) will not happen for you in just one day. Take it slowly and enjoy the progress that you're making. Are you still reading your bookmark twice a day?

Day 6
The Morning Session

Good morning! I can't even begin to express what an honor it is for me to share all of these teachings and lessons with you. Thank you so very much for doing this.

Today, we're going to build on our "bird's eye view" and learn a new game we simply call...

A Different Way Back

Ingwe, co-founder and Grandfather of Wilderness Awareness School, always reminds us of a tradition he was raised with in Africa, "To walk in your own footsteps means death." He tells us this over and over again. Every time I think I understand it, I learn that there is even more to it.

What does it mean exactly? "To walk in your own footsteps means death." Well, where he was raised in Africa, there are many predators that watch and wait for patterns to emerge. When they know which way you always go, they simply sit and wait for you to come by. This is very helpful information for avoiding encounters with cougars and muggers. There is also a much larger teaching in this lesson.

There are two ways (at least) we can look at the deeper meaning of this lesson. Ingwe always encourages us to think of both. The first is to remember to look at the ground you walk on (not forgetting to look around you, too!). This certainly helps us notice tracks, especially if we take it literally and accept that it may mean our death! So remember this and always make sure you know what you're stepping on.

The other way to think about this is quite different. Never go back the same way you came. This is an important perspective, and I'm going to ask you to think about it and practice it for the next two days. For most of us, with our time restrictions, our roads and sidewalks, this can be rather challenging. But trust me, it's well worth it!

Lost Coffee Shop
(Quite different than Lost Valley)
by Matt Wild

Recently, after spending the night at a friend's house, I woke up early and walked to the local coffee shop. As I was leaving the store, hot coffee in hand, I decided to go back a different way than I came. It was a little town and there weren't many options. Not sure which way I would go, I wandered half way around the building and found a little alley between shops. You know the kind—full of dumpsters, broken glass and loading docks for the store's deliveries. Because I can never resist the opportunity to investigate prime raccoon habitat, I was immediately absorbed in the alley's ecology. What I suspected was the raccoon's nightly trail led roughly in the direction of my friend's house, so I followed it. Through several alley ways I had never taken the time to notice before, holes in fences, a local park (Is that Coyote scat?) and the spaces that would be shadows at night. I ended up just two blocks from my friend's house.

I had fun exploring but didn't realize how much I had learned about the town until a couple of weeks later. I was driving through that same town and traffic was backed up. I can't stand sitting in traffic. Plus, it was taking the time I had reserved for getting coffee. I didn't have time to wait in traffic, get coffee *and* make it to my destination on time. Because I had taken the time to explore prior to that day, I had an advantage. I made a quick right off the main road, cut through the vacant lot and wove my way in and out of the dumpsters and loading docks, parked the car, got a cup of coffee and was back on the road in no time. I actually saved time!

This may seem like a rather insignificant event, but the point is that practicing going a different way is easy, fun and always gives you a deeper understanding of your area. Getting coffee is just a bonus.

This is a great game to play, and I love to share it with other people. Why? Because it's *rewarding*! Seriously, this will only take you a few minutes each day and I guarantee you will learn more about your area than you can imagine.

Just Go a Different Way

It can be anything from going way out of your way and exploring a new "back road" home from work to simply walking on the other side of the street. At home, it might even be as simple as going outside via the back door and walking around the house or apartment. It's important to internalize this idea and make every effort, in the next couple of days, to go everywhere a different way than the way you normally go.

If you have extremely limited options, then find a way to make it "new." For example, when you walk from your bedroom to your bathroom, what do you always look at? If I were a cougar in your house, where would I hide and wait for you? Look at something different - actually force yourself to do it. It may be hard for you to believe, but I assure you that you get stuck in ruts of awareness (or maybe unawareness).

It's when we are in the places that are most familiar to us that we "tune out" and focus only on what we know. If I were a hungry cougar I would have a better chance of catching you off guard on your front doorstep than I would out in the woods. Let's just hope cougars don't figure out how to turn doorknobs!

Remember to have a good time today and *go a different way back!*

The Evening Session

Thanksgiving: Trees

Take a deep breath, and let's reach our senses up a level in the Thanksgiving Address. Let us direct our humble attention to the **trees** All of them, the saplings and the old growth, the natives and the cultivars, the little scraggly trees in the parking lots of the city and the forests on the mountainsides that create their own weather. Let your mind travel upwards along the posture of their trunks and out along the gestures of their arms. Think of their wood and the oxygen they breathe out. They provide so much for all living things and we know we could not survive without them. Think with that feeling of uplifted heart on trees you know and love; trees throughout your life that have made a lasting impression on you. Then take a moment to give them thanks.

Reflecting on the Week

Tonight's writing exercise is kind of an easy one. I know you've been spending a lot of your time practicing and playing these games. Tomorrow is your day off from this, so just relax and take the time to reflect on how you've been doing. Although it might not seem like it, if you've been doing what we're asking you to, you've already learned a heck of a lot!

- Take a few minutes to write about what you did today.
- When did you go a different way?
- What new nooks and crannies did you discover?
- Was it hard, or awkward to change your habits?
- Did you get lost?
- Had you ever really taken the time to get to know your area in this way?
- And finally, how's your trigger working?

Write a bit about it, and have a great day off tomorrow!

Day 7

The Morning Session

Well, hello again. Did you take the day off? It's pretty hard to turn that awareness off once you turn it on, don't you think? That's a good sign! We'll start up again nice and slow. Keep going a "Different Way Back" today and let's hear from Jon Young about things to help us observe Nature in new ways. Try to incorporate these ideas into the Different Way Back mentality.

Go and Ask the Baby
by Jon Young

When I talk to students and apprentices in my travels, I encounter some common threads in the stumbling blocks that slow progress in this training. One of the most common is the belief that what we are doing here is difficult, or that it is so technical that only a few have the skill to "master" the techniques I am talking about. I wish to assure you that what I am asking you to do in this program is extremely natural. So natural that children and babies do them automatically.

Let's pick up where we left off when we were children and babies and exercise our bodies and minds in a most natural way.

Along the way, our mind will rebel with notions of boredom, discomfort and other awareness "Rites of Passage," as I have come to call these aggravating "thought programs" that run when triggered. If you have the ability to ignore these and persist, you will succeed. Your body, deep mind and memory all know how to succeed at breathing, eating, heart-beating and other natural functions. Your body also knows how to sense the natural environment.

To demonstrate the kind of naturalness that lies behind the exercises, and to help set the tone for the kind of approach you may want to take, learn from a baby…

My son Liam was born in the late spring. During his first fall living in the Northwest, we experienced soft rains almost every day. Whenever he got really cranky or cried about something, I only had to bring him outside. The moment his skin and other senses detected the feel of the coolness of the air, the moisture and the feeling of the rain, and the sounds of the drizzle, he would stop crying and tune in. It was simple, yet profound. He loved the outdoors then, and he still does now.

Sometimes we would step off the porch and out from under

the roof to experience the water which would form little droplets on the fine hairs of his arms and face. He would look up into the night and blink a little bit at the drizzle. His hands would reach out and open and search the air around him to sense the rain. He would thoroughly experience the rain.

When he seemed satisfied and calm, which usually only took a minute or two, we would head back into the house. His body would tense, and he would actually lunge back towards the outdoors. He always wants to go back outside if he hasn't gotten his fill. He would sometimes cry again and tell me in that manner that I had not given him enough time for his needs.

We would go back outside and stay until he was satisfied. Only then could we go back in. Sometimes, I would have to let him touch the wet grass, or the bark of a large Douglas-fir in the front yard.

When he grew a bit older and learned to toddle and make recognizable sounds and gestures that told me of his intent, I realized that he wants to be outside all the time. He is simply more comfortable with the sky, earth and grass than he is with the carpets, chairs and counters of a house. He wants out. When we experience wind, he likes to take his hands out and spread his fingers and kind of work them as if he is massaging the air itself. He really likes the wind.

When a bird flies over he gets really excited and almost shouts in surprise and points with his finger, hand and arm thrusting toward the birds passing by. Dogs, other babies and children playing do the same thing for him. He loves when deer are visible, or a frog, or a spider on a web. He can look for very long periods at the things that move and crawl.

He loves to be outdoors. He knows how. The wind is not a source of discomfort for him, it is a sensation to be experienced. The birds are exciting, even starlings and crows. They feed him. He cannot even talk, but he knows how to be natural.

You do too.

What I am asking you to do is to simply allow the baby and child in you to remember how to be natural again. Please have no judgments and remember that "trying" is not necessary here. We are simply being natural in nature. The only reason we need "lessons" is to give us enough excuses to break the patterns that we have developed over the course of our growing up and education that have separated us from our naturalness.

Just Be Natural

Use your trigger to help you remember these ideas today. Excuse yourself from being a grownup when you're triggered, and drop momentarily into baby consciousness. Put your hand in the air to feel the breeze, or let yourself suddenly break into a skip and hop over a sidewalk crack, or stoop down to watch an ant… Let the child in you assert itself.

Get Into the Forests Again
-D.H. Lawrence

When we get out of the glass bottles of our ego,
And when we escape turning Like squirrels in the cages of our personalities
And get into the forests again,
We shall shiver with cold and fright
But things will happen to us
So that we don't know ourselves.
Cool, unlying life will rush in,
And passion will make our bodies taut with power,
We shall stamp our feet with new power
And old things will fall down,
We shall laugh, and institutions will curl up like burnt paper

THE EVENING SESSION

Good evening! I am so glad that you've made it back here safely and we can learn some more!

Thanksgiving: Birds

Today, let's turn our minds to the space in and above the trees: to the birds that so easily draw a child's eye up to the sky. Many cultures the world over say that it is the birds that raise our spirits and remind us of "unseen powers." I know that for me, no matter what kind of mood I'm in when I hear birdsong, I am always reminded to smile. Were birds in your child's mind today? Take the time to think about the ever present wildlife of the sky – the LBJ's (Little Brown Jobs) that twitter and leave their tracks in the bobbing branches they just left, the raucous urban crows and starlings that always seem to play, the waterfowl in flocks and families, and of course the soaring raptors that watch us from the high trees of the roadsides and rule the skies with their stately wheeling flight patterns. Write a brief letter to the **birds** What do you want to thank them for?

Reflecting on Being like a Baby

Did you allow yourself to drop into child consciousness when you were triggered today? Did "cool unlying life rush in?" How far did you let yourself take it? Did you crawl around on all fours at the office? Throw a tantrum? Eat ice cream? Or were you more subtle? Did your friends, family, or colleagues think you were nuts or join in the fun? Jot down some notes on what happens to you and the world when you "escape turning like squirrels in their cages."

Opening Owl Eyes

What we're going to do in the "focus" time tonight is a practice we call "Owl Eyes." You may know a similar exercise that Tom Brown, Jr. calls "wide angle vision," but take your time to do this one over again. Owl Eyes is about expanding your visual perception from a focal point to a wide circle that emanates out from it. It's about learning to concentrate on everything all at once in a quiet, peaceful, open gaze.

We'll start in a very easy way. Find a place where you can stand up and have some room on all sides of you. It can be indoors or outdoors. Make sure that you are not facing anything closer than ten feet away. Hold your arms out in front of you and wiggle your fingers a bit. Keep your eyes focused on something in front of you, but notice that it is easy to see your wiggling fingers. Slowly, move your hands farther apart and don't move the focus of your eyes. See how wide you can spread your arms while still seeing the movement of both hands. Pretty cool, don't you think? Try it again with your hands moving up and down this time. This is the field of vision that your eyes monitor *all of the time*! It's your peripheral vision.

Pretend you are a great-horned owl, or a little screech owl, or whatever owl you want to be. Owls' eyes are stuck in place in their sockets, because they are so big. Pretend you can only look straight ahead.

Notice that your peripheral vision is wide enough to see the sky or ceiling, the stuff to your left and right, *and* the ground or floor at the same time. You can see a whole half hemisphere if you let yourself relax into it.

The exercise is to just sit back and relax and take in everything in front of you as a scene. Just breathe softly, sit very still and let your eyes be like the owl's eyes: still, large and absorbing of all that is in front of you. If you grow tired, close your eyes and rest.

Imagine yourself as a patient, silent and very content owl sitting in the sun with soft pine branches swaying gently in a breeze to lull your mind to peace. Try it for five minutes and come on back, OK?

So, what do you think? Take some time now to write about it.

DAY 8
THE MORNING SESSION

We'll start today with a story about the benefits of Owl Eyes.

Old Brunswick Buck
by Matt Wild

In my writing a few days ago, I mentioned an organic farm I used to visit on the edge of New Brunswick, New Jersey. I really loved to hang out there and watch things happen. There was so much life there! It was as if all of the wildlife that had been in the entire city 200 years earlier had moved into these few acres and agreed to give each other enough space to live. Never before or since have I seen so many mammals and birds of prey living in such close proximity to one another.

On the edge of one of the old farm fields stood a big, old white oak where it seemed, more times than not, there was a red-tailed hawk sitting and waiting patiently for lunch to stir the grasses and give away its location. My favorite place to sit was about 30 yards from the tree (far enough so that I didn't have to hurt my neck to watch the hawk) with my back up against an old and forgotten stone wall, looking out over the field with my legs lying across a red fox trail that ran parallel to the stone wall. On the other side of what remained of the stone wall were the woods: American beech, spicebush, white oak, red oak, black cherry, and many others. And I will never forget—more *Rhus radicans* than you could shake a jewelweed at!

I used to go there and try to catch a glimpse of the red fox. I would get there before dawn and position myself up against the stone wall, waiting for that moment when the fox would come trotting down the trail and hop over my legs. I waited and waited. But that's a story for another campfire. I learned many things while I sat waiting for that fox (which I never saw, by the way).

Every morning that I waited for the fox, a small herd of white-tailed deer would cautiously make their way out to the middle of the clearing (that's where the biggest patch of red clover was) and graze for 30-45 minutes before retreating to the safety of the woods.

I knew, from tracking there previously, that there was a buck in the area also, but I never saw it out in the field. Why not? I couldn't figure it out. I knew that bucks are much more shy than

After deciding that I'd rather track than wait to see the fox, I continued to arrive early in the morning and began mapping the deer trails. I had recently been shown how to tell the difference between the tracks of a buck and a doe. I thought that was just the coolest thing in the world and spent tons of time journaling deer tracks and trying to figure out which was which. Needless to say, I spent many hours with my nose to the ground, dirtying the knees of my pants.

Jon Young had told me over and over again how important Owl Eyes is while tracking. "It's not just Owl Eyes that's important, Matt, it's pretending to be an owl. Actually become an owl in your mind. You can even do it while you're moving around."

Certainly, they were wise words. But I was doing something much more important…I was telling buck tracks from those of a doe!

I got so hung up on the details of the tracks that I began to ignore all other senses and everything that was happening around me. Of course, I didn't notice I was doing this and still nodded in agreement when Jon reminded me to pretend to be an owl.

"Yeah, yeah, I know, Jon. Look at these journals!" I was so proud of myself. I had mapped every deer trail, run and push-down in the area and used different colors for doe and buck trails. Pretty cool, eh?

I discovered that the buck did, in fact, go into the field for the clover, but did so in a different place. He took his time, actually lying down in a greenbriar thicket at the edge of the field and waiting there until he knew it was safe to go out.

One morning I stumbled upon his tracks in some grasses. It was early morning and the grass was still springing back to place in each of his tracks. I looked back at my own tracks doing the same thing. *Oh my gosh! These tracks can't be more than five minutes old! I'm gonna see the buck…I'm gonna see the buck…*, I sang to myself as I moved down his trail. I couldn't wait to tell Jon. Who needed Owl Eyes when you could see tracks and recognize the subtle differences?

After a short distance he began walking on a worn trail and I could see more of the details of his tracks. I couldn't wait to see him. I had been waiting and working for years to actually track an animal to where its foot was still in the next track. Man, was I going to have some bragging rights!

I tracked him for about an hour but could never manage to catch up. I decided that I was taking the wrong approach and should start looking for the subtle pressure releases in his tracks to see which way he was looking, and then I could save some time by cutting him off. Not a bad theory, maybe, but it was way,

way beyond my skill level. Too stubborn to do anything else, I got down on hands and knees and studied every single track. I didn't look at anything else. Of course, I couldn't see any pressure releases, so I spent another hour or so staring at every track, and making notes in my journal.

I tracked him through the thickest of thickets, where it seemed he was hiding from something. I even found a place where he had hunkered down and crawled low enough to leave a belly drag mark! Boy, he was a sneaky one! *I'm gonna see the buck...I'm gonna see the buck...*

I continued tracking him on my hands and knees, being careful not to make too much noise and let him know I was there. I looked at the ground where I was about to place my hand to make sure there weren't any noise makers in the way. Guess what I saw? My own hand print! Humm...that's strange.

For the first time in two hours I looked up to see where I was and remembered the world around me. To make a long story short, I discovered that this darn buck had been circling around, over and over again, in an attempt to lose *me*. I suddenly remembered that I had ears and realized that every bird within ear shot was announcing my location.

Oh...well maybe I'm not gonna see that buck after all. I backtracked my foolishness only to realize that all those times the buck lay down to hide, I was only yards away! He was hiding from *me*! Can you imagine my embarrassment?

I couldn't believe how unaware I had been. I was focusing so much on the tracks that I didn't notice the deer. How's that for not being able to see the forest for the trees? On that day, I vowed to start thinking about this whole "Become an Owl" thing.

I didn't tell this story to make a fool of myself. (Although, I think I did a pretty good job of that, too.) I learned a very valuable and priceless lesson that day, and I hope I can save you from the same mistake.

Using Owl Eyes

Today, when you're triggered, notice: are you paying close attention to something? If you are, open out into a wider "owl eyes" awareness. Look around and listen. This works not only for physical stuff, but for your social and intellectual world as well. If you're staring at a deer track or a computer screen, open up to the buck in the bushes or the activity in the office. If you're tight into a conversation, open up to see the surrounding body language, not only of the person you're talking with, but of others nearby. If you're caught in a thought, open up to its wider context. If you're absorbed in an urgent task, open up to what else important you might better bo doing! Hopefully, in the next two days, you'll be able to internalize "Becoming an Owl" a little bit. Just take it slow and try to "relax into it" every chance you get. Have a good day.

THE EVENING SESSION

Thanksgiving: Weather

As you probably guessed, I'd like you to add some more to the Thanksgiving Address. Let's direct our minds to the **winds, thunder, rain and clouds**. All of these things remind me of new and fresh beginnings. The wind sweeps away, the thunder humbles, the rain washes away, and the clouds protect. I encourage you, once again, to write a brief letter to express your gratitude.

Reflecting on Owl Eyes

So, what did you think of Owl Eyes? This is one of those games that I never get tired of. The better you get, the more room there is to grow. Tonight, I'd like to ask you to *not* just write about what happened when you used Owl Eyes.

- Write about how it made you feel.
- What is it *like* to notice more?
- Does it calm your mind?
- Does it put you more in touch with your other senses, too?

See you tomorrow.

DAY 9

THE MORNING SESSION

Good morning. We're going to be working on a couple of different things today.

The Way You Walk

Today's first exercise is to be conscious of the way *you* walk. Use your trigger to remind you of how you are "holding" your body. How do you sit? How do you stand? How do you travel? Notice which leg you favor and where you hold your tension. Notice if you cock your head to one side or another. If you have a pet at home, imagine it's watching you the way animals watch each other. What would it see about "the way you walk?"

Then, when you've noticed your natural way of walking, Combine this with Become the Owl and you'll be a different person today! When that trigger goes off for you and you are reminded of how you walk, take it one step further. Actually "Become the Owl." Feel the wind in your feathers, the sunshine or rain on your head. Feel your upright posture.

Becoming the Owl

Try it. Walk around. At first, just walk around like you normally do. Don't even think about Owl Eyes. Notice the way your feet hit the ground, the way your legs and body move when you walk. Does your head go up and down? Do you drag your feet or hop from one foot to the other? It's important that you don't try to change any of these things for today. Just observe and get ready to write about it tonight.

After a few minutes of that, relax into your Owl Eyes and walk around some more. Finally, actually Become the Owl in your mind. As silly as this may sound, I want you to go and perch on something in the house. Find a chair, table, counter or couch that will support your weight. If you're uncomfortable at all, pick a place where you can lean your back up against something. Squat down, pick your heels up a little bit and rest your forearms on your upper thighs. Keep your back straight and lock your eyes in place. Become the Owl. Turn your head slowly and look around the room. Remember to relax your eyes—it should not be a strain. After a few minutes of that, walk around the house while you're still an Owl. Go on and have some fun!

Make sure you leave enough time after this morning's exercise to sit, breathe and get ready for your day. Don't ignore this! It's important. Becoming the Owl will make you very, very empathetic to the things around you. If you don't take the time to make the transition to the rest of the day, you'll give yourself an awful headache. This part of the exercise is just as important as any other. I'll talk with you tonight. Remember, you'll need a full hour.

THE EVENING SESSION

Thanksgiving: The Moon

Let's also add one more layer to the Thanksgiving Address.

You may have noticed that the Thanksgiving Address moves your mind from the ground of the earth up through the waters that lie on the face of the earth, through the low lying accessible plants, up along the vertical postures of the trees, into the air where the birds draw our attention, further into the winds and clouds that define our atmosphere, and now we zoom way out into the celestial spheres. Sometimes you can't "see" the moon or sun or stars, but they are always there.

I'd like you to direct your attention this evening to the **Moon**. The Iroquois people say that the Moon "holds hands with" all of the waters, pulling the tides in their daily and monthly cycles, and therefore has a special bond with the women of the world. Many civilizations recognize the moon as a feminine or Yin power, quiet, shining white light, secretive, reflective. I, myself, am always overjoyed to see the moon light my way at night and cast moon shadows. What do you love about the moon? Recall some times when the moon has been particularly compelling, and write your image with thanks.

Reflecting on Becoming the Owl

The faster one goes, the more strain there is on the senses, the more they fail to take in, the more confusion they must tolerate or gloss over, — and the longer it takes to bring the mind to a stop in the presence of anything. Though the freeway passes through the very heart of this forest, the motorist remains several hours journey by foot from what is living at the edge of the right of way.

— *Wendell Berry*

You've been doing these exercises for a while now and Becoming the Owl is a powerful one. Please write about how it affected you today and compare it to yesterday.

- What did you find out about the Way You Walk?
- When were you able to Become the Owl?
- What is the difference between Owl Eyes and Becoming the Owl?

Fox Walking Practice

Tonight's "focus" time will be spent "Fox Walking." No writing tonight, but spend the time practicing this walk. I really love this one. I practice it every day.

Stand up, be still and relax. Let your knees bend ever so slightly and adjust your hips to feel comfortable. Breathe deeply and relax more fully. Lift one foot and use it as if you were trying to find a sharp object on the ground in front of you without stepping down on it. You just sort of tap lightly with your foot here and there before letting it settle down. Pretend you have eyes on the bottom of your feet and make sure you are not going to step on anything.

When you find a place to put your foot down, make sure it is no more than 12 inches in front of your other foot. Place the ball of your foot down first, then your toes, and finally your heel. *You still don't have any weight on the foot at all.* Test yourself by picking it up—you should not have to shift your weight at all. Put it down again in the same way as before.

The next step is to *slowly* shift your weight to that front foot. Pretend you are gliding along train tracks and don't let your head bounce up and down at all. Carefully pick up your back foot and begin the process again. Yes, you will be walking very, very slowly. That's perfect.

Try to do this so carefully as to minimize the sounds your feet make. Move slowly at first, but eventually build up speed. Try to use your peripheral vision and gaze at the horizon while you move along. Be conscious.

Try this now and give yourself as long as you can to keep on practicing. Try it inside first, then give it a shot out in your yard. Have fun with it, then come on back inside.

Write down what you think of Fox Walking. Was it fun? Boring? Challenging? Tell me all about it.

DAY 10
THE MORNING SESSION

I hope you had fun last night.

Let's add one more dimension to how we use our bodies and our movement. Here are some thoughts from Jon Young to inspire you to practice Fox Walking with fox consciousness today.

Stealth
By Jon Young

Have you ever sat in a park and just watched the visitors? You might have noticed that many of them never look up from the ground and that they almost slam their feet against the ground when they walk. Their heads move about on their shoulders because their bodies lean slightly forward as they walk, and they rise on their toes with each step. If there are several people together, they tend to talk to one another rather loudly, since the noise they are making as they tramp along is difficult to hear over. People look down at the path to avoid obstacles. Most animals and birds hide from this commotion, or run for dear life.

From the many talking circles I have lead, I have learned that people believe that if they don't look where they're walking, they will trip. This may seem logical, but it assumes that there is only one way to walk. Actually, there are many. I find that people usually do realize that when they are looking down, they are not really paying attention to what's going on around them, but are thinking about other things. Their minds are busy and their senses are only alert to the most obvious signals. For them, the world is like Sean's—they only see garbage, tree roots, and a few crows, which are always flying away.

Our logo for Wilderness Awareness School is a red fox, gazing at you with "soft eyes"—unalarmed, unconcerned—simply aware of your presence. This is the ultimate goal of every student of nature—to catch a red fox unaware, and to be so at ease in the wilderness that the fox does not bound away in alarm.

Foxes are some of the most acutely aware creatures in the forest. They have to be, for their lives depend on it. Their meals are tiny and quick, and those who prey on the fox are big and mean. When a fox walks along the edge of the forest, he's certainly not looking at his feet, or chatting with his mate about whom they saw at the water hole last night.

It is a simple matter to improve our ability to see wildlife by

It has been said repeatedly that one can never, try as he will, get around to the front of the universe. Man is destined to see only its far side, to realize nature only in retreat. Yet here was the thing in the midst of the bones, the wide-eyed, innocent fox inviting me to play, with the innate courtesy of its two forepaws placed appealingly together, along with a mock shake of the head. The universe was swinging in some fantastic fashion around to present its face, and the face was so small that the universe itself was laughing.

Loren Eiseley,
The Immense Universe

giving some basic thought to our conduct in the field. In order to really see and feel the woods for what they are, you must enter them quietly. Pay attention to the noise that you make with each footstep. After you become aware of how loud you are, it is easy to move with more stealth. Native people tell their children that they should walk as if they were walking on the face of their most revered elder. Indeed, her name is Mother Earth. After doing this for even a little while, the next time you are in the woods with people who are unaware of the commotion they create, you will be astounded at the amount of noise you yourself once accepted as "normal."

Walking with Stealth

Think about Jon's words for the day and focus on Fox Walking with a stealthy approach as much as possible. Whenever you're triggered, check to see if you're out in the full sun in the center of attention, or off in the shadows watching others. Are you talking or listening? Are you making a commotion or being stealthy?

I'll see you tonight.

The Evening Session

Thanksgiving: The Sun

I'd like to ask you to think about the **Sun** The Iroquois people say the Sun is our eldest brother. I've always liked that image. It's amazing to think of how dependent we are on the Sun. Cosmologists say that four and a half billion years ago, the earth and all its elements were created out of its dust. Our days and nights are shaped by it, as are our seasons. Its heat fuels all life, and its light gives us eyes that see. Even in the dead of dark winter, I like to feel the heat in my hand is "harvested sunlight." Have fun writing the Sun your letter of gratitude.

Reflecting on Walking with Stealth

How did Walking with Stealth go today? It's amazing to watch how unaware people are of their bodies, isn't it? Did you feel yourself remembering how to move in this "new" way? Keep working on this and notice how your awareness changes. Jot down some thoughts about it.

- When did you consciously choose to be stealthy today?
- What did you observe about people's walking habits – do they look down?
- What did you notice about sound levels – how they rise and fall with the loudest and quietest noises around?
- Did the effort to be stealthy make you feel like predator or prey?

Jack was bent double. He was down like a sprinter, his nose only a few inches from the humid earth. The tree trunks and the creepers that festooned them lost themselves in a green dusk thirty feet above him, and all about was the undergrowth. There was only the faintest indication of a trail here; a cracked twig and what might be the impression of one side of a hoof. He lowered his chin and stared at the traces as though he would force them to speak to him. Jack crouched with his face a few inches away from this clue, then stared forward into the semi-darkness of the undergrowth...He closed his eyes, raised his head and breathed in gently with flared nostrils, assessing the current of warm air for information. The forest and he were very still....

Then again he stole forward and cast this way and that over the ground. To Ralph, he explained: "In the forest, when you're hunting, not when you're getting fruit, of course, but when you're on your own.." He paused for a moment, not sure if Ralph would take him seriously.

"Go on."

"If you're hunting sometimes you catch yourself feeling as if.." He flushed suddenly. "There's nothing in it of course. Just a feeling. But you can feel as if you're not hunting, but— being hunted, as if something's behind you all the time in the jungle."

—William Golding,
<u>Lord of the Flies</u>

DAY 11
THE MORNING SESSION

Today we're going to give you some fun exercises from Jon Young to develop your senses. Read and play around with each of the following exercises. While you're doing this, you'll be moving around a bit. After you've brought it all together and practiced using all of your senses while moving, you're going to spend the focus time outside, just sitting in one place and engaging each of your senses. You're already used to Owl Eyes, so here we go....

Ears of a Deer

Deer have amazing hearing ability. They can hear so much. How about using that same kind of relaxed and whole view that you practice in owl eyes and just let your ears take in the whole field of sound around you.

Visit the sounds to your left, then in front of you, then to your right and finally behind you. Listen above and below. Listen to yourself breathing. Just let your ears wander. Notice that when you focus your mind on a particular location, the sounds from that direction grow louder. What does it feel like to be a deer with huge ears that can flick in all directions?

Skin of a Baby

Your skin is sensitive again as it was when you were a baby. Just drift into a relaxed state and let your skin speak to you. What do you feel in the way of warmth or coolness. Visit the various parts of your body with your mind and see what you feel.

You will notice all of a sudden that there is a little breeze when you thought there was no breeze. You will notice that you are sitting in a way that makes some part of you unhappy and you will shift your position. Your skin has a lot to say about heat, moisture level and air movement. Learn to listen to your skin. Go from head to toe, again in a slow and relaxed mental journey. You will probably get a nice rejuvenated feeling from this and the other exercises combined.

Pretend you are experiencing the sensations from your skin for the first time. Everything is new and informative.

Nose of the Bear

Bears have an amazing sense of smell. What can you smell right now? Pretend you are a bear searching for something sweet.

Walk around and search the air, slowly swinging your face back and forth as you sniff out the sweets. You may be surprised what you smell.

Do the same now for something smoky, or something with a strong scent of vegetation. See what happens when you pretend you are a bear.

Developing a Taste for Nature

When you tune in to the flavors that are in your mouth, really tune in to them, you will find that there is always something there. Ingwe says that you can taste wood smoke on the breeze, and the coming of rain, and the nearness of salt water.

Your taste buds are linked deeply to your awareness of what is good for you and not. (I don't mean chocolate bars.) When you sit and eat an apple or a carrot, or a slice of rich bread, close your eyes and imagine that you are trying to remember everything about the flavors and textures you're experiencing in your mouth as you eat. Chew the bite you take slow and long, twenty or thirty times, and really experience the fullness of the flavors.

You will notice that "carrot" is actually made up of many different kinds of tastes.

Even when you haven't eaten recently, you will notice tastes in the air and in your mouth. Tune in to these and imagine you are tasting things for the first time.

The Power of the Wolf

Wolves use their eyes, ears, nose and other senses all simultaneously to a great degree. Their eyes, ears and nose are all equally important and equally powerful. They have amazing senses.

This simultaneous sensory power creates a synthesis of awareness in us. If you practice all five senses together, a sixth sense will emerge that seems to be like a combination of all the other senses, yet still separate somehow.

Imagine you are a wolf, listening to the bird calls in the distance, scenting the breeze, feeling the breeze on your fur, ears and wet nose, tasting the air, and gazing into the distance watching for movement—here and there focusing in on a detail or movement.

Move slowly with all your senses engaged. You will find a powerful relaxed calm emerges. Move a bit, quietly and gently. Stop. Look left, right, behind and above. Look ahead again.

Remember to smile. You aren't sneaking, you are exploring and relaxing. This is natural, not contrived. Just have fun. If you feel like moving quickly, do so (just don't make too much of a habit of it). This will be greatly enhanced when you pretend you are some animal or another, or perhaps a child free and happy, wandering the landscape as if for the first time.

Todays Challenge

Today, we won't use the trigger. Instead, several times today, take time out to sit still. Choose anywhere to sit, as long as you're comfortable. Try to stay put at last 15 minutes. While you're sitting in one place, practice engaging each of the senses separately. Then start combining them. While you're in Owl Eyes, add Ears of a Deer. Stay in both of those, then add Skin of a Baby. Strive to have all five senses going at once.

Try to keep yourself comfortable in the beginning and remember to just relax and enjoy them. There is no right or wrong way to do these exercises. You can create variations and just play around with them.

I suggest that you set aside a few minutes in the morning, at lunch, and in the afternoon indoors or out. Especially try to practice them outside as you walk about and stop here and there.

Practice each sense separately for awhile, then start combining them. Strive to have all five senses going at once. Remember to pretend you are the animal in each exercise, or use another animal that better represents the sensory experience for you.

The key to developing the sixth is to add movement while practicing all the other senses.

THE EVENING SESSION

Thanksgiving: The Stars

The last true *level* of the Thanksgiving Address is to think about and thank the **stars** The stars always seem to remind me of how very small I am…how insignificant my problems are. They always remind me of the hope for the future. How do they speak to you?

Reflecting on Using All Your Senses

Write some notes about how this exercise went for you today. Were you able to engage

- Ears of the Deer
- Skin of the Baby
- Nose of the Bear
- A Taste for Nature
- The Power of the Wolf

DAY 12

THE MORNING SESSION

Getting Back to the Basics: Remember, You Already Knew this Stuff as a Kid
By Josh Lane

When you think back to childhood, can you remember playing games like Simon Says? Wasn't it so much fun to try to perfectly match the movements of the other players? Or to try to psyche them out with your movements if you were Simon?

There is a deeply instinctive aspect within people that loves to imitate, and to see others imitating. If you ever get a chance to watch The Great Dance: A Hunter's Story (available from our friends the Foster Brothers, at SenseAfrica.com), you will see how traditional San hunters in the Kalahari use imitation while tracking, to get deeper into the mindset of the animal they are trailing. These trackers really "become" the animals they are trailing, and they use a powerful blend of gesture, facial expression, and imagination - what we call the "storyteller's mind" - to tune into the story of the tracks.

In general, just look at how much importance today is placed on entertainment in the form of movies and television. All these types of media are ways of sharing stories. We thrive on stories, and they inform our day-to-day interaction. Imitation and body language are the building blocks of storytelling, and offer a powerful way to convey emotion and empathy. A good storyteller brings the audience into the story.

In fact, our sensory awareness and social cognitive systems are built on this ability. We each have within our neural networks something called "mirror neurons." These magic neurons are a key to socializing, and also to learning.

Basically, if you see someone smile, your neurons that are responsible for smiling will also fire. Even if you don't crack a full-blown smile, the electrical impulses responsible for smiling will fire on a subtle level, triggering slight muscle movements and perhaps even a shift in brain chemistry. Read Mirroring People: The New Science of How We Connect With Others by Marco Iacoboni if you want to learn more about this fascinating field.

Pretty wild, right? In a sense, we are constantly mimicking and imitating others around us, even on a subconscious level. Deceptively simple, imitation is a power tool for tracking and enhancing connection.

We can consciously engage with this natural tendency to play and mimic as a way to support our deep nature connection journeys. The best part – it's really fun!

An Invitation to Imitate

Today, your mission is to use your trigger to remind you to apply your abilities of imitation to their fullest. Imitation helps you get fully into your senses, and builds your observation skills in a powerful way.

Disclaimer:

That's right, we're giving you permission to unleash one of the ultimate tools in the kid's tool box of instinctive awareness connectors. This tool, however, can either be used like a fine chisel or like a chainsaw. The art here is balance.

The trick is finding the right balance of ninja vs. clown. Being subtle can be useful at times. Your challenge is to combine your imitation ability with your awareness of proper timing and place – and also gift yourself with the space to get fully into the process.

OK. . . Back to Today's Mission:

Perhaps you'll be in the office, subtly imitating the body posture of someone you are near or talking with. In fact, a lot of us already do this, unconsciously, during conversations. Now is your chance to have some fun with it. Note: It's probably better to err on the side of the ninja, when mimicking in the work environment.

Maybe you'll be outside today and hear a bird sound – if you can whistle (or sing), try imitating the bird, even crudely, a few times.

You might see a robin striding on the lawn, searching for worms – ever imitate a robin's halting run? It's really fun! Puff out your chest, head up, beak out, wings back, and let fun (that was a typo; I meant "run," but I had to leave it)!

THE EVENING SESSION

Thanksgiving: Life Energy That Gives Us Vitality

When we look around us, we can see that everything is constantly in motion. Plants are growing, and animals are moving about. Even as you read this, your heart is beating and your lungs are breathing in and out, all without any conscious effort on your part.

Even on a sub-atomic level, small particles of matter and packets of energy are moving around us and through all things. Energy is at work, and something is acting upon and vivifying us in each moment.

We take in this energy in so many ways, from the food we eat and air we breathe, to the rays of sun that warm our skin each day. Take some time now to reflect with gratitude on the various forms of energy that are supporting your life.

Reflection: Imitation

What were you drawn to imitate today?

How did imitation affect your emotions? your senses?

What did you enjoy imitating?

Did this exercise cause you to pay deeper attention to things you might not otherwise notice consciously (facial expressions, body language, posture)? If so, what did you notice?

Day 13

The Morning Session

"Groundhog Day"
by Josh Lane

As we open our awareness and expand into the senses, the patterns around us and within us begin to take shape in our consciousness. Many of these patterns have always been there, of course. Now the light of our conscious awareness begins to shine on them. Hidden patterns become evident, just like footprints that are lit up by the sun in the late afternoon – sometimes it takes just the right angle of light to see tracks that have been sitting there the whole day.

A pattern implies a certain level of order and causation: there is some cause, a need for the pattern to form. When a pattern is repeated, a "rut" or "wear pattern" forms. Sometimes these wear patterns manifest in our physical environment, and offer us fun possibilities for tracking. If you live in a house with an old floor or a carpet that's been around for a while, you can easily start finding wear patterns around your house.

Go and spend five minutes doing this – I bet you'll find worn linoleum or hardwood floor where you stand in front of your kitchen sink, and probably around the refrigerator too. I've even seen buildings with the noticeable grooves of human footsteps worn into the stone stairs, from the passage of thousands of feet over the years. Cat owners may find worn, greasy marks about ten inches off the ground, where their cats are rubbing their faces on the corners of doorways. Go take a quick look around your house right now for any evidence of repetitive wear patterns.

What did you find when you looked for patterns in your house? This is a fun way to track. If you do this outside, you could find a lot of interesting things, too. You might find a smooth branch that a bird lands on over and over. Or, a worn patch on the fence where a raccoon is clambering around each night. Once I found a small oval of smooth dirt in the center of an otherwise well-manicured lawn. Eventually, I found the cause – a pet rabbit that lived outside would use that spot for his favorite place to sit. You never know what you'll find if you start looking.

These kinds of "ruts" can occur internally as well. Sometimes we get into ruts in our day-to-day habits and thoughts; this offers a chance to track ourselves on the inner level. "Know thyself" is the old injunction. If you've ever seen the movie Groundhog Day, Bill

Murray's character ends up repeating the exact same day, over and over, and doesn't know why. He eventually learns to expand his horizons and meets life with a new perspective. Then everything finally changes for him. The more we track ourselves, the better we can understand our own choices, behaviors, and ruts. We can learn more about how to move towards our goals by understanding our inner needs and blocks.

The deep nature connection journey spans this inner world as we discover our own essential natures, and the patterns that have woven into our experience through our lives. With this in mind, today is a chance to track your inner landscape.

Use your trigger today to remind you to pause and observe your inner state. Notice any thought patterns, emotions, and also your body posture each time you remember your trigger. Note any tension in your body. Are you getting into any ruts?

THE EVENING SESSION

Thanksgiving: The Ancestors

Take some time now to reflect on your family lineage, and the story of the greater human family. Ponder the unique histories, aspirations, and traits that have been passed on through your family.

Genetic science is now telling us that all of humanity stems back from an original ancestral lineage, rooting from the San people of the Kalahari Desert region of southern Africa. Since then, the human family has dispersed and diversified around the globe, with myriad cultures arising as the family tree has spread out.

In some mysterious way, all of these unique contributions of your ancestors have moved through time to meld into the fabric of your life, allowing you to be present here in this moment, to be reading this right now.

Reflect back, starting with your most recent known ancestors, and then travel back further, beyond the horizon of time, to ancestors of the distant past, whose names and stories may now be unknown. Remember your link in this chain of life, and that one day you, too, will take a place in the ranks of the ancestors in the minds and hearts of the future generations. Write some words here in contemplation and gratitude of the ancestors who have supported us all to be here today:

Reflection: Inner Tracking

How did your quest to "know thyself" go today?

Did you learn anything new about yourself?

Was it easier for you to observe a particular aspect of your being – thoughts, emotions, or physical attributes? Spend a few minutes writing your observations here.

DAY 14
OUR FINAL DAY

Well, this is it folks—it's our last day.

What I'd like you to concentrate on for our final days is putting this all together: use all your senses at once to see patterns in the whole. Really tuning in to what your eyes and ears and nose and skin are telling you will make you alert to the connections between things in the "wall of green." Putting all your sensory antennae out all at once promotes the use of a particular part of our brains that "ties things together." Uniting all of our senses enables you to see the patterns and tendencies that unfold Natural Mystery.

Here's a story.

Chuck's Woodshed
by Matt Wild

Believe it or not, just as I began writing the paragraph above, a winter wren started calling from outside my house. The morning sun just came over the horizon to turn these Pacific Northwest skies light gray again. By listening carefully, I can tell that the wren is very excited and afraid, and that it's sitting pretty high up in the huckleberry bush growing out of that old cedar stump.

Because I have taken the time to notice before today, I remember that there's a little trail underneath that bush that leads to my neighbor's woodshed. I ask myself, "What would be on that tiny little trail that could really scare the heck out of a winter wren?" Well, the last time I saw a wren that scared, it was because of a house cat. "Ah-hah! Of course! Just a couple of weeks ago, around this time of day, I saw that old feral cat sneaking around my woodpile right near that stump. It's probably heading over to the woodshed. It rained really hard last night so I know that shed is just full of mice."

Makes sense, right? But what if you were sitting with me here in my cabin this morning? We were stoking the fire and heard the winter wren. I said, "Oh, that's just that old gray and white cat. Probably going to Chuck's woodshed." That could seem a bit far-fetched, don't you think? But it's actually very simple and logical and there's nothing magical about it. It's rooted in knowing your surroundings through firsthand experience. It is simply the result of taking the time to walk slowly, noticing what's around us, listening to the birds, asking good questions—and giving ourselves permission to play in the woods.

You can do this in your own yard. What takes shelter under your porch? What comes by your garbage can or dumpster to smell for tasty morsels? Where does the red-tailed hawk hang out near you? And, a very important one for urban, suburban and rural areas alike—where is the closest raccoon to you? Right now, where is that raccoon?

You might not be able to answer these questions right away, and that's just fine. Nobody expects you to, so don't go getting down on yourself if you can't. Don't think for a moment that I could have translated the winter wren's alarm call if I hadn't been living on that same piece of land for a whole year. Not just living there, but exploring, playing, studying and always asking myself tons and tons of questions. It has taken me years to be able to monitor the birds outside with my ears while doing other tasks at the same time, but every single moment of it was fun. I cringe to think of all the messages I miss because I get too wrapped up in my "busy mind."

I only know about that feral cat because I have been walking slowly, listening and sitting at my Secret Spot. Because I have spent hours staring at the maps of my area, exploring the trails (in my mind, on foot and on hands and knees), investigating and scratching my head in frustration many, many times. It took me two months to figure out that the trail from my woodpile went to my neighbor's shed. Then, another eight months to figure out why sometimes there were no mice and other times there were tons.

This is not a process you can rush, but you can chip away at it a little every day. Just be kind to yourself and keep asking yourself questions. They will lead to even better questions. Once, living in Eugene, Oregon, I asked myself, "Where is the closest raccoon?" I found it within a few weeks and followed what I thought would be its trail, the shadows that connected garbage cans, dumpsters and alleyways. It led to an apartment complex next door to my apartment. Within another few weeks, by making simple observations, I discovered that the automatic light next door turned itself off at 2:00 a.m. and the raccoon and her young ones came by at 2:05—every night. Once I saw the raccoons surprise a passing house cat looking for food in the garbage (the cat was looking for food in the garbage, not me). I watched carefully and noticed the way the cat reacted.

Months later I was at a friend's house in Boulder, Colorado, next door to a middle school. It was 10:55 p.m., and I was outside waiting for the moon to rise. A feral cat came running in my direction (not seeing me) and was behaving exactly the same way as the cat who had run from the raccoons. I thought to myself, "I'll bet there's a raccoon over there behind that fence." Guess what?

At 11 o'clock, the automatic light over the school turned off and a big, huge raccoon came ambling out from behind a garbage can (not the fence I thought it would) and crossed the parking lot in the deepest of shadows.

Taking the time to notice, question, study and remember everything that you see and hear will bring you to a place where you can make these "educated guesses" about what's happening. That's all they are, educated guesses. Sometimes you'll be right and sometimes you'll be wrong. But you will always learn something and it is always, always fun to guess and pretend you know.

Looking for Patterns and Tendencies

Think about these things for the day and see what mysteries unfold to you. If you've been living in your place, or taking your route a long time, you've probably already added up a lot of clues, begun to see some "trails that all action leaves around itself." Let your trigger remind you to "tune in" to all your senses. When you put the sights and sounds and smells and feelings together, sometimes, you can suddenly see a pattern emerge.

What patterns and tendencies you see will depend a lot on where you live, and how you travel, as well as on what season it is, and what time of day.

Also some of us are disposed to happen to be interested in different kinds of mysteries. Some will see patterns in the lay of the land – for instance, how the waterways connect throughout the hills and valleys. Some will see patterns in the vegetative communities. Some will look for trails and tracks – evidence of routes people and wildlife take. Some will be weather watchers, noting the shifts in the clouds and winds and humidity. And some of you – those with more time on your hands and dirt in your feet – will be trackers, looking for the who, what, when, where, and how of prints and signs in the dirt.

THE EVENING SESSION

Thanksgiving: The Spirit That Moves Through All Things

The final layer of the Thanksgiving Address for you to write about tonight is what the Iroquois call the **"Creator"** and Stalking Wolf called "The Spirit That Moves Through All Things." No matter what your belief about it, or your name for it, some force seems to unify this world in which we live. A physicist might call it "the energy that dwells in all things."

To tie together all the levels of the Thanksgiving Address, turn your mind to the idea that in our world, everything is hitched to everything, and send your thanksgiving to this amazing natural mystery.

Reflecting on Patterns and Tendencies

Write down patterns or tendencies you noticed today. Take your time and think about it. What you write here will be telling. It will show you what you have a passionate desire to learn more about.

Secret Spot

Our final reading is by Jon Young about what we call the "Secret Spot." A Secret Spot is simply a place to go in the woods, or even your back porch, and sit. It doesn't have to be all that special to start with. You make it special, and secret, by sitting in it—time after time.

The Best Teacher is One Place
Jon Young

People who know me well have heard me give this same answer to many different questions—not because I am losing my train of thought, contrary to what some might say, but because there is truly only one good answer to the many questions about the deep learning of naturalist skills. The foundation is the same for all:

What makes a great naturalist?
What makes a great tracker?
How did they become "natives"?
How did they become good teachers?
How did they become good storytellers?
How can we become great outdoor instructors?
How can we learn to understand the language of the birds?

In one way or another, my answer always contains something of the following:

"Find one place you can get to know really, really well. This is the most important routine you can develop. Know it by day; know it by night; know it in the rain and in the snow, in the depth of winter and in the heat of summer. Know the stars and where the four directions are there; know the birds that live there, know the trees they live in. Get to know these things as if they were your relatives, for, in time, you will come to know that they are! That is the most important thing you can do in order to excel at any skill in nature. Nature and your own heart are your best teachers, but your body, mind and spirit all have to attend class, and do the homework. There is no replacement for this experience!"

One of the most critical elements in the routine of visiting a single place and getting to know one area well is really just taking the time to listen to the wind, to check in with your heart—that is, your feelings—and allow yourself to just be.

Imagining a Secret Spot

For your last reflection, I'd like you write down your thoughts about one place to make your Secret Spot. If you choose to go on to the next level of the program, your Secret Spot will become a very good friend of yours.

On the next page:

- Describe a time in your life when you had a Secret Spot.
- Describe some of the most exotic and wonderful places you've ever been that you'd like to adopt as your secret spot.
- Describe some places not 30 feet from your house where you could enjoy sitting quietly day after day.
- Describe a few real locations that would work tomorrow for your secret spot—places not too far away from home, where you could sit pretty undisturbed, and go to in dawn and dusk; places that maybe include some cover and some open space and maybe a little water.

Secret Spot

Name:
Date:

A Final Request

There's one more thing. We left a couple blank pages in the very back for you to write one final reflection to help us make this course better for the next generation. Please, we would appreciate your thoughts about yourself, your explorations, and how this course worked for you when you send us your Field packet.

Reflecting on the past two weeks

Wait a few days, then look through all you've written here over the past two weeks. Then write a bit about how these two weeks have affected you.

- Did the trigger work for you?

- Which of our stories made a lasting impression?

- What have these exercises done for your sensory awareness?

- What have they done for your consciousness of natural mystery?

- What did you think of the Thanksgiving Address? Have you put all twelve layers together and thought about them as one big thing to be thankful for?

- Will you find a secret spot and practice sitting in it next?

Part Two was designed to represent the whole of the Kamana Nature Awareness Trail. If you choose to go on with Kamana Two through Four, you will experience twelve awareness Field Exercises throughout the duration of the program. Each of these exercises is meant to be focused on for 30-60 days. At the end of each exercise, you write a Field Exercise Reflection paper, which you send in with your Field Pack. You also complete weekly Naturalist Inventories. They are based on the Thanksgiving Address and are designed to keep your awareness focused on many aspects of the natural world on a consistent and regular basis. Exercising your awareness rhythmically over time is the only way it will grow and expand. Each Field Pack includes work from both the Awareness Trail and the Resource Trail.

See the Appendix at the end of this book for a detailed description of Kamana Two, Three, and Four; and a Registration Form to sign up for Kamana Two.

Thanks again for completing this part of the program. It has truly been an honor to write this. We look forward to sitting around the fire with you sometime.

Part Three
Resource Trailhead

Chapter One

Welcome to Resources

Jungle lore is not a science that can be learned from textbooks. It can, however, be absorbed a little at a time, and the absorption process can go on indefinitely, for The Book of Nature has no beginning as it has no end. Open the book where you will, and you will find it of intense interest, and no matter how long or how intently you study he pages, your interest will not flag, for in nature, there is no finality.

—Jim Corbett, *Jungle Lore*

A Note from Jon Young

Every great tracker and naturalist develops over years of practice, skills of keen observation and artful questioning. When a naturalist looks at an unfamiliar plant, or when a tracker looks at the ground or landscape, they pick up a myriad of details in a single glance. Jim Corbett, the legendary tracker of man-eating tigers from India, had the mysterious ability to read the mood of the big cat from its footprints. Tom Brown, Jr., "The Tracker," could decipher the entire story of a junco's dance in the snow.

What these men were both born with was an insatiable curiosity and a never-ending sense of wonder at the natural world. With these essential ingredients, they were able to shape themselves into skilled observers who were keenly aware of the subtle nuances of their surroundings. Through these skills and the burning desire to know, these two trackers achieved the status of living legends, each in his own time.

A tremendous amount of experience and learning went into making these men highly effective "processors of information." The end result of their experience and skill was an ability to make seemingly magical deductions about the world around them.

A hugely important part of their learning was the resources that were available to them. In Jim Corbett and Tom Brown's early years, their resources would have included a respected elder, maybe a field guide or two, and nature itself. Today, we may have to search harder for "nature itself," but we are living in an exciting time in history for resources to study the world of nature. Never before have there been so many good sources of information and wisdom at our fingertips. From books and videos to CD's and movies, a journey into the natural world is ours for the taking.

A Note from Paul Houghtaling

In the exercises that you are working on in the Nature Awareness Trail Head, you are focusing on developing a *keen* awareness of your surroundings. Through the Resource Trail Head, we will focus on developing a *penetrating* awareness, one that links background studies with your observation skills to help you gain a deeper understanding of what you are seeing. Here, you will mine the gold from the Information Age and apply it in a skillful and efficient manner to the study of the natural world.

Field Guides can become a mentor to you. The key lies in the power of your questions. Your questions give you a focus for your attention. That is what this part of the program is about—questioning and research skills that empower your senses to learn deeply.

Along this trail of the course, we will introduce you to *dynamic research* skills for mining resources. Though the times may have changed, the process behind this course is an Ancient way of perceiving and raking in information for you to utilize as a naturalist and tracker.. These routines are refinements on the same way in which Jon Young was mentored as a young man by Tom Brown, Jr. In addition, while the tools have changed some over the years, it was recently understood that the techniques in this course are the same as the ones that Tom was himself mentored with. This course also incorporates feedback from Native peoples from around the world. The lessons behind the words and exercises here are Ancient and common to us all, just reformatted for a Modern era.

If you really want to acquire these skills for yourself, they are available for you here. The reading and exercises have deliberately been made easy and repetitive because we learn best through repetition. Try to avoid the old "I-Know-That-Already-Syndrome." Even if you do know the answer that is being looked for in an exercise, do it anyway, because it is a foundation that will be built upon later, and there may be a lesson behind-the-scenes that may not be obvious.

Anyway, it is all here for you to do. There is nothing left now but to get down to it! Grab your *Seeing Through Native Eyes* tapes, *Reader's Digest: North American Wildlife*, and a cup of tea or coffee. It's time to get busy and take a look at some different hazards that you will need to know about in the outdoors as we take the first step toward exploring natural mystery through native eyes.

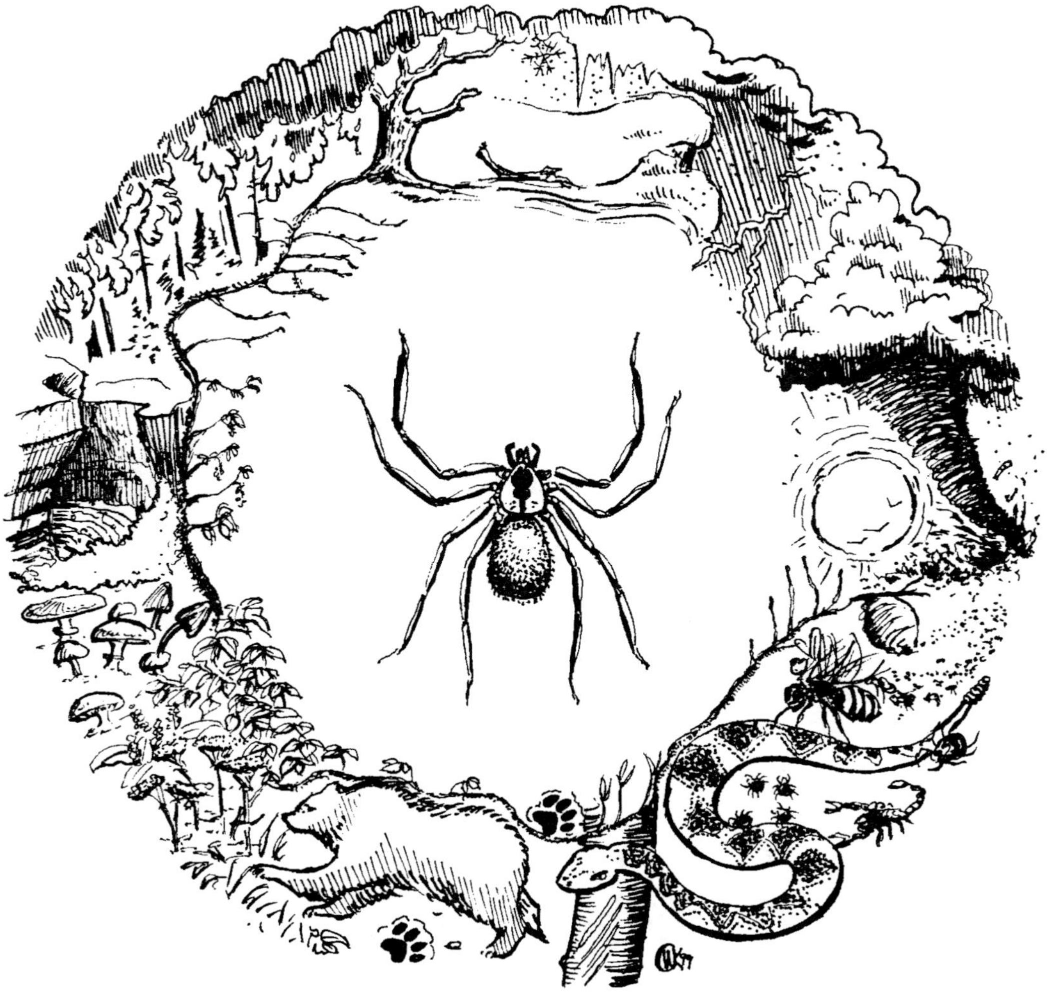

Chapter Two

A Little Bit of Knowledge...

Listen to Disc One of the *Seeing Through Native Eyes* disc series before or while you are completing this chapter.

If a little knowledge is a dangerous thing, no knowledge can be downright lethal—to both human beings and the natural world. There was a time when the human animal knew and respected its place within the natural order of things and had respect for the delicate, dynamic balance maintained among all living things, as well as for potential threats to safety posed by certain fellow creatures. This knowledge and respect have largely been forgotten or ignored by many, with the knowledge of spider bites replaced by the knowledge of sound bytes, and we are much the poorer for it.

For anybody who wants to be an outdoors person, the first things for you to learn about are those things that can actually hurt you. "Actually" hurt you? Yes. There are many things that we commonly believe can hurt us that really pose little threat. There is a lot of misinformation, misconception, and fear surrounding the wilderness. Frequently, it is the things that can pose a real danger to us that give rise to these mistakes. For instance, if something is potentially harmful to children, it will often become an emotionally charged issue for parents and the community. A good example of this is mountain lions that live on the fringe of the suburbs. There is no need for fear of mountain lions to go unchecked, for that can cause more harm than good. Therefore, here we place a strong emphasis on differentiating between the real hazards and the commonly believed hazards—those that exist only in the mind.

It is important that we take a look at those things in our environment which demand our respect for one reason or another—respect, not fear. We often fear what we do not understand, and we only understand what we have come to know on a first-name basis. Even the most fearsome, dreaded creature loses most of its menace when we come to know and understand it in a close and intimate way. Once we have discovered where a black widow spider prefers to live, we will be wary and aware when we visit its favorite haunts. We need not fear or automatically kill this or any other creature without real justification.

Reptiles

Appreciating these animals often begins with a fondness for friendly little lizards or long-legged frogs. And as unknowns become knowns, apprehension is transformed into genuine admiration.

—Introduction to Reptiles and Amphibians
Reader's Digest: North American Wildlife

Reptiles are an interesting—and often misunderstood—group of animals. In many respects, reptiles are very different from people and the furry mammals that we are most comfortable with. They are usually covered with scales or bony plates. They lay eggs. They are also cold-blooded, which gives them behavior that can appear strange as they lie in the open to warm their bodies in the sun. Reptiles include a fair bit of diversity and a wide range of "designs" such as the water turtles and land tortoises, lizards with legs and lizards without legs. There are large lizards and small ones. There are dark ones, bright ones, and those that change colors. There are all manner of snakes, huge crocodiles and alligators, and many other things that fall into the world of reptiles. In the end, however, out of all this diversity, relatively few reptiles in the United States are hazardous. The majority of them are harmless and most are actually beneficial to man. Even the poisonous ones will usually flee without incident if given the chance.

Snakes are one group of reptiles that have traditionally received a bad reputation. Today, in fact, they are becoming more and more scarce. This is due to many factors such as loss of habitat, their habit of lying on warm roadways to soak up the heat, as well, perhaps, as the increased use of pesticides which has led to a drastic reduction in the variety of insects and shelter that once supported snakes. Another factor that has led to their decline is their bad public image. This is a place where you might help: helping people to understand and appreciate snakes and the important role that they play in the world.

In our western mythology, religions, and colloquial expressions, the poor snake seems to have gotten a lot of bad press. It seems that the snake is almost always cast in the role of the villain. The biblical story of Eve and the Serpent in the Garden of Eden is a good example of this. Common expressions portray the snake in a not-so-glamorous light, as well. "You low-down, dirty, rotten sidewinder!" was a favorite way of cursing at someone in the days of the Old West (at least in the movies!). "He's nothing but a snake in the grass!" refers to someone who is thought to be underhanded and a cheater. In mythology, the serpent often represents the Underworld and the realm of demons.

However, native cultures respected snakes and a few tribes featured them in certain religious ceremonies. The Mayan culture built temples precisely aligned with the angle of the sun, so that at certain times of the year, the movement of the shadow cast by the pyramid-shaped structure seemed to cause a great snake to crawl along the temple's side. The Serpent Mound near Louden, Ohio, is thought by some to have been constructed by ancestral members of the Hopi Snake Clan during the course of their migrations. The largest serpent effigy in the world, it is almost a quarter of a mile long and twenty feet wide, depicting a snake with seven curves in its body, its mouth closing around an egg, which is thought to represent the village of those who constructed this great snake.

The Big Black Snake that Almost Killed Grandma
by Jon Young

There is a story in my family that underscores the publicity problem that our snake friends suffer from. My grandmother would tell this story throughout the year, but—like snakes themselves—it was most likely to appear during the summer months.

Back when she was still living on her father's farm, Nanny Bird (as we called her) was sitting outside on the lawn when she heard a fearsome rattling sound under her chair. She looked down and to her dismay saw "a big black rattlesnake, all coiled up and ready to strike."

"A black rattlesnake, Grandma?" I would ask the first few times that I heard the story. "Yes! Black as night!" she would say. Then, as the story goes, she jumped up on her chair and began screaming for help. According to Nanny Bird, a farmer named Jim appeared and valiantly slew the fearsome beast that was about to make short work of her.

I always had a problem with this story because there is no such thing as a black rattlesnake in the part of New Jersey where she lived. I couldn't be so bold as to directly accuse my grandmother of such a mistake so many years after it had happened, though—especially after the story had grown to truthful proportions in the minds of so many in the family who had heard it for so long. This story rested in the back of my mind as an unsolved naturalist's mystery. Did Nanny Bird have a rattlesnake on her farm and in her fright confuse its color? Was it really a black rat snake, which was a snake that was common around the farms of New Jersey at that time? If it was a black rat snake, though, what was the rattling sound that she had so clearly described again and again?

My sophomore year in college, I had the opportunity to work with a beautiful black rat snake. He was a strong six-footer, but was very docile most of the time. He only bit me once or twice and that just served to startle me. After all, a snake like that will only make a scratch.

Early one summer afternoon, I had the rat snake in a carrying box to take to a snake presentation I was giving. It was about 85 degrees and humid—perfect snake weather. I put the case on the passenger seat of the car and drove off. As I was stopped at a traffic light, I heard a rattling sound coming from the snake's box. Now, I had been around snakes my entire life, but for one moment I had to ask myself, "Do black rat snakes rattle? If not, how did a rattlesnake get into my snake cage?"

After thinking a bit, I discovered that there was some dry paper in the back of the box and the rat snake's tail was vibrating wildly against it in a clear imitation of a rattlesnake. This is a defense strategy for the rat snake which causes potentially dangerous animals to be warned off by the "rattle" of its tail in dry leaves. It is very effective—unless, of course, Farmer Jim should come along with a shovel…

Anyway, to end this story, as I drove the rest of the way to the class, it struck me that this was the answer to the riddle of "The Big Black Snake That Almost Killed Grandma." Those many years later, the answer finally came. It was just a large and agitated black rat snake like mine on a hot summer day, doing its rattler imitation—and doing it too well for its own good.

Spiders

Another creature that has historically received a bad reputation is the spider. How many times have you heard when you were younger and at summer camp or some other place that someone woke up from their night's sleep and blamed some strange bump on their arm on a spider that had bitten them in the middle of the night? That never did sit quite right with me. I've often wondered,

"Why would a spider want to do that?" Spiders don't typically feed on the blood of larger animals like mosquitoes do. Instead, they feed on insects that they hunt or trap in their webs. While I need to confess that I don't have a definite answer to this, I still need to wonder: What would cause a spider to crawl onto somebody and bite them without being disturbed or provoked? While spiders do, at times, bite people, perhaps this is just a summer camp myth....

Something else that may have contributed to people's displeasure with spiders is the habit of some types to weave webs in the corners of buildings, shelves, and windows. With age and some household dust, these webs can begin to look somewhat ratty and are often viewed as a sign of poor housekeeping on the part of the person whose home the spider lives in. Upon taking a closer look at one of these webs, though, you will probably find that there are several insects caught in the web—some wrapped in a cocoon of spider silk—that might otherwise be flying about your home.

Spiders in the outdoors do the same thing. Here in western Washington, in the summertime, you can drive down the roads in the early morning while the dew is still heavy and sparkling in the sun and see countless spider webs. They are woven between the phone and electric cables that stretch from one utility pole to the next along the road, and between the branches and twigs in the forests. One can look out across a field of grasses and shrubs and see literally hundreds, if not thousands, of spider webs shining like round diamonds in the sun. Think of all the mosquitoes and other insects that those webs catch! It can really make one wonder how many mosquitoes and other insects there would be, especially in an area as infamous for its "moist" climate as Washington, if it weren't for spiders. After you have finished with this chapter, you may want to look around your own home to see if there are any spiders there. If you find a web, look at it closely. Resting still and patiently in the corner of that web you will probably find the spider that wove it.

Before you go check your home for spiders, however, please remember what I wrote at the beginning of this chapter: "If a little knowledge is a dangerous thing, then no knowledge can be downright lethal." Since there are spiders around whose venom is strong enough to kill some people, you should take this saying literally. Truth be told, out of the many types of spiders in the United States, there are only a very small handful whose venom is strong enough to harm people. What are those types of spiders that you would need to be careful of? Pages 280 and 281 of your

Reader's Digest: North American Wildlife (which we also refer to as Reader's Digest Guide or just RDG) covers common spiders of the United States. Take a moment now to read the section titled "Arachnids" on page 280. In the space below, give the names of all the types of "arachnids" it says are venomous.

Let's focus in now on one type of venomous arachnid. Keep your *Reader's Digest Guide* open to pages 280 and 281 so that you can see the pictures and read the descriptions that it gives. Since the RDG says that they live only in deserts, you don't need to study the scorpion unless you live or spend a lot of time in the desert. The same thing goes for the tarantula, unless you live in the "arid to semiarid areas" of the South/Southwest. For our purposes here, what we are looking for is a creature that is widespread. The map next to the black widow spider shows that it is found across most of the United States, and the description below the picture of it says that it lives in "nearly all land habitats, including houses." This certainly makes it worth getting to know! What about the other venomous spider from your list above: the brown recluse? Take a look at the map that is above its picture. In what parts of the country does the map say it is found?

Interestingly, the map is not quite up to date. Perhaps as a result of its tendency to hide in clothing and the advent of moving vans that can carry people's clothing and belongings across the country, in recent decades the brown recluse's range has expanded greatly to cover most of the United States. Read the section that describes where it lives, too, and you will see that it—like the black widow—is widespread and found indoors as well as outside. It would be a good idea to know something about both of them, wouldn't you agree?

Study the pictures of the black widow and the brown recluse for a few moments. What is a good question that comes to mind about these two? As I am reading in my own Reader's Digest book, here is what I want to know: how can I tell these two apart from other spiders or insects? Mark the page that you are on now and close your RDG for a moment. Can you remember what the illustrations of the black widow looked like? Could you draw a picture of the black widow as it was shown in the book? Without opening your book again, use the space below and make a quick sketch of the picture as you remember it. Don't worry about how good it looks—just give it a go!

Now, open your *Reader's Digest Guide* again and take a look at the picture of the black widow spider. Is there anything that you did not include in your sketch? Doing this myself, what I noticed was that its abdomen is much larger than it appears to be in the picture that I drew. What I did remember to include, though, was that it is shiny and black with a red hourglass shape on its underside. To fine-tune the picture that you drew above, study the picture from your book again, mark your page, close your book, and make any quick changes to your picture of the black widow spider. *Don't be too detailed*, either. This isn't art school!

Okay, that was fairly simple. After all, the black widow's appearance is pretty unique. What about the brown recluse, though? There seem to be an awful lot of spiders around that are brown—how can you tell which one of them might be a brown recluse? Try doing the same thing that you did with the black widow in the space below, this time making a sketch from your memory of the brown recluse (good luck!).

In doing this myself just now, I noticed that in the picture there is a small line with a check-mark pointing to a small dark spot on the brown recluse's otherwise light-color back. In the section of the text next to the picture labeled "What to look for," it said that the head usually has a "violin like" mark. That section also said that the head was "rather flat." That helped me a lot to focus my attention when I was studying the picture. In comparing my drawing with the one in the RDG, though, I noticed that I drew the legs rather short and stumpy instead of long and thin. How does your drawing compare with the one in the book? Compare your drawing for a few moments and then, as you did with the black widow, mark your page, close the book, and update your sketch of the brown recluse spider that you drew above. Once again: Don't be too detailed! When you are finished, keep your book closed and make a few notes next to the picture to highlight some of the spider's unique features that will help you to remember what it looks like. Go back and do the same next to your sketch of the black widow.

How large would you say these spiders are? Are they the same size as one another? How do they compare with the size of the tarantula on page 281? From the illustrations on both pages, it appears that the black widow, scorpion, and earthworm are the same size. Now, in all probability, in real life they aren't all the same size—but how big are they? The description of each spider has a category that gives its actual size. After you've read each description, again mark your page, close your RDG, and now draw a circle below for the black widow, tarantula, and brown recluse that shows the approximate size of each. In addition, relate their size to something common such as a coin. Is it the size of a dime? A nickel? Bigger than a quarter? Write that comparison next to the name for each circle that you draw.

It appears that the black widow and brown recluse aren't very large. In fact, they could probably fit into some pretty tight places. Like I said before, the brown recluse is known to live in the old clothes that people put into storage. The description of where it lives says that the brown recluse can even live under rugs! Where else can they live, though? From reading the description next to the picture, I'm beginning to get the sense that they prefer to live in places that are tight where there might be lots of insects to feed on. The RDG says that they live in "woods and brushy areas in leaf litter and low vegetation; indoors in closets, under rugs, and blankets." A common link between these places does seem to be that they are both tight and likely to have insects for them to feed on. It certainly makes me want to give my blankets a vigorous shaking when I dig them out of the cedar chest to be sure that there aren't any unwanted visitors! Can you imagine some other places where you might encounter a brown recluse? Would a woodpile be a likely place? What about a shelf in your garage? Does it sound as though you are likely to find a brown recluse in a web in the corner of your living room? In the space below, write down a few short notes on where you would imagine finding a brown recluse spider. Do the same for the black widow.

Brown recluse:

Black widow:

Now that we have done all of this, I'm beginning to wonder what is so dangerous about these spiders in the first place. What would happen to me if I were to be bitten by one of them? Would I fall over dead immediately or become paralyzed? Would I be hospitalized while my liver disintegrated, as can happen if one were to eat just a tiny piece of one of the country's poisonous mushrooms? Would I just get a stomachache? Are there spiders that are dangerous only to certain people who might have an allergy to them? As someone who leads workshops with groups of adults and children, that is a question that I definitely want to know. Beyond all of these questions, too, is another question: what do I do in case of a bite from one of these spiders? How do I treat it? Referring to my *Reader's Digest: North American Wildlife*, I've noticed that the answer is not there. Places where I would turn to find the answers to questions would be the health department, medical resource books, and the library. One book that we highly recommend all students at Wilderness Awareness School become familiar with is the Peterson Field Guide to *Venomous Animals & Poisonous Plants* by Steven Foster and Roger Caras. While our RDG may not tell us how poisonous our spider friends are, I do feel that I know the black widow and brown recluse spiders much better, which brings me back to a statement from the beginning of this chapter:

We often fear what we do not understand, and we only understand what we have come to know on a first-name basis.

When we come to understand something in this way, then, what replaces the fear? Some might say empathy, some love, while others might say respect. Whatever it is, it is a healthier attitude and a part of learning to see through native eyes.

AFTER LISTENING TO DISC ONE AND COMPLETING CHAPTER TWO

1. What is the East attribute?

2. What is the natural learning cycle?

3. What is the best thing to teach us common sense?

4. Why are hazards important to learn first?

5. What are some benefits of nature connection?

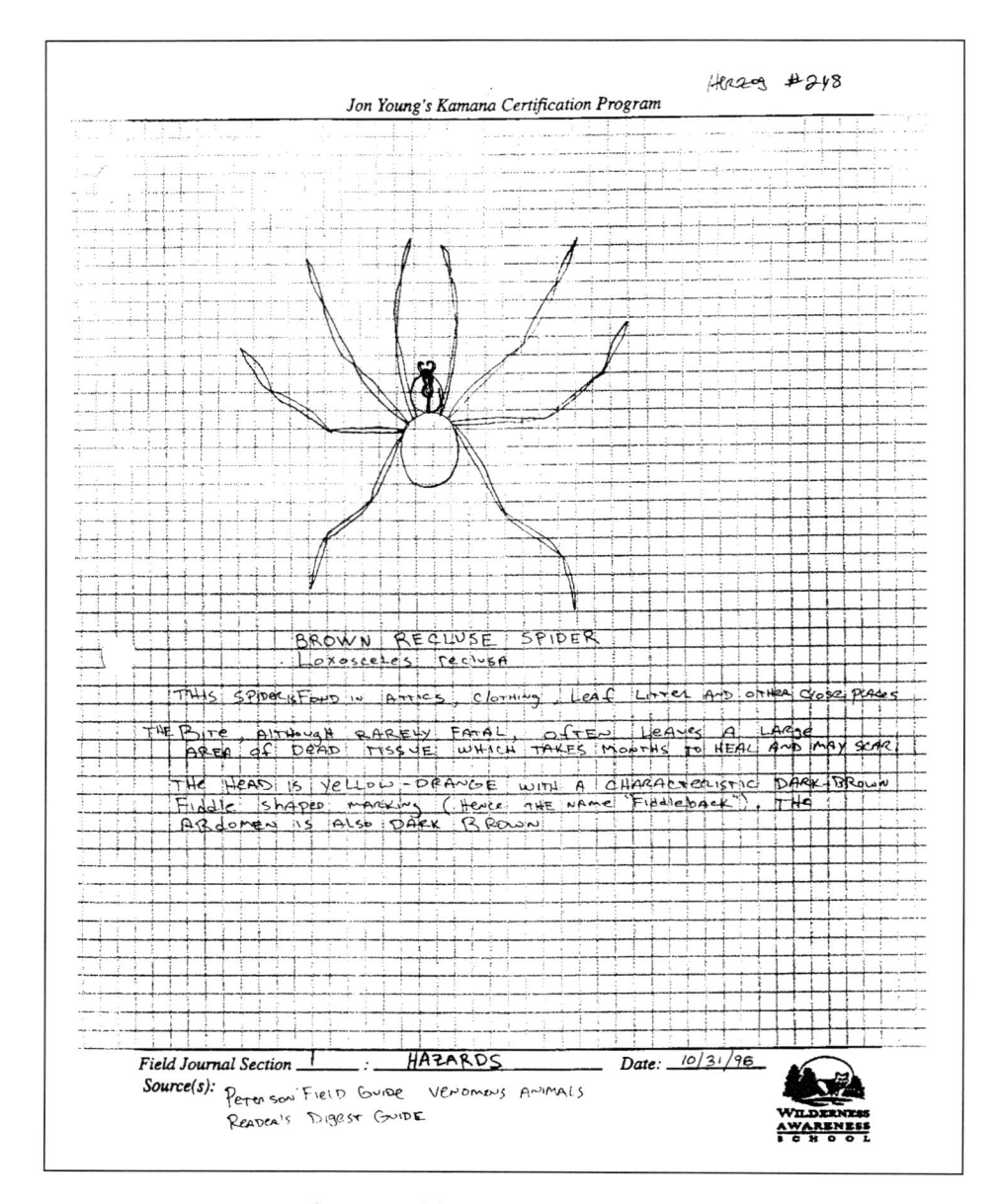

Kamana Resource Trail Journal by Kamana Four graduate Carl Herzog
You'll begin focused advanced journaling in *Kamana Two*.

Create a Hazards journal page. Use your RDG.
Please take no more than 20 minutes to complete.

Name:

Date:

Species Name:

Scientific name:

Source(s):
Reader's Digest:
North American Wildlife

Sketch and color the species

Range Map

Important facts:

KAMANA
NATURALIST TRAINING PROGRAM

Chapter Three

Adventures In The Back Yard...

Listen to Disc Two of the *Seeing Through Native Eyes* disc series before or while you are completing this chapter.

As a kid, I can remember how much fun it was to go to my grandparent's house during the summer time. Both Grandma and Grandpa Smith were avid gardeners, and the yard around their house was always filled with good things to eat. They would send my brother, sister, and me out to collect whichever garden food was in season at the time, or to investigate some mystery from nature in the garden.

Looking back, I can see how these errands gave us a chance to connect with nature in lots of little yet profound ways. It's amazing how something as basic as a garden in the suburbs can provide such a life-expanding experience. Below, I'll share a bit more about the lessons of the garden, and how the "errand principle" can help us to connect with our local ecology.

It seemed as if every summer, just when the New England coast had grown hot and an evening rain was imminent, Grandpa would say, "Listen, do you hear that?" We would listen, hearing a mysterious trilling sound coming from the trees. "Those are my favorite tree frogs. Have you ever seen one? They can change color, you know. I've never known anyone who could find one. . ." With one sentence, Grandpa had given us both a connection with those frogs, and a challenge to seek them out. It took a long time just to figure out where these little ventriloquists were calling from, and much longer to actually spot one.

Beyond the tree frogs, it was amazing how much life there was jammed into that one parcel of land in the middle of the suburbs. In fact, my grandparents' house stuck out like a sore thumb in the middle of the neighborhood – all the rest of the homes had sedate, well-manicured lawns, sparsely planted with a lone maple tree here and there. Not my grandparent's place, though. Since they moved onto the property in the 1950's, they had steadily planted trees, built up the soil with mulch for garden beds, and even gathered unique and rare New England plants, such as the prickly pear cactus, which they continued to propagate and share with their friends. As a result, any trip into the garden (which was really the whole property) was always an adventure.

Along with other birds, cardinals and song sparrows frequented the yard. One spring, I can vividly remember hearing a raucous pulse of tense-sounding bird calls, which I went to investigate. Several bird species were clustered together, all alarming about 20 feet up, positioning themselves in a tight umbrella shape just above a predator in a dogwood tree. It turned out to be a raccoon making the rounds during the nesting season, looking for eggs and nestlings.

Another time, I was walking quietly through the bamboo nursery and almost stepped on a doe that was bedded down for the day. One never knew what mysteries the garden could be hiding. By simply being sent out on errands in the garden, I bumped into all kinds of spontaneous nature connection moments along the way.

Those moments of pure curiosity also make for the most powerful memories, the kind that build a really authentic and lasting sense of place. I'll always have fond memories of that garden and the time I spent there with my family as a child.

Since then, I've come to believe that simply creating the space to "get out there" in nature in an unstructured way is one of the greatest gifts we can give to ourselves and others. Having an errand to accomplish gives us an extra reason to step out the door and open to those connections. The errand may or may not even be completed, yet it opens an opportunity to explore and reach into the greater world of nature. We use this "errand principle" quite a bit in our nature connection programs, with great success.

In the next section, you'll have a chance to go on an errand of your own.

Catchable Critters and Gatherable Super-Connectors:
Berries, Lizards & Crayfish
by Josh Lane

When you were ten years old, did you love to catch critters? Or gather berries? Or jump in mud puddles, play hide and seek, and climb trees? If you spend time outside with kids around this age, you'll notice that these activities instantly generate a lot of enthusiasm.

Jon Young points out this phenomenon in his Reclaiming Our Natural Connection series, and we have to wonder if this kind of behavior is "hard-wired" to emerge at this stage of life. It's almost as if these activities add light to a person's being, or flip an inner switch that turns on hidden resources of vitality and quickness – probably because of how fun it is!

If you feel yourself getting stuck in a rut, and need to get the bounce back in your step, these "super-connectors" are indispensable – no matter how many revolutions around the sun you have experienced.

If you didn't get to do these types of things as a kid, no worries. Now's your chance! We're going to send you on some errands, just like Grandma and Grandpa might do. Of course we fully expect you to get into mischief on the way there and back. This is your chance to go on some adventures of your own.

We've noticed several categories of critters and catchables that are especially effective at opening up this playful energy. We call these the "motivating species." These species cross many kingdoms and genera of the natural world, and it's good to keep an eye out for them in your studies of nature. Of course, from this perspective, you can cross out the word "studies" and replace it with "play and connection." This is important!

Motivating species awaken our inner hunter-gatherer instincts. The sweetness of berries, the thrill of catching a frog or crayfish, and the challenge of climbing a tree – these are all things that awaken our bodies and instincts, and bring us into the moment with energy and enthusiasm. A few sure-fire motivating species that we've identified are:

- Frogs
- Salamanders
- Lizards
- Snakes
- Crayfish
- Fish
- Wild berries

See Coyote's Guide to Connecting with Nature for more about the motivating species.

Another category of motivators include "actionable" things such as:

-climbing trees and rocks
-swimming and finding water sources
-hiding, running, silly games
-throwing rocks and sticks at targets
-building forts and primitive tools, baskets
-anything that engages the body and instincts

PART THREE: THE RESOURCE TRAILHEAD   138

Since the "motivating species" can be found across the board in many different aspects of nature (including animals, plants, trees, and more), you may notice some overlap with what you are learning here with the other chapters of the Kamana Resource Trail. Remember, the key to identifying motivating species is to simply ask, "Does this species enliven my senses? Does it build energy in my curiosity? Is this species something I could easily catch or gather if I were ten years old?"

Use the first list above as a reference, and flip through your field guides to select some local motivating species in your area. Look at the range maps and habitat descriptions to see who lives in your area. Pick at least five different species.

Try to include one local version from each of these categories: one lizard or snake, one frog, one salamander, one local raspberry or strawberry, and one invertebrate. If you can't find anything from one of these categories in your area, do your best to pick something that would motivate you personally to search for on your next adventure.

List your local motivating species here, for now just filling in the species name and including the page number and book title of the field guide(s) you are referencing:

1) Species Name:
Page#
Field Guide:
Major Field Marks:
Habitat:

2) Species Name:
Page#
Field Guide:
Major Field Marks:
Habitat:

3) Species Name:
Page#
Field Guide:
Major Field Marks:
Habitat:

4) Species Name:
Page#
Field Guide:
Major Field Marks:
Habitat:

5) Species Name:
Page#
Field Guide:
Major Field Marks:
Habitat:

Now that you've got a list of local motivating species, it's time to learn more about them. Take a few minutes to look deeply at the pictures of these species in your field guide(s). Close your eyes and see if you can picture each species clearly in your mind's eye, one at a time.

Field Marks:
Could you identify each species in the field, or at least some of the major "field marks" that makes this species unique? Now, go back to your species list above and add in notes on any major field marks that would help you to identify these species in the field. Use your field guides to help you with this. Try to find two or three unique features about each species.

Habitat:
Now, read the descriptions in the field guide about where each species lives. Picture them in their natural habitat in your imagination. Add notes of the preferred habitat for each species onto your list above. Think of places in your local area where you might actually be able to find them.

Putting it All Together:
Draw a picture that includes all of the species you listed in it in some way. Have fun with this!
Looking at the second list, you could include interesting elements of your local landscape in your drawing that you want to explore - maybe a creek, or a good climbing tree. This will help you to get some ideas for fun places to go and motivating species to look for on your next adventure. Put this drawing up over your desk or on your fridge to help remind you about the adventures that are awaiting you!

Let's Take This Outside. . .

So, now what? Time to get outside. Depending on the season, pick something from this list and go search for it on the landscape. Allow yourself time to create an adventure out of it.

Take the long way, allow your curiosity to divert you as you wander to and from your destination, and have fun! In the end it's about connection, so let yourself connect through play and excitement.

Gift yourself with permission to explore as a child would, with senses and imagination open to the possibilities of the landscape. It's okay, too, if you never end up actually finding what you were originally looking for. The goal is to get out there and let your curiosity guide you. We'll be waiting for you with a few questions for later.

(Hint: Don't over think this. Even a walk in the backyard can be an adventure. . . if you let it be.)

Reflection:

What did you choose as the focal point or "errand" for your adventure? Did you find it? Did this adventure lead to any new discoveries?

What happened along the way that connected you with nature? Did you let yourself get dirty, mucky, or splash puddles?

What was fun for you about this adventure? What did you do that brought you more fully to life?

Did anything hold you back? If so, what was it? Could you give yourself permission to do this again in a deeper way?

What could you do for your next adventure?

AFTER LISTENING TO DISC TWO AND COMPLETING CHAPTER THREE

1. What is the SouthEast attribute? Why is this energy important in life? In mentoring?

2. What is a core routine? What are some examples of core routines in nature connection?

3. Why is the sit spot the ultimate core routine for nature connection?

4. Why is so important to share our stories from nature? Who can you ask to be your nature story-sharing buddy?

5. Why is it essential in mentoring to facilitate connection first, rather than immediately imparting information on a subject?

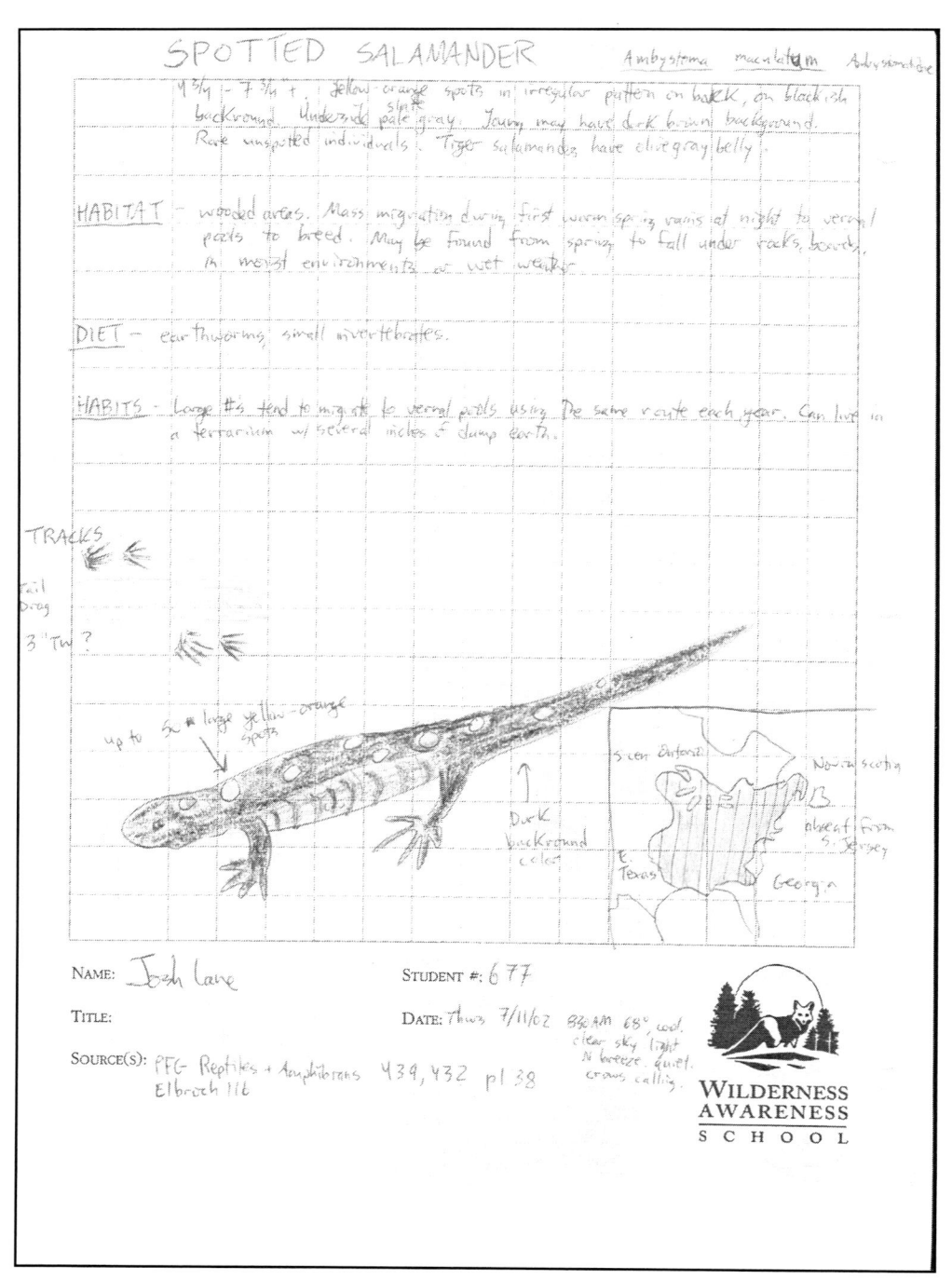

Kamana Resource Trail Journal by Kamana Four graduate Josh Lane

Create a Motivating Species journal page.
Please take no more than 20 minutes to complete.

Name:

Date:

Species Name:

Scientific name:

Source(s):
Reader's Digest:
North American Wildlife

Sketch and color the species

Range Map

Important facts:

KAMANA
NATURALIST TRAINING PROGRAM

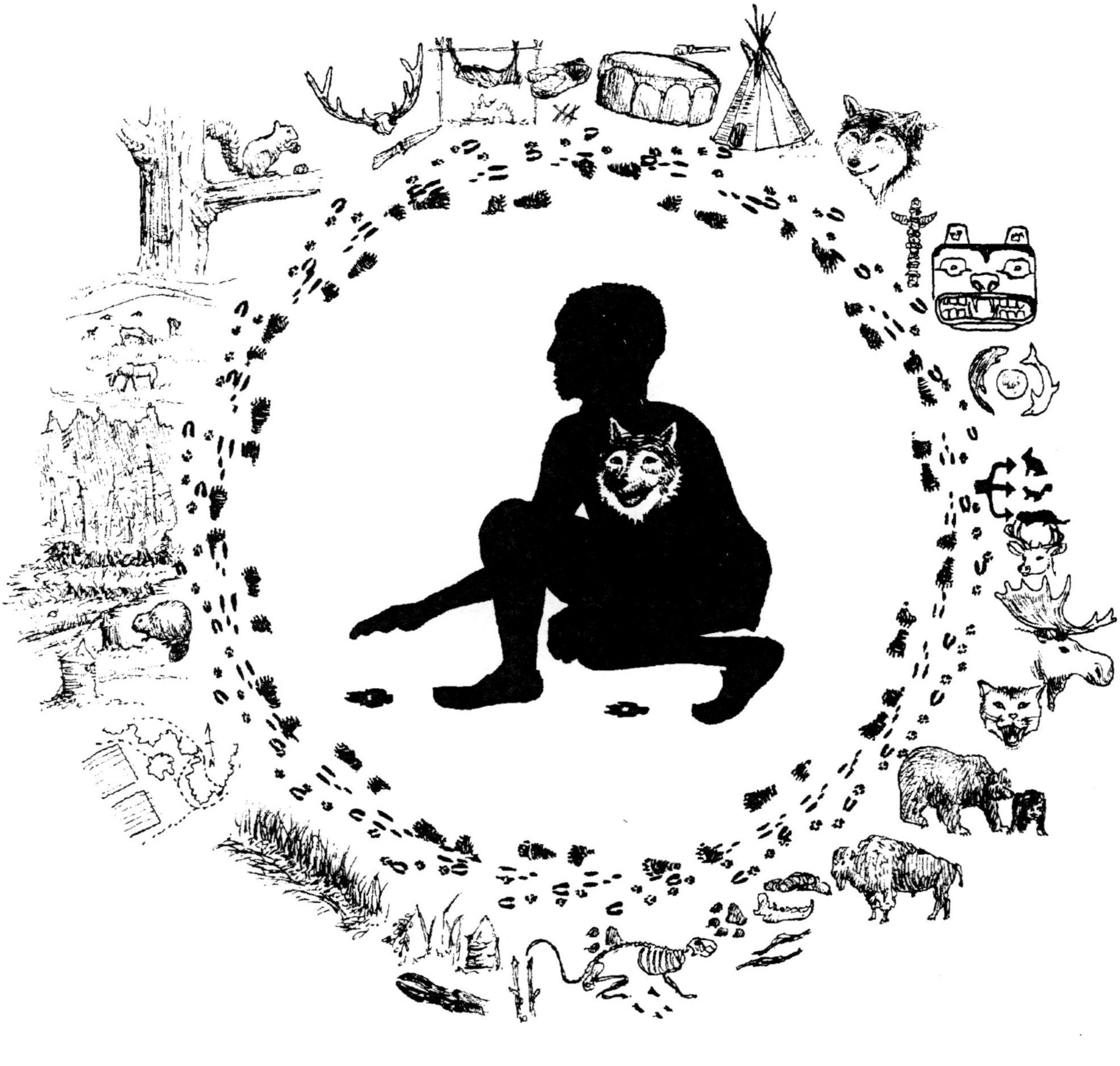

Chapter Four

A Way to See

Listen to Disc Three of the *Seeing Through Native Eyes* disc series before or while you are completing this chapter.

In the world of nature study, mammals may be some of the toughest beings to get to know. For instance, in looking at the study of wolves, Barry Lopez, author of *Of Wolves and Men*, sums it up well when he writes:

> Let's say there are 8,000 wolves in Alaska. Multiplying by 365, that's about 3 million wolf-days of activity a year. Researchers may see something like 75 different wolves over a period of 25 to 30 hours. That's about 90 wolf days. Observed behavior amounts to about three one-thousandths of one percent of wolf behavior (0.003%). The deductions made from such observations would represent good guesses, and indicate how incomplete is our sense of worlds outside our own.

Granted, wolves move a lot, inhabit the wilderness, and are very elusive. There is a real truth to Lopez's words, though, that applies to all other mammals—and, really, all life forms that can move. It speaks to our ability to understand them and their habits: We need to have some way to "see" into the lives of the animals in order to get to know them.

When it comes to observing nature, one might think that birds are harder to know than mammals. After all, birds can fly and therefore have more places to hide, whereas most mammals have to walk where they're going. Believe it or not, birds are actually some of the easiest beings to find and observe in nature, so much so that the most popular participant sport in the United States over the past few years has been bird watching. This is made possible because birds are anchored to specific, limited territories. They also call and sing, traits that help us to know where they are and what they are up to, something that mammals tend not to do.

Perhaps the most helpful aspect of bird behavior to the naturalist, though, is that most birds need daylight to be active. The reasons for this are many, and really just boil down to common sense when you look at them from the perspective of a bird. Flying is difficult and dangerous, as it requires defying gravity, moving at fairly rapid speeds, negotiating wind gusts, and other things that birds encounter regularly that we don't think of. Throw obstacles such as branches, hills, wires, and buildings into the mix, and its easy to see that birds encounter some very dangerous conditions—all while moving very fast. This danger would be multiplied a thousand-fold if birds couldn't see where they were going. After all, if you can't see obstacles, you bump into them and get injured, and birds don't like that any more than you or I would. As a result, *most* birds fly by day.

Of course, not all birds are active during the daytime. There are some birds—owls and a few others—that are the exception to this rule. Take a closer look at the owl, though, and you will notice that it sits *real* still. That's because it has to. Owls may be one of the most elusive animals to study, partially because they are nocturnal, and partially because their slow manner of flight and adaptations for cautious nighttime maneuvering put them at a disadvantage by day. Therefore, owls tend to be secretive to limit their daytime exposure to unexpected and dangerous encounters, and they otherwise lay low until darkness returns.

Many mammals think a lot like owls. They are nocturnal and secretive. They choose the cover of darkness or of the thicket and move with great caution. Within these general tendencies, however, there are variations in the habits of mammals from one type of mammal to the next, and there is even variety amongst individuals. An example of this is deer. Often one will see a particular doe and her offspring together on a regular basis, out in the backyard, a neighbor's field, or along the roadside. While we often see these individuals together, one might wonder—where is the buck? In general, we *never* see the buck, and if we do, which buck are we seeing? Is it the young, inexperienced buck, or is it the old and wise ghost of the forest? The bottom line here is that in order to peer into the lives of mammals, we need a way to observe them.

Tracking is a means to look into the lives of mammals and other elusive animals. There are definite challenges with tracking, however. The first challenge is related to the fact that tracking is a fairly complex language to learn. It requires some background knowledge and a lot of focus and mentoring. It also requires that there be plenty of convenient places to track and time spent actually out there practicing—what many trackers refer to as "dirt time." One first step in tracking is learning to identify tracks in a given area. In order for a person to do this, it is important to know what animals may be found in that place. A large part of the art of tracking is the process of elimination, which is made easier by your background knowledge. For example, tracks are always an indication of the size, weight, movement, behavior, mood, identity, physiology, and direction of the being that left the tracks. When we understand how tracks indicate size, we can say to ourselves, "There are only four kinds of animals in this area that would make tracks of this size."

After that, the list of options becomes smaller and smaller based on your knowledge of the weight, type of movement, behavior, and other aspects of your remaining choices. How quickly you are able to do this depends greatly on your ability to ask questions that will help you to thin out your field of options. As a result, the ability to ask good questions is the tracker's greatest skill.

If there are so many things to consider when learning about mammals, where is a good place to start? A good place to start is with a good book on mammals—your *Reader's Digest North American Wildlife*. Pages 42 through 75 in your book cover common mammals in the United States, from moles to bats to the great mammals of the oceans—whales. One section that will benefit your overall understanding of mammals is the introduction on pages 42 and 43. Go ahead and read it now.

In reading this introduction myself, I've noticed that these two pages are jam-packed with information that is very important for a tracker to consider. I'd recommend that you take some time to read this section a few times to yourself, and make some notes on it in the space below. Once you've done this, I've got something that I want you to take a look at.

"Whodunit?"

I came across these tracks a few days ago out at my favorite local tracking spot.

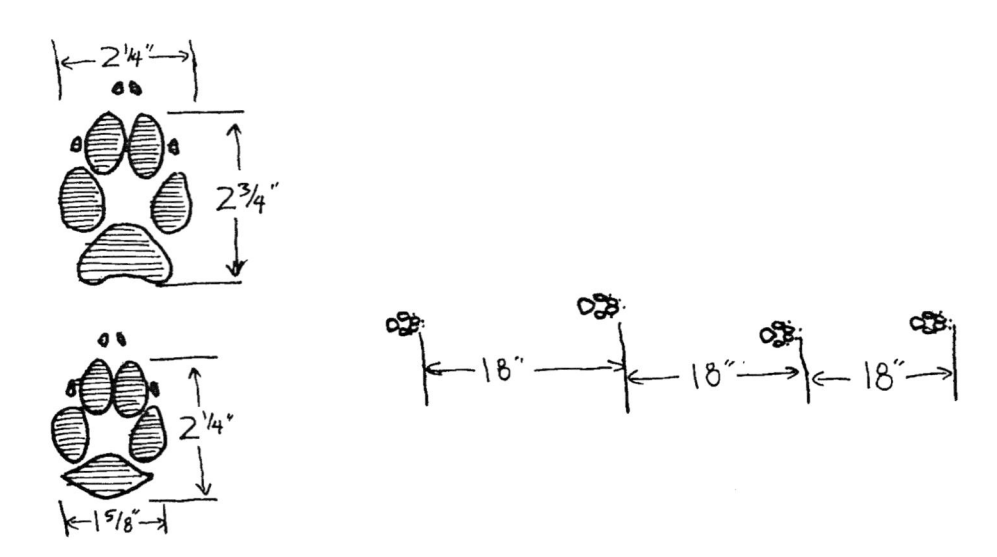

What do you make of them? Take a moment to study the tracks and then, without looking, make a quick sketch of them in the space below based only on what you can remember.

How does your sketch compare with my drawings above? No, I'm not asking for comparison in the sense of it being "good" or "bad." Instead, does your sketch include all of the same features as my drawing? Ask the following questions: How many toes does it have? Does it have a heel pad? If so, how large is it? Are there any marks where claws may have scratched the ground? What I've noticed from my sketch is that the tracks each have four toes, a mark from a triangular-shaped heel pad, and that, yes, there are marks from claws. Compare your sketch and the one that I drew for a moment and then make any quick changes to your drawing to include anything that you may have missed.

Where do we begin to understand what they are telling us? The first question that usually comes to mind is "Who made these tracks?" Now keep in mind that when I said "local tracking spot," I was referring to a place near my own home here in western Washington. There are many mammals commonly found here, ranging in size from the tiny shrew to the enormous elk. Because of the wide range of possibilities, I've found that asking "What type of animal could *not* have left these tracks?" is the easiest way to narrow down my options.

Many of the descriptions of the mammals in the RDG have a small picture that shows what their tracks look like. After you have assured yourself that you have included all of the important features, take the time to compare your sketch above with the tracks of each mammal described on pages 44 though 75. In looking through these pages myself, I've noticed that some mammal descriptions do not include track illustrations. As a result, when you are going through these pages, spend a moment with each mammal, but focus your attention on those that include pictures of their tracks. To help us narrow down our possibilities, even if you think you already know who made these tracks, make a list in the space below of what mammals could *not* have made our mystery tracks. Include on your list the names of only those animals that showed pictures of their tracks.

Obviously, the deer and their relatives can be ruled out as possibilities. Deer don't have toes at all (at least not "toes" as we would think of them). Instead, they have hard cloven hooves for feet. Based on the track illustrations in the RDG, it seems that there are only a few animals with four toes on each foot with claws that show in their tracks: the foxes, coyote, and wolf from pages 62 and 63. Which one is it, though? Here in western Washington, it is possible to find all three. A piece of knowledge about each

PART THREE: THE RESOURCE TRAILHEAD 152

of these animals that helps greatly here, however, is the size of the animal. All three of our options are greatly different in size. Read the descriptions for each of these animals now: the wolf, coyote, and the red fox. We chose the red fox because its range is the broadest of the foxes. Pay special attention to the category that is titled "Length." Once you have read this, mark your page in the RDG and close it. In the space below are three sketches of different sizes. On the line below the sketches, label one of them "wolf," another "coyote," and another "red fox." Base your labeling only on the measurements that you read in your book.

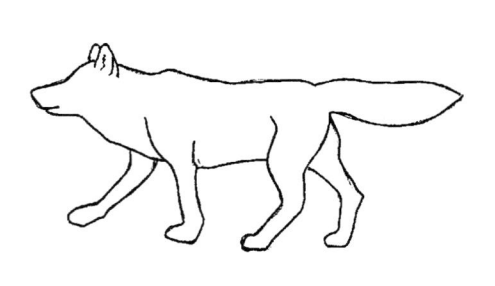

Looking at these three sketches, it is easy to see how different the sizes of these animals really are. Ask yourself this, though: How else are these animals different? Yes, from just glancing at the pictures in my RDG, I can see that the red fox is bright red, and that the wolf and coyote are dusky gray. However, as the following story will attest, identifying mammals is not necessarily this cut-and-dried.

Some time ago, I was on my way home from a friend's house. It was late at night and I was the only person on the road. As I was stopped at a traffic light, the green eye-shine of an animal standing next to an empty lot caught my attention. As I moved toward it, it turned and ran, but not without pausing to take a quick glance back at me. In the dim yellow light of the street lamp, I could see that it was some type of wild dog. It was fairly short—its exact height was not easy to tell because it was still about half a block away. It was a dusky shade of gray with rusty orange mixed in, and had a long tail.

I followed this animal as it meandered down the neighborhood streets, scent-marking trees and sniffing about. It didn't seem too concerned about my presence. The more I looked at it, though, the more I wondered what type of animal I was looking at. Was it a coyote? Was it a dark-colored red fox (the description in the RDG starts by discussing its many different "color phases")? Could it have been a gray fox? I memorized what the animal looked like: gray fur with rusty highlights, reddish legs, whitish throat, and long tail with black on it. When I arrived home, even though it was very late, I opened up my RDG and other field guides to compare what I had seen. I went through the specific features that I could recall—the grayish fur, the rusty legs, the long tail—and checked with each picture in the field guides to identify the animal I had seen.

Now I want you to do the same thing for the three mammals we have been working with: the wolf, coyote, and the red fox. Focus on one of them at a time, and study the illustration first. After a few moments, look away from the book. Can you still see the picture? What does the animal look like? Return to the book again and read the description of the animal and then look back to the picture. Again, take just a minute to study and then mark your page and close the book. Now, return to the sketches above that you labeled earlier and color in the distinctive features for that animal. If you have colored pencils, markers, or crayons, go ahead and use them here. If not, just shade with your pencil or pen and indicate what the colors are. Don't be afraid to change the shape of the sketch to reflect a distinctive feature of the animal. For instance, if the text says that the coyote often has its "tail held between its legs when running," draw that into the picture. Again, do this for the red fox, the coyote, and the wolf. Make some brief notes next to each picture, too, that will remind you of the most unique features of that animal with an arrow pointing to each of those features in the picture that you have colored in.

After spending some time going through this process myself and consulting my roommate on what I had seen, I narrowed my options from three down to two. There were coyotes in our area, but the features did not quite match up, especially given the height of the animal. What type of fox could it have been, though? Looking at the maps for each of my choices in the RDG, neither fox is supposed to be in the area. It seems to be fairly common, though, that range maps are only approximations of the actual ranges of plants and animals. Given this in conjunction with the growth of farmlands and suburban areas that have opened up the dense forests and given animals ways to travel into new areas, it seemed likely that it could be either one of my options. In fact, it was fairly well known that there were red foxes in the area. Gray fox? With further comparison with the animal that I had seen, it turned out that it was indeed a gray fox! What ultimately convinced my that it was a gray fox was the dark stripe on its long tail which, if you compare the pictures yourself in your RDG, you will see that the red fox does not have. Since that time, I've actually seen several gray foxes in the area, as have many others. It looks as though the range maps will need to be updated! To be fair to the range maps, they are just as I said above: approximations of where animals and plants are to be found, and on the whole, they are close enough to help you to realize what animals might be living in your area.

In the maps below, shade in the ranges for each: the wolf, coyote, and red fox. As you have before, first look at the maps in your RDG and then picture what you can remember of each map in your mind. Do this before you shade in the maps below.

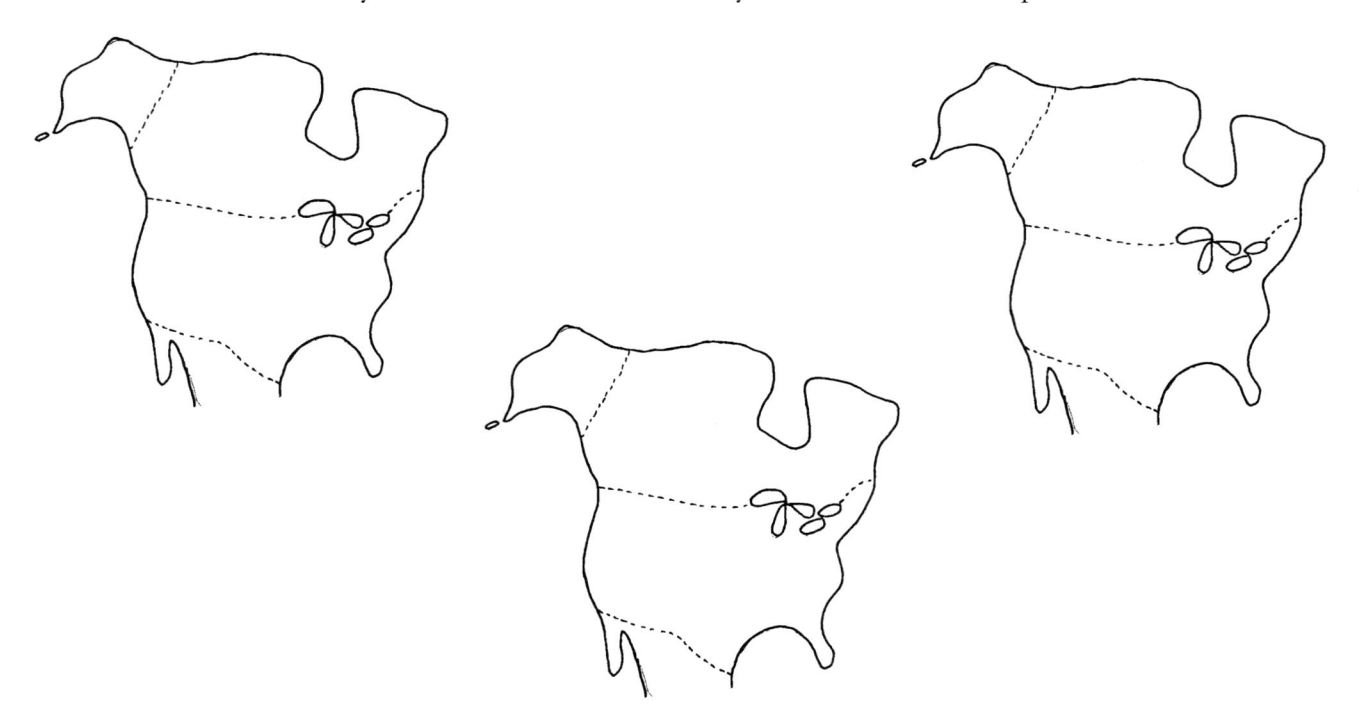

Based on the maps that you've just shaded above, is it reasonable to believe that each of these mammals could be found in your area? Put a light "X" through the maps that are nowhere near the area where you live. For example, if you live in Louisiana, chances are that you won't find gray wolves. As a result, you would want to put a light "X" through the map to signify that it is most likely not something to consider. Since animals do move and can expand their range, however, double check with each animal to see if there are any habitats in your area where they could live. Reading the description of the coyote given next to its picture, I can see that it says they prefer "prairies, open forests, and brush." The map shows that there are no coyotes in the eastern United States, but aren't there open forests and brushy places in the eastern part of the country? There are abandoned fields and hillsides, too, that are grassy like a prairie, so maybe it is at least possible there could be coyotes there. To be sure, go through and read the description for the wolf, coyote, and red fox again. When reading, imagine a setting like each one that it describes and imagine that animal there. As you've done before, mark your page (pages 62 and 63 of your RDG), close your book, and then write some brief notes on the types of places where the red fox, wolf, and coyote live next to their maps that you shaded above.

Wow! This has been a lot of work! Does your head ache a little bit like mine does right now? Believe it or not, though, what we are doing right now is actually preparing ourselves to be trackers by getting to know the animals that we want to track.

When I have worked with people who have studied tracking under various teachers and with various books, I have found their abilities to work with common everyday tracking information hampered by their lack of a naturalist's basic understanding of mammals. Knowing what mammals are found in an area and their ecology, physiology, and other information add up to create the animal's behavior and way of thinking—its personality. Reflect now on what you've learned already about these three mammals that we've studied here: the red fox, the coyote, and the wolf. Through just these few pages of questions and study, you've grown in leaps and bounds in your ability to track on your own. Certainly there is more to learn about an animal: What does this animal eat? When is it active? How much does it weigh? How does its body move? How many young does it have and at what time of year? Since not every animal has good eyesight as people do the question that is perhaps of greatest interest to the tracker is, "What is its most dominant sense, the sense that it views the world through?" Is it scent? Hearing? Maybe it is the sense of touch? Many of these questions may still be found in the descriptions in your RDG. Other questions may require a more specialized source, and for that we recommend two books from the Peterson Field Guide Series: *Animal Tracks* by Olaus Murie, and *North American Mammals*, by Burt and Grossenheider. Both of these sources will serve you well in your quest to learn the language of mammals and tracking.

Speaking of tracking, let's go back to the beginning of the chapter to the set of tracks that started this entire adventure—the mysterious dog tracks. Based on what you've learned so far about the red fox, coyote, and wolf, which one do you think could have made the tracks? Now, this is only a tendency, but the length of a walking stride for a dog is generally a little over half the length of its body. Can you recall how long a wolf is? Referring back to your drawing of the wolf that you did earlier may help. Chances are that the size of the tracks and the distance between each step is too small to be a wolf, wouldn't you agree? The length of the stride for a wolf would be much longer. That leaves us with the red fox and the coyote. Which one do you think made the tracks? Study the length of the stride and compare it to the size of the fox and the size of the coyote. When you look at it in this light, the fox is just too small, which leaves only one animal that makes sense: the coyote!

This is just a beginning, though, and as any tracker will tell you, no story in nature can ever be fully completed by its reader. As the late and great tracker from the Himalayas of India, Jim Corbett, wrote in his book *Jungle Lore*, "the book of nature has no beginning as it has no end." To quote another great naturalist, John Muir, "when you pick anything up by itself, you find it hitched to everything else in the universe." This is the mindset of the tracker, and yet another part of learning to see through native eyes.

AFTER LISTENING TO DISC THREE AND COMPLETING CHAPTER FOUR

1. What is the South attribute?

2. Why is a mentoring culture important?

3. What are the benefits to tracking with other people?

4. What is a holistic tracker?

5. How are using your senses important for tracking? What are some tools of listening that you can use?

Coyote : Canis latrans
(Brush Wolf)

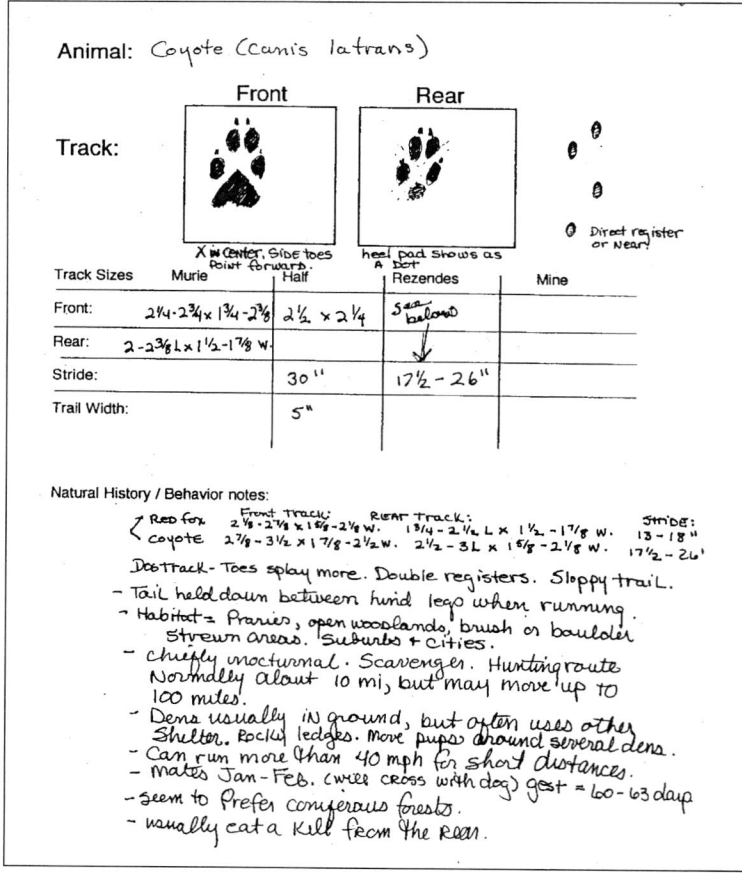

Diane Gibbons

Jon Young's Kamana Certification Program

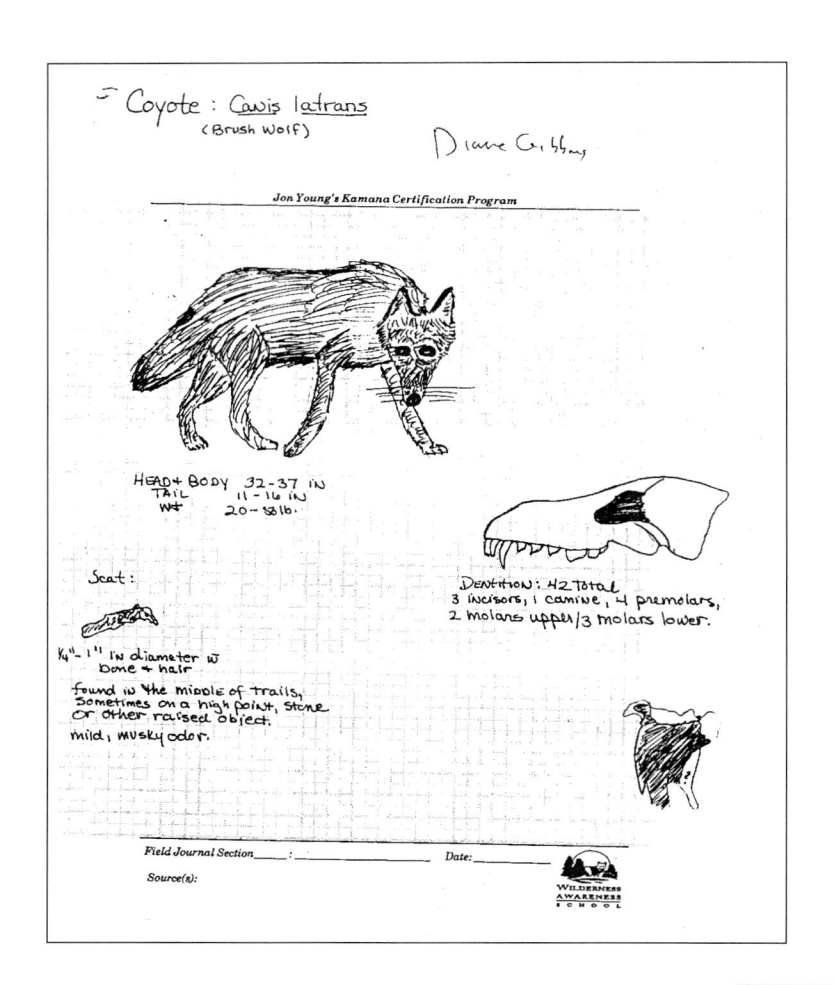

HEAD + BODY 32-37 IN
TAIL 11-16 IN
Wt 20-38 lb.

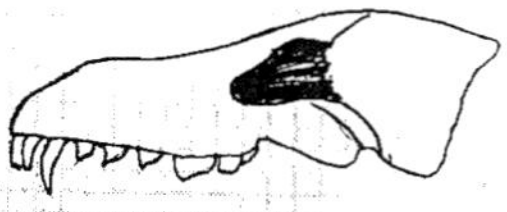

DENTITION: 42 Total
3 incisors, 1 canine, 4 premolars, 2 molars upper / 3 molars lower.

Scat:

1/4"-1" in diameter w bone + hair

found in the middle of trails, sometimes on a high point, stone or other raised object.

mild, musky odor.

Field Journal Section ____ : ____ *Date:* ____

Source(s):

WILDERNESS AWARENESS SCHOOL

Animal: Coyote (Canis latrans)

Track:

Front	Rear	
		 Direct register or Near!
X in Center, Side toes point forward.	heel pad shows as a Dot	

Track Sizes	Murie	Half	Rezendes	Mine
Front:	2 1/4-2 3/4 x 1 3/4-2 3/8	2 1/2 x 2 1/4	See below ↓	
Rear:	2-2 3/8 L x 1 1/2-1 7/8 W.			
Stride:		30"	17 1/2-26"	
Trail Width:		5"		

Natural History / Behavior notes:

	Front Track:	Rear Track:	Stride:
Red fox	2 1/8-2 7/8 x 1 5/8-2 1/8 W.	1 3/4-2 1/2 L x 1 1/2-1 7/8 W.	13-18"
coyote	2 7/8-3 1/2 x 1 7/8-2 1/2 W.	2 1/2-3 L x 1 5/8-2 1/8 W.	17 1/2-26'

Dog Track - Toes splay more. Double registers. Sloppy trail.

- Tail held down between hind legs when running.
- Habitat = Praries, open woodlands, brush or boulder strewn areas. Suburbs + cities.
- chiefly nocturnal. Scavenger. Hunting route normally about 10 mi, but may move up to 100 miles.
- Dens usually in ground, but often uses other shelter. Rocky ledges. Move pups around several dens.
- Can run more than 40 mph for short distances.
- Mates Jan-Feb. (will cross with dog) gest = 60-63 days
- seem to Prefer coniferous forests.
- usually eat a kill from the rear.

Kamana Resource Trail Journal by Kamana Four graduate Diane Gibbons

Create a Mammals journal page.
Please take no more than 20 minutes to complete.

Name:

Date:

Species Name:

Scientific name:

Source(s):
Reader's Digest:
North American Wildlife

Sketch and color the species

Range Map

Important facts:

KAMANA
NATURALIST TRAINING PROGRAM

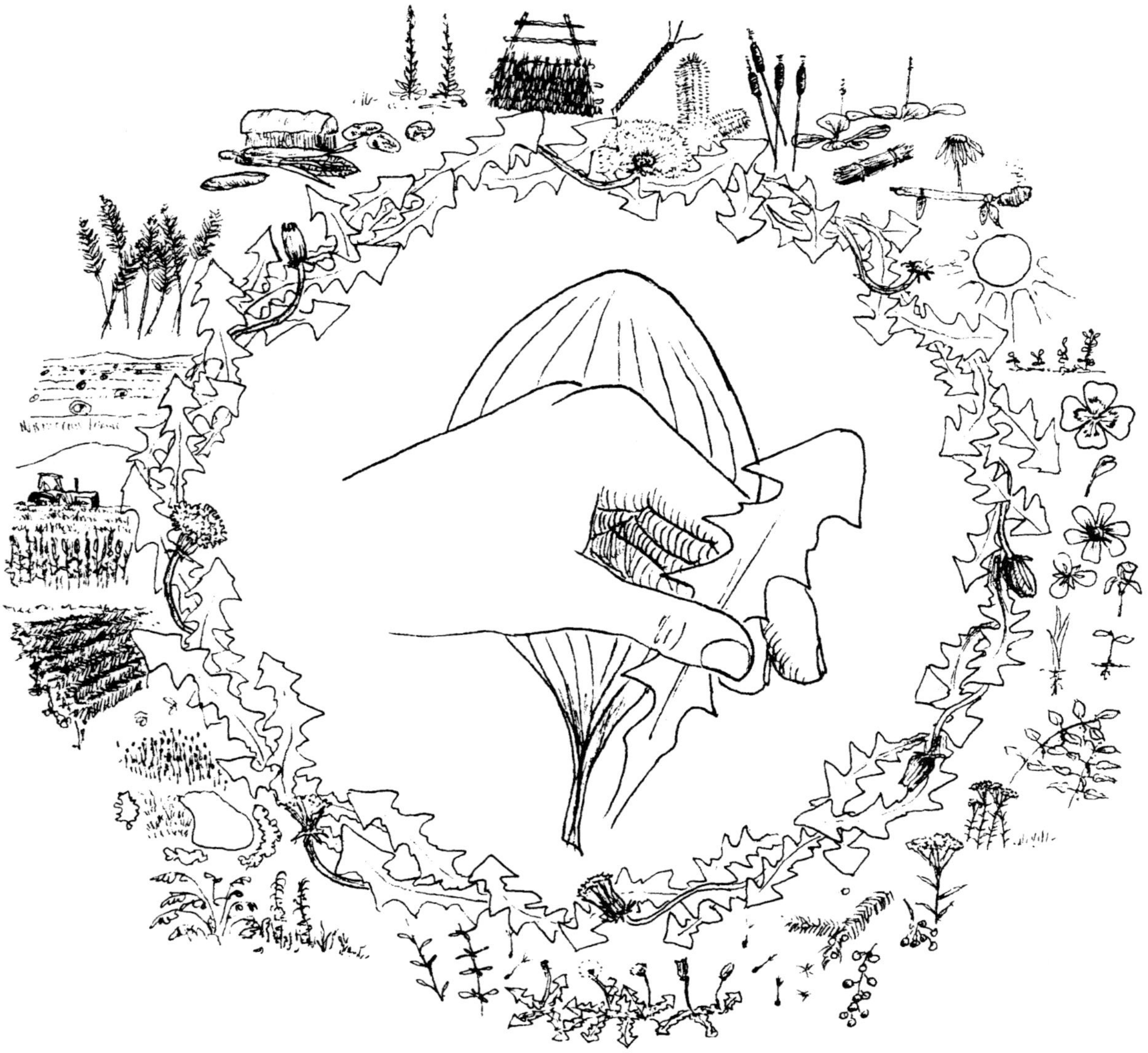

Chapter Five

The Movable Feast

Listen to Disc Four of the *Seeing Through Native Eyes* disc series before or while you are completing this chapter.

One of the most recognized leaders of the Apache is Geronimo. During the 1890's, Geronimo and his people were some of the last to resist the reservation system. In the process, they led the army on a non-ending chase throughout the American Southwest that lasted for over 18 months. When it ended, the only reason Geronimo surrendered to the U.S. Cavalry was the fact that the army had captured some of the women and children from the families of Geronimo and the men he traveled with. If it were not for this leverage, perhaps it is possible that they would still be out there.

When Geronimo and his men made their stand against the U.S. Army, what allowed them to beat such odds for so long? The army had sent its best general in field tactics along with its best soldiers, who were armed with the army's best artillery and their best horses. All of these forces were in pursuit of Geronimo, who was on foot with bows and arrows and only a handful of men, with their families hidden away to keep them out of danger's path. The army had Comanches, and even some Apaches, to scout ahead of them in search of evidence of where Geronimo and his men had gone. Often they would follow Geronimo's trail to his campsite and feel where he and his men had slept the night before—only to find that the ground was cold. They were gone. Whereas the previous day the army had been only five hours behind Geronimo, today—even on horseback—they were ten hours behind. The army would send their scouts ahead once again and ride hard all day—only to find at Geronimo's next campsite that they were now *fifteen* hours behind.

What was going on? For one thing Geronimo and his men had spent a lifetime learning everything about the land. It was said that Geronimo knew the animals so well that he could use their strategies as his own. He and his men would hide in the same thickets as the deer. They would seek places with a clear view like the goats. He would adapt his running style to match that of the coyote, which moved straight as an arrow and would eat up the miles at a surprising speed.

More than these things, however, Geronimo and his men knew how to literally eat on the run. They were able to pick this handful of leaves, that bunch of seeds, scoop up a couple of something else, and just munch as they ran. Talk about fast food! They never built a fire or so much as set up a shelter, instead sleeping in the open so that they could be off on a moment's notice, running again at that slow, efficient coyote-trot—walking, trotting, walking, and trotting some more. They could cover a lot of country this way. While they did this, the cavalry men on horseback had to stop, build fires, set up tents, unpack all of their provisions, cook their food, and care for their horses—and then pack everything up again in the morning and resume their pursuit.

It was this knowledge of the animals, the plants, and the landscape of their area that helped Geronimo and his handful of men elude over 5,000 of the army's finest for over a year and a half. In addition, these same traits were shared amongst all of the Apache. As a result, I think that the Apache people were the ultimate wanderers: they had nothing to tie them to anything. It is for these reasons, too, that I think the Apaches—and the nomadic hunter-gather types like them from around the world—are just about the freest people on Earth.

—Jon Young

These events between the Apache people and the U.S. Army occurred over one hundred years ago, but they still have great relevance today. True, you may not be evading the army, but wouldn't you like to make an occasional salad from the wild greens growing right in your own backyard, or forage for your own food? Would you like to learn which plant grows right along with poison ivy and provides welcome relief from its unpleasant side effects? Native people living close to the Earth have always relied on plants for the vast majority of their everyday needs. The plant kingdom is like a huge shopping mall of foods, medicines, and supplies for tools and crafts. In fact, if you chose to do so, you would find that the plants that grow in your region would provide for almost all of your needs.

Just as you wouldn't expect to find a loaf of bread at the hardware store, however, when you are "shopping" in the plant kingdom, it is important to know where to go to find what you need. Once you think you have found the plant you need, it is crucial to be absolutely certain that you truly have the right one, for your life may very well be on the line if you do not.

An example of a plant that I often use when introducing people to edible plants is one that we should all be familiar with: dandelion. *Dandelion?* Yes, dandelion! Would you believe that this "weed" is one of the best sources of vitamins and minerals available? It is iron-rich and oxidizes the blood, which means that it actually helps your muscles work more efficiently, allowing you to work or play harder for longer. Actually, the name "dandelion" has its roots in French, and translates to English to mean "the tooth of the lion," implying that those that eat dandelion regularly will grow to be as strong as a lion's tooth! Dandelion is a truly wonderful plant, and I try to eat at least one fresh dandelion leaf a day.

You Are What You Eat

When I reach to pick a dandelion leaf, there are two things that I watch for: the presence of herbicides or other toxins, and my own certainty that what I am reaching for is really dandelion. One of the places that I never harvest plants or berries is from the side of heavily traveled roads. Toxins from exhaust, motor oil, and tire rubber wash off of the roads when it rains and, unless there is a gutter to catch it, run into the ground alongside the road. The levels of these toxins are usually not enough to prevent plants from growing there, but I simply don't want to take the risk of putting these substances into my own body. Another potential danger is the presence of herbicides. If a lawn is sprayed with chemical weed killers, I certainly don't want to ingest those herbicides myself. Yuck!

I am also wary to be sure that the plant I am reaching for is, indeed, dandelion. As was discussed on the tape that you listened to, many edible plants have a similar "counterpart" that is poisonous. Dandelion is no exception. "That's crazy," some might say to this. "There is no way that I am going to mistake a plant like dandelion. I see it every day." You know, I've thought that exact same thing. After all, dandelion grows most everywhere, right? Roadsides, parks, lawns, sidewalk cracks. Who *doesn't* know it? Something that I have noticed, though, is that I see more of its poisonous look-alike along the roadsides than I do dandelion. I see more of them growing on lawns than I do dandelion, too. A good thing to do right now would be to actually check your knowledge of dandelion. Take a brief moment and look at both of the plants pictured on the next page. Circle the one that is the dandelion.

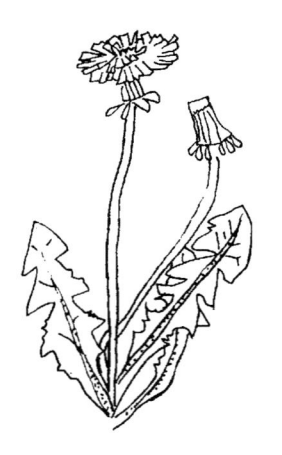

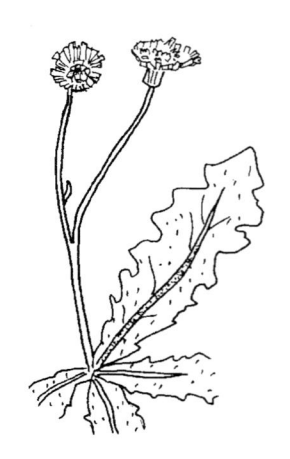

If you circled the one on the right, you chose the wrong plant. Now, if you had eaten it, the effects would have been far from deadly. Most likely the most severe result would be a mildly upset stomach that would stay with you for awhile. Regardless of which plant you circled, though, ask yourself this: Why did you circle the plant that you did? What parts of each plant informed you when you made your choice?

"A Rose by Any Other Name…"

As with mammals, birds, the faces of family and friends, there are certain characteristics of plants that will help you to distinguish one kind from another. One of these things is *not* the name of the plant. Just because I've been speaking on these pages here about a plant named "dandelion," does that necessarily mean that we are thinking about the same plant? In his tragedy, *Romeo and Juliet,* Shakespeare wrote the oft-quoted line, "a rose by any other name would smell as sweet." Of course, this line was included as part of the love scene wherein Romeo is professing his devotion to his forbidden love, Juliet, but it speaks a truth that applies directly to our subject here: different people may have different names for the same thing. For instance, if you and I are talking about the same animal, but you call it a horse and I call it a cow, how do we know that we are talking about the same thing? Unless we both know some of the details of the animal we are talking about, and unless we have an example of the animal to point at, we might spend a lot of time feeling bewildered. This is not an uncommon occurrence when it comes to plants. In fact, in different areas of the country, whole groups of people can have a name for a plant that is common amongst themselves, but that nobody outside of their region will understand.

An example of this is the plant coltsfoot. Coltsfoot is a plant that was introduced into North America from Europe and is fairly common throughout the eastern United States. It is typically found in places where the soil has been disturbed and that also have a good deal of moisture—roadsides are an excellent example of such a place. This plant has been renowned for centuries for its pleasant taste and ability to clear the lungs of congestion. In fact, much like the candy-striped pole outside of barber shops, pharmacies in Europe a hundred years ago had signs on their storefronts that had a picture of coltsfoot on it to let people know that it was a place to buy healing herbs and remedies. While many people back then might have recognized the plant that we call coltsfoot, there were many different names for the plant, some of which survive today. Names such as coltsfoot, son-before-father, foal's-foot, and coughwort, are just a few. As a result, two people using different names can be talking about the same plant. To make things a little more complicated, here in the western United States, there is a very different-looking plant that also goes by the name of coltsfoot. As a result, it is possible that two people using the same name can be referring to two different types of plants.

What is the point here? For your own safety and confidence, knowing the name of a plant is one of the *last* things that you need. It is far better to know the details of what a plant looks like and where it grows. What having a name will allow you to do is consult books to learn more about the poisonous, edible, or medicinal properties of the plant, as well as allow you to see if there are any plants that look like it that you need to learn about.

What are those things that you "really have to look for?" If we were able be outside to look at an actual plant together, that would be ideal—especially if it were summertime and all that we had to do was walk out to the lawn or a nearby park. Your *Reader's Digest: North American Wildlife* has some great illustrations of plants, though, so that will have to suffice. Open your RDG now to page 464. In the bottom left-hand corner of the page you will see a picture and description of our plant, the dandelion. Take a moment to study the picture of the dandelion. Look at the picture and then mark your page and close the book. Remember, too, that if we could, we would rather do this with you with a real plant, lying on the grass where we could touch it, bend it, and smell the dandelion's strong summery scent. Use your imagination and make the picture of this plant come to life while you are studying it (you may even want to lie down on your floor when doing this just to make it that much more real). In the space below, draw a quick sketch of the dandelion from what you can remember of the

I can't tell you how many times someone has come up to me and said, "There's this really neat plant I saw the other day. Can you identify it for me?" I ask them where the plant is, and it's in the woods by their house which is a half-an-hour's drive away. Since that is a little far to travel, I ask them to describe it for me. "Well, it's purple." I need more detail than that. I start pinning them down. Sure, the flower's purple, but they aren't sure what petals are when I ask them how many it has, let alone what the leaves looked and felt like, where they were growing on the plant, and where the plant itself was growing. I ask them to go home, sketch it, and bring me the drawing. They do this, but I still won't be able to identify it for them because they haven't included the important things, the things that you really have to look for.
—Jon Young

picture. Don't use any colored pencils or markers just yet. Instead, just create a simple drawing, and remember that the point here is not to create artwork, but to capture the most important features of the plant!

Now that you've made a sketch of your plant, open your book again to page 464 and read the description of the dandelion. How tall is it? Yes, the book says that the dandelion is from "1 to 20 inches tall." How tall is that *really*? Hold your hand about twenty inches above your table or floor. Grab a ruler if you need to, but don't worry about how exact your measurement is here. Just know that twenty inches is equal to about a foot and a half. Remember, though, that twenty inches is the higher end of the scale, with the lower end all the way down at one inch. Drop your hand down to that height now, and you'll see that there is quite a lot of variety in the size of the dandelion! Just for the sake of having it handy, write the size of the plant next to your picture.

Turn again to page 464 in your Reader's Digest Guide and go back to the description of the dandelion. In the text, there is a section titled "What to look for." Read that a few times to yourself and then mark your page and close the book. Ask yourself this: What were those features it said to look for? In the space next to the picture that you drew above, write down some brief notes on each feature that you can remember with an arrow pointing to each part of the plant that you are describing. As an example, if you were doing this for a western coltsfoot, you might write "large hand-like leaves" and draw an arrow connecting that description to the plant's leaf in your picture. Do this now for the dandelion.

Could you remember them all? It seems somehow strange that a plant so very common can have so many parts to remember, because we all know dandelion, *right?* It's okay if a few things slipped your mind. It can take awhile to get the hang of this. If you got them all, then good going! Even if you did remember all of the features, though, take a moment to re-read the description of the dandelion on page 464 just to be certain. If there are any things to look for that you didn't write down, write them next to your picture now.

By now, your picture is most likely finding itself surrounded by a ring of descriptions and arrows, each pointing to a different part of your plant. Let's take a moment and reflect on the picture that you've created. What you've done is essentially create your own field guide description. If we were going to publish this, we'd want to make sure that everything was in the proper order. One thing that we've yet to do is touch up the picture that you drew at the beginning of all this to make sure that it really reflects what you have read and written down yourself. Using what you have learned about the flowers and leaves of dandelion from writing it next to your picture, study the illustration on page 464. Turn back now to the picture that you drew. How does it compare? Are the leaves in your picture really "deeply toothed?" Are they really "clustered at the base?" Instead of changing the picture that you have drawn already, simply make some quick sketches in the spaces remaining next to your picture to show these things. If you find that you've already covered all of them in your picture, then good going once again! When doing this, use some colored pencils to color in the features of your plant and give it some life! Remember, though—don't copy from the picture in your RDG! The point is to do this from memory.

Now that we've done all of this work to identify dandelion, how do we recognize the plant that looks like dandelion but that, instead of making you "strong as a lion's tooth," can make you sick? It's not as difficult as you may think. As you did at the beginning of this chapter, look over the two plants that are pictured below and circle the dandelion.

Knowing the plants makes all of the difference, doesn't it? While you may not know exactly what the specific characteristics of the look-alike plant are, knowing the dandelion makes it obvious which one is which. If I asked you now to list the features that informed you when you made your decision like I did the first time that you did this, you would be able to easily list features of the leaves, stem, and flowers that were different. I'll bet that we could even take a ride in the car now and have a blast pointing these plants out to each other as we drive.

The End of the World?

Is this all that there is to know about plants? No. The business of studying the world of plants is never-ending and employs thousands of botanists, foresters, herbalists, florists, farmers and gardeners around the country. In all of the work we have done so far, we have not even touched upon whether or not there are any uses of the dandelion as a medicine, or how to go about eating the leaves. If you want to learn more about these things for yourself, we recommend that you use the following field guides for your region:

Peterson Field Guide to *Wildflowers*
Newcomb's Wildflower Guide

Peterson Field Guide to *Venomous Animals & Poisonous Plants*
Peterson Field Guide to *Edible Wild Plants*
Peterson Field Guide to *Medicinal Plants*

Since there is no all-encompassing field guide, it is usually necessary when studying any topic that you refer to several sources for your information. Use these books together when studying your plants, and remember to go through the same process of studying the picture or text, closing your eyes, and then drawing or writing based on what you can remember. At Wilderness Awareness School, we call this process "learning to see with your mind's eye." What it means is essentially testing your own skills at recalling sights, sounds, smells, and such from your memory. If you take the time to do this through all of your naturalist studies you will develop a phenomenal ability to store information about wildlife or about places you have been to and be able to recall minute details from just a quick glance at an object or place. Hence, from now on in this book, when I refer you to your "mind's eye," it is this process of studying, closing your eyes, and then drawing what you can remember.

A Room with a View

Now this may seem like a funny time to ask a question like this, given that we've already taken the time to study the dandelion, but have you ever seen a dandelion in the "wild?" If so, where are some of the places that you have seen them? Have you seen them deep inside a dark forest? On lawns? In parks? In the space below, make a list of some of the places where you have seen dandelions growing.

Take a look at the list of places that you have just written. What do all of these places have in common? Yes, grass might be a common feature, so you may want to write that down later. What do dandelions and grass have in common though? Think of it from the plant's perspective: If I were a plant, what would my needs be? Plants don't move around like animals do, so they don't need a lot of space to find their food—or do they? What do plants "eat?" It is generally common knowledge that part of the miracle of plants is that they feed on the light that the sun provides. They don't have to hunt or shop for their food—their food comes to them! In turn, animals, birds, and other things that move are able to eat because they feed on the plants (or feed on other creatures that eat plants). Keeping in mind that plants "eat" the light of the sun, how much space do they need to find enough of that food to sustain themselves? Just as a wolf needs a certain amount of land to roam in order to find enough food to keep itself fed, a flower needs to have a certain amount of access to the sun's rays to keep itself fed. Think again about all of the places where you have seen dandelions growing. The map drawn below shows a corner of a typical suburban park. It may even be someone's backyard. Take a moment now and, thinking of the places where you have seen dandelions growing before in terms of the plant's needs for food, shade in the places on this map where you feel they would be most likely to be found.

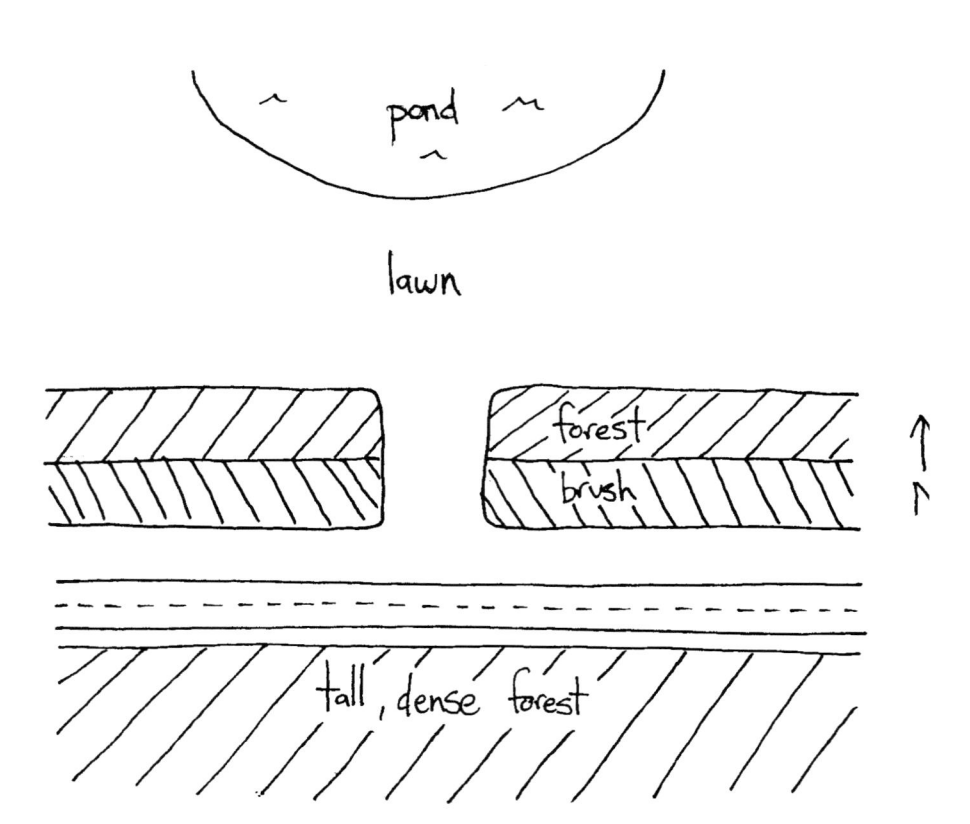

What do these places have in common that allows dandelions to grow there? If you were to interview a dandelion on what it wants, it would probably say something along the lines of, "What I'm looking for in a home is something with a good view." Thinking like a plant again, a "good view" wouldn't mean a place with a scenic view of the mountains as much as it would mean a place that offered it a good, unobstructed view of the sun for as much of the day as possible. Yes, dandelions need sunlight—and lots of it—to grow. Think again of the places where you have seen them growing. Cracks in sidewalks, roadsides, lawns, parks—these are all places where there are no trees, tall grasses, or buildings to block dandelion's access to the sun. Turn back now to page 464 of your Reader's Digest Guide and re-read the section titled "Habitat" that describes where dandelion grows. Using your mind's eye now, write the places where your RDG says dandelions prefer to live.

Can you see how our conclusion about dandelions preferring open spaces is reflected in the list of habitats that is given in the RDG? Sunlight is like a common thread that runs through the whole list. To comment on that list of habitats, I'll add that when it says "woods" and "swamps," those types of woods and swamps are not darkened by heavy shadows. Both of these places will have a lot of sunlight shining through to the ground. Now, I have to admit that in doing this myself, since I know that dandelions need lots of sunlight to grow, I was a caught off guard a little when I read that dandelions grow in the woods. I was not expecting to read that. What it forced me to do, though, was travel back into my memory—even as I sat here on my bed writing on my laptop—and recall places in the forests where I have seen dandelions grow. From my memory, I could recall that I have seen dandelions growing in the woods, but that they were all places that allowed a great deal of sunlight to reach the forest floor. It is seeking the common links between one experience with dandelion and another that will enable you to see through the dandelion's "eyes."

As you may have noticed through using the map above, maps can be a tremendous tool to help us to learn about plants. Through combining maps with your knowledge of the needs of the plants and trees as we have just practiced, you can even try your hand at predicting where you will be able to find certain plants—just from looking at a map! This is something that I enjoy practicing frequently. I have a large map on my wall that shows the contours of the hills and valleys. I placed this map right next to the door and often stop to look at it whenever I enter or leave my bedroom. As my friend Matt (who wrote the daily Nature Awareness

Trail exercises you have been working on) will attest, there are dirt stains on my map, too, that follow the trails that I will take on my journeys to see if my predictions are correct. It is all the same process that you have just gone through by plotting on your map where the dandelion will grow based on what you know about the dandelion. With some experience getting to know the other plants and your area, you may want to try this same thing. Before you begin your journeys, however, make sure that you know how to avoid getting lost. Refer back to the notes that you made at the beginning of this chapter and listen again to Tape Three of the *Seeing Through Native Eyes* tape series for Jon's discussion on learning to orient yourself in the woods.

We are about at the end of our own journey that we have taken together through the wide world of plants. I know that the world of plants may seem huge. There are so many things to study and know that the question that I have heard most often is "where do I begin?" I hope that your work in this chapter has helped to give you that first step. Before I turn you loose to wander through the world of plants, though, there is one important consideration that we have not yet discussed.

Wild Carrot Salad? Don't Even THINK of It!

As you continue to learn about plants, the wealth of knowledge and the lure of free and nutritious foods that they offer will undoubtedly grow more and more appealing. After all, who *wouldn't* be turned on to an idea like this? Certainly, it is great to take what you have learned through your studies to go and experience this new world for yourself. When you first begin to forage or gather wild plants, though, the one family to stay away from is the carrot family, also known in some books as the parsleys. There are many edible and poisonous members of this family that are hard to distinguish. One of them is water hemlock—the most deadly plant in all of North America. You could take one small nibble smaller than half the size of your pinky fingernail and be dead in only minutes, and people have even been known to die from simply handling these plants and then handling food without first washing their hands!

In certain parts of the country, there is also a plant called elderberry. The hollow stems of this plant make very good whistles and are even crafted into very fine flutes. It just so happens, though, that water hemlock grows in those same places as the elderberry and looks a lot like it. People have been known to cut the stems of the water hemlock—thinking that it is elderberry—and died from blowing on those whistles.

The same principle goes for mushrooms, only to a much, much higher and more complicated degree. There are hundreds of stories that circulate around the naturalist's rumor mill of people—even certified experts with decades of experience—who have poisoned themselves, and often several others who trusted them, by eating what they believed to be an edible type of mushroom. The distinctions between edible and toxic mushrooms can be so minute and complex that it takes a microscope to study the details of the mushroom's tiny spores to be absolutely sure what type of mushroom it is. I heard one story about an elderly couple who had enjoyed studying nature together for their entire lives. After eating a salad mixed with a highly toxic mushroom that they had picked, however, their final days were spent together in a hospital room waiting for a liver transplant, because the poisons in the mushroom had begun to dissolve their livers. Since first hearing this story—and several others by now, too—about people's misadventures with wild mushrooms, I've decided to not eat wild mushrooms—there are too many places for disaster to slip in and really ruin my day (as well as the day of my close friends and family). Please, however, study and enjoy them all that you want. In my eyes and in the eyes of Wilderness Awareness School, though, the risks that come with eating wild mushrooms are just too great. Leave them where they grow.

There are other poisonous plants, but either they don't kill you outright, or they don't look like another edible plant. Remember that the carrot family does have many edible members, though. Remember the story of Socrates dying from drinking a cup of hemlock tea? That tea was made from poison hemlock, which is another member of the carrot/parsley family. Originally, it was found only in Europe, but it is now quite common here in North America, too. Don't jump to any conclusions about anything with the name "hemlock," though. I often brew a tea that is delicious and exceptionally high in Vitamin C from the needles of the hemlock tree, of which there are several types found across North America. So, remember your Shakespeare: "A rose by any other name would smell as sweet," and be informed about your plants. Get to know them first, and then study their uses—and don't touch the parsley.

Despite these words of caution, enjoy the plants. We have things to learn and appreciate from the plants that we find in the grocery store, the plants that we grow in flower beds and gardens, the many varieties that grow in the wilds, and even those that dwell in the cracks of the sidewalk. The next time you find yourself lying in a meadow, forest, or lawn soaking up the rays of the sun or listening to the songs of birds, look around you, too, and notice the many types of plants that surround you. Just as feeling the warmth of the sun and listening to the birds are a part of awareness, so, too, is seeing and recognizing the variety of plant life that is around you, and it is an important part of learning to see again with native eyes.

"Interested in learning to make your own herbal remedies with the plants that grow around you?"

Kamana design editor and herbalist John Gallagher created the **Herbal Medicine Making Kit** to show you how simple it is.

Each kit comes with *Roots and Branches, an Herbal Home Study Course,* at no extra charge.

LearningHerbs.com

Herbal Medicine Made Simple.

AFTER LISTENING TO DISC FOUR AND COMPLETING CHAPTER FIVE

1. What is the attribute of the SouthWest? Why is it important to embrace the energy of the South-West?

2. How does wandering lead to connection?

3. What is the difference between connection and awareness?

4. How does the Art of Questioning help with deepening connection?

5. What's the importance of experiencing your landscape with a bird's eye view and of mapping that area?

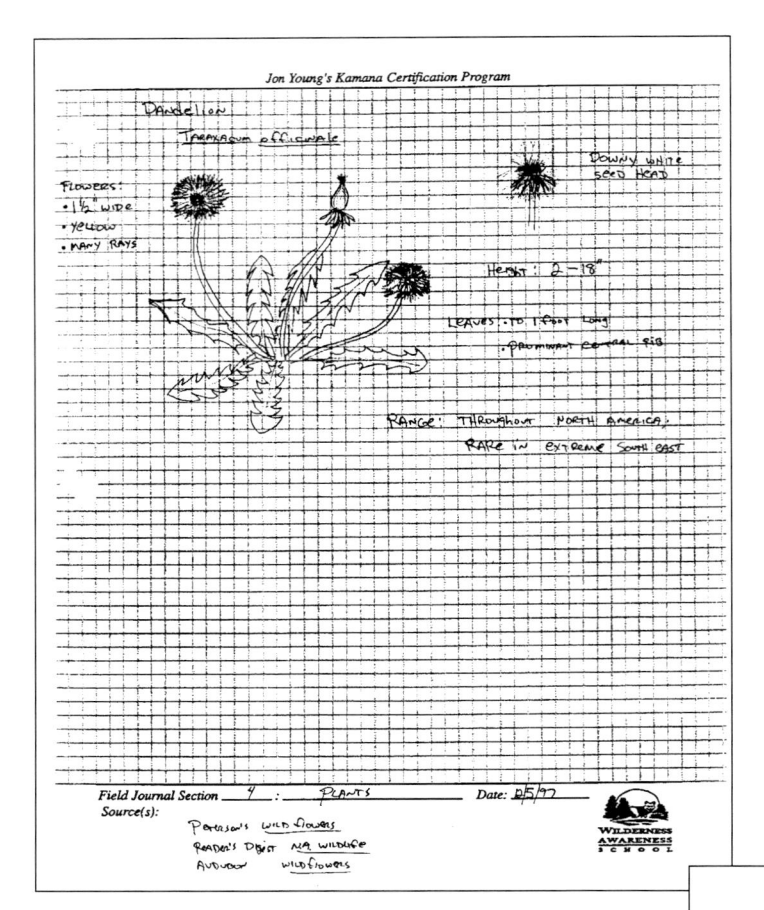

Jon Young's Kamana Certification Program

Dandelion
Taraxacum officinale

Downy white seed head

Flowers:
- 1½" wide
- yellow
- many rays

Height: 2-18"

Leaves: to 1 foot long
- prominent central rib

Range: Throughout North America; rare in extreme south east

Field Journal Section __4__: PLANTS Date: 2/5/97
Source(s):
Peterson's Wild Flowers
Reader's Digest N.A. Wildlife
Audubon Wildflowers

WILDERNESS AWARENESS SCHOOL

Dandelion, *Taraxacum officinale*,   Herzog, #248   12/4/97
Asteraceae, Sunflower family

Habits
- Seeds are wind dispersed
- Lawns, waste places, fields, road sides

Identification
- 7-2-3
- Leaves are basal, deeply toothed
- Prominent tap root
- Solitary flower from Spring to Fall, occasionally in winter
- Stem hollow, milky

Edibility
- Young leaves, gathered before flowering, can be eaten raw or boiled for 5-10 minutes; change water once if too bitter
- White part of leaf below soil is the best part
- Young flower buds (early spring) can be boiled for several minutes or pickled
- Flowers can be dipped in batter and fried or boiled in two water changes
- Roots (fall to early spring) can be slowly roasted until dark brown and brittle, and ground into a coffee substitute
- The root is edible by roasting in a hotter oven for less time
- Flowers and leaves are rich in vitamin A and C

Medicinal
- Tea of fresh root used for liver, gall bladder, kidney, and bladder ailments; diuretic, digestion tonic, constipation
- Dried root thought to be weaker
- Dried leaf tea a folk laxative
- Root is experimentally to be hypoglycemic, weak antibiotic against yeast infections, stimulates bile flow, weight loss
- Tea of fresh leaves is a mild tonic

Sources:
Peterson's Edible Wild Plants
Peterson's Ecology of Eastern Forests
Peterson's Medicinal Plants
Newcomb's Wildflower Guide
Tom Brown's Guide to Wild Edible and Medicinal Plants
Audubon Field Guide to North American Wildflowers

Kamana Resource Trail Journal by Kamana Four graduate Carl Herzog

Create a Plants journal page.
Please take no more than 20 minutes to complete.

Name:

Date:

Species Name:

Scientific name:

Source(s):
Reader's Digest:
North American Wildlife

Sketch and color the species

Range Map

Important facts:

KAMANA
NATURALIST TRAINING PROGRAM

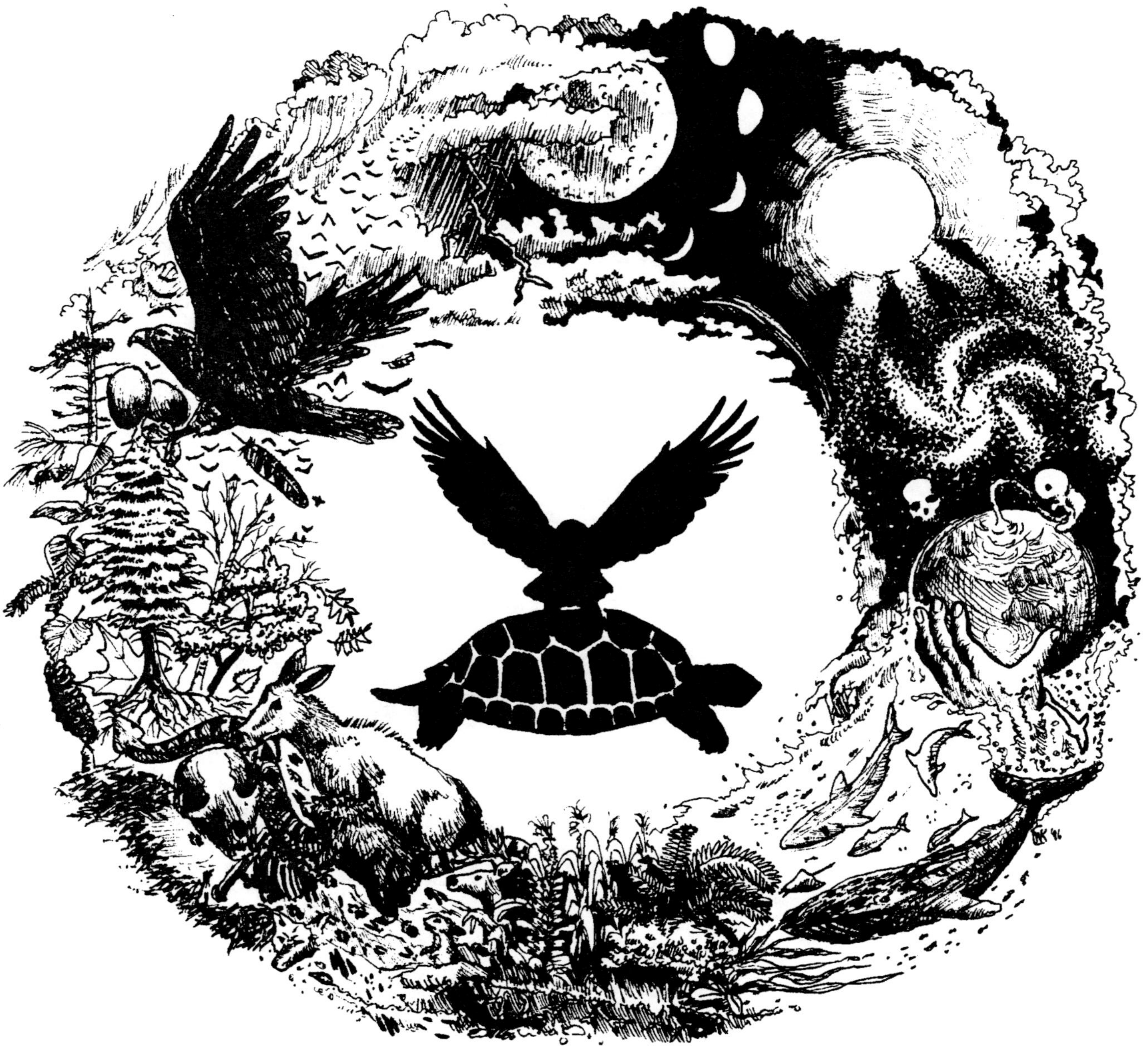

Chapter Six

Step Back and Take a Closer Look

Listen to Disc Five of the *Seeing Through Native Eyes* disc series before or while you are completing this chapter.

While driving home one early-summer day, I spied a robin on the ground struggling with what I thought was a worm. I stopped and moved closer to the bird on foot. With patience, I made my way close enough to the bird to see the many shades of color on its head, its bill, and finally—as I strained to see through the grasses and leaf debris on the ground—I glimpsed what it was struggling with: a small garter snake. I remained nearby quietly and watched out of the side of my vision as, after much struggle, the robin stopped the snake's movement. It then carried off its prize, no doubt enough food for all of its young.

Later that same day, I heard a commotion in the brush along the side of a sand trail in the Pine Barrens. With curiosity and patience, I again approached closely, being sure not to further agitate noisy birds. As I closed in, I noticed that the towhees were pointing their distress toward a certain point amongst a group of laurels, and I recognized their alarm as one concerned with a threat to their own young. When I finally made it close enough to see into the laurels, my patience was more than rewarded by what I saw: a medium-sized pine snake in the process of fitting its mouth over the head of a fledgling towhee. Wrapped in the coils of the snake, the bird had since breathed its last. It was now the snake's turn to feed on birds.

During a stay in a friend's home here in Washington one recent spring, I heard the distinct howls of a small family of wolves from across the large beaver pond beyond their back porch. The very next morning, I was up bright and early to comb the area for their tracks and sign. As it turned out, there were four wolves that stayed there for what appeared to be three or four days. I recognized this family from the summer before when I had spent a great deal of time tracking them. There was a large male who weighed in at close to 100 pounds, a "largish" female who weighed close to 85 pounds, and two young wolves—one male and one female—who were slightly smaller and like awkward teenagers not yet used to their fast-growing bodies.

In my quest to learn more about these wolves I consulted a local and well-known wolf biologist. From him I learned that, while there may be plenty of other things to feed on in an area, the one deciding factor that kept the wolves interested in sticking around there and not heading someplace else was most likely the presence of elk. Following that line of thought, then, had there not been elk in those mountains, then those wolves would probably have gone to another place where there were elk. Similarly, I've learned that in other areas of the country, it is often the presence of moose that is the deciding factor. In my experience with these wolves, I had observed where they had brought down a deer and the remains of many, many rabbits. I had seen in their scat that at certain times of the year the wolves had dined on berries, and at one point even corn. The question that I held in my mind now, though, was "what were they eating now, in the early spring?" for little was available after a long and tough winter.

As I searched and searched for evidence in the dim light of the early morning, I found a large, fresh scat that was placed just in the right place on the trail that I followed to tell me that it was, indeed, from a wolf. I examined the ground near the scat and found the gentle compressions from its feet around the scat to pinpoint its source. It had come from one of the younger wolves—and it was composed entirely of the skin and parts of frogs!

There have been many experiences in my years as a tracker that have shown me over and over the importance of reptiles and amphibians in nature. These animals are themselves important—and fragile—strands in the web of life. As such, they are always important to some aspect of your awareness as a naturalist, so you should always be on the watch for them. For instance, I always know when I am in a healthy ecosystem when I see many and varied members of these two classes. It is these animals that indicate health to me. An unfortunate side effect of being an indicator of a natural area's health these days, however, is that both reptiles and amphibians often appear on many endangered and threatened species lists. Knowing that sets off many loud alarm bells in my mind when I think about the health of the land. A good question, though, is "what links these creatures to nature's health?" Why is it that knowing frogs will tell me if things are unbalanced? It is the fragility and sensitivity of these animals that makes them good indicators, for if just subtle things are off balance, it will be these creatures that will feel the effects first. By getting to know these animals, you can read the health of your environment, too. You can really help your local region by getting to know these animals. They can teach you a great deal about your neighborhood.

—Jon Young

Knowing about the animals that will tell us about the health of an environment is a good place to start. Ask yourself, "What *is* a reptile?" "What *is* an amphibian?" Well, we know that they all at least have slimy skin, right? Not exactly. It is actually a fairly common myth that all reptiles and snakes are "slimy." Even if you already know that such a statement is not true, do you know anybody who holds to that belief, or have you heard other people say that? Pages 158 and 181 of your *Reader's Digest: North American Wildlife* have good explanations of what distinguishes reptiles and what distinguishes amphibians from other types of animals. Using your mind's eye, read those descriptions and create two lists in the space below—one listing the characteristics of reptiles and another that lists the characteristics common to amphibians.

Reptiles   **Amphibians**

There are a lot of things that make amphibians and reptiles unique! What are the types of animals that fit these descriptions? Take a short glance back at pages 158 and 181 now and add to your list above the different types of animals that are classified as reptiles and amphibians. You only need to be general here in your listing: "turtle," "frog," or "alligator"—no specific names such as "spring peeper" just yet.

Bird-a-thons and Frog-a-thons

Over the years, the Audubon Society has trained tens of thousands of people to become amateur bird watchers, or "birders." Through the organized efforts of the Audubon Society, these people have contributed a great deal to preservation and conservation work through the years. Bird-a-thons, Christmas Counts, and other annual events nationwide utilize the many thousands of eyes that are out there recreationally making observations of birds. From these events, statistics and information are published that have become important to the decision-makers who decide which real estate is to be set aside for preservation as parks and wetlands for future generations. Lately, too, there are trackers who have been contributing important knowledge about mammals for similar purposes. What is being done for the reptiles and amphibians?

Several years ago in the area of New Jersey where Wilderness Awareness School was based, we started an annual event in our area called the "Frog-a-thon." We used it to raise money to support our youth programs, while at the same time raising grassroots awareness of the frogs of the state. This happened because of the experience of some of my students searching for wood frogs breeding at a pond in a local park that I knew from my childhood. It had been just a few years since the last time I had been there to see the frogs, but they had disappeared entirely from that place. The wood frogs were gone, and nobody noticed. No one knew this had happened except those few students and me, though, because this little-known vernal pool was off of the beaten trail. In fact, to my knowledge, this writing is the one and only record of their having been there at all. This inspired more earnest outreach to train more people to understand what was SUPPOSED to be in the places around their homes. In time, this earnestness inspired the creation of this very Kamana program as a way to reach more people to help them to learn about the wildlife in their very backyards.

The Great Toad Migration

Speaking of the wildlife in our backyards, there is a mystery that I need some help to solve. When I was a child growing up in the suburbs near Albany, New York, there was an event that happened every summer that I have yet to figure out. To set the stage, my home was located on a typical suburban block, with neighboring houses on both sides, across the street, and on the other side of my backyard. Across the street from that backyard neighbor's house was a golf course that had a very large water trap that was complete with a large fountain and a ring of cattails around it. Every summer—around July or so, if I recall it correctly—I would go out into my backyard and find myself surrounded by what I believed at the time to be toads. It seemed like there were hundreds of the small brown creatures, and they were all moving in the same direction as they moved toward my home. They were tiny—about an inch long—with smooth tan skin and a black stripe next to their eyes. Back then as a little kid, I just assumed that since they were brown that they had to be toads and that they must have come from the water trap at the golf course. Often I would walk around, pick some of them up, and bring them onto my back porch where I would sit down and plunk them into a large glass jar that I had filled with water. I would usually spend a long time after that building a small raft that I thought they would like to float on when they got tired of swimming. After all, don't all toads like to swim? Unfortunately, many-a-"toad" perished in that glass jar due to my young boy's short attention span.

Thinking back on it, I'm not so sure that a toad would really enjoy being plunked into the water like that. Or would it? Do toads like to swim in water? Is it more likely that I was plunking frogs into my jar? Your RDG has some good descriptions of frogs and toads. Read what it has to has to say about them on page 181 in the sections titled "Frogs and Toads" and "Tips on Identifying Amphibians." Read the blue-highlighted section titled "Frog or Toad?" on page 188, the description of "True Toads" on page 190, and the descriptions of "Treefrogs" and "True Frogs" on pages 192 and 194, as well. Using your mind's eye and the space below, make a list of the things that make a frog a frog and a toad a toad.

Frog: **Toad:**

Now, help me out with my mystery—*please* (I know that someday, somewhere somebody out there will have the answer to the Great Toad Migration). I need you to make your best guess now about the small brown guys that hopped across my backyard. Go back to the place above where I described the frog/toad, and, using your new knowledge about frogs and toads, write what you think they were in the space below. Write a few notes about why you came to that conclusion.

Hmmm. It seems as though maybe they were small brown frogs that I was plunking into my jar. Oh well. I wish that I had known that when I was a kid. I also wish that I knew what type of frogs they were now. Sifting through my own RDG, I'm noticing that there aren't any frogs or toads described in there that really match my memories of the frogs from my backyard. If it were any of the frogs in the book, though, I think that the wood frog is the closest match. What do you think? Since I can't quite figure it out, perhaps it is my memory that is flawed. That usually seems to be the case when I can't find something that I've seen in one of my field guides, so I just have to go back and look at it again or wait until the next time that it crosses my path. It may be that I'll just have to go back there and take another look someday. Perhaps I'd better make that trip home quickly, though. The last time that I was back at my parent's home in New York during the summertime a few years ago, I noticed that there were a lot less of the tiny tan guys with black eye-stripes hopping across my backyard than there were when I was a boy.

Thinking about frogs in my backyard, I'm wondering now what type of frog is in *your* backyard. Aren't you? Turn now to the descriptions of "True Frogs" on pages 194 and 195 of your Reader's Digest Guide. Look at the range maps for each of the frogs on these two pages to see which ones are found in your area. Write the name of each of the frogs that the range maps say live in your area in the space below. Do this now.

Look at the list that you have just made. It should have at least one type of frog listed. If not, review the range maps again and choose one that is the closest to your area. If you have more than one type of frog listed in the space above, choose one and circle its name. This is now your "backyard frog."

Read the section titled "True Frogs" again. In the space below there are a few categories of things to pay special attention to from the section that you are reading. Make some notes about each aspect of frog behavior or things to watch for to help you to identify a frog. Don't get too detailed about these notes. Instead, use your mind's eye—reading and then picturing what you have read in your mind before re-reading the section again. Do this now.

Color:

Identification Tips:

Frog Calls:

Now let's take a look at your backyard frog. The more that I think about the frogs that I found in my backyard, the more uncertain I become that they were wood frogs. Take a look at the wood frog. Now, I didn't describe my backyard to you very well, but it is essentially a large lawn with some red maples that create some good shade from their branches high above. More or less, though, the yard is just green grass. The description of where the wood frog lives says that they prefer "damp shady woodlands." That hardly describes my backyard, nor does it describe the first hole at the golf course across the street that those frogs would have had to have crossed. Maybe the golf course is not where they came from. The mystery seems to have deepened! Getting back to your backyard frog, though, read the description of where your frog lives. Read it a couple of times and then mark your page and close your book. Can you picture any places around your home or in your area that you have seen that fit that description? Write some of those places that seem like they would make a good home for frogs in your area in the space below. If you cannot think of any such places, then just write what you can recall from what you read in your RDG.

Now let's take a look at what will help you to identify your frog. The most useful thing to you would actually be a tape of frog calls, which you should be able to find or order through your local bookstore. This would be a very helpful thing because frogs don't generally make themselves very visible. After all, if people enjoy frog legs, what animal in the forest wouldn't? Frogs are on everybody's menu! As a result, with the exception of their booming nighttime calls and choruses, frogs tend to keep a low profile. Even when frogs are calling, though, they have a trick up their sleeve that helps them to stay hidden even when they are making a lot of noise—frogs are master ventriloquists. There have been times that I have heard the call of a frog and set out in search of it only to be standing right next to it and unable to find it. I'll look to where I think the sound is coming from, but no frog. Where is it? One moment the sound is coming from one place, the next moment it has moved—but the frog hasn't! I don't know how it is they do it, but it is a marvelous, if not frustrating, skill. Nevertheless, a tape of frog calls should be at the top of your shopping list. It will at least help you get close!

Since we can't include a frog or a tape of frog calls with this course to sing for you, the next thing to pay attention to is what your frog looks like. Regarding the frogs that I saw in my backyard, I can't remember ever hearing them call. I guess that is something else to look into the next time I'm home. I did get to play with them a lot, though, and look at them. What does your frog look like? Use your mind's eye to study the picture of your frog and then make a quick sketch of it in the space below. Use your mind's eye and read the description of your frog. Write the important things that you need to look for next to your sketch and include an arrow that points to that feature on your picture. Write its name next to your picture, too! Do this now.

Did you include the size of your frog in your sketch? How big is that size in reality? Sometimes it is hard to gain a real sense for how large something is by a couple of numbers. Look for something nearby that is close to the size of your frog and study it for a moment to gain a sense of how big your frog is. Imagine that object turning into a frog and staring at you as you hold it in your hand. Now, how big is your frog? Some frogs can be really huge, while others are really tiny! If you didn't include the size of your frog next to your picture above, jot that down now.

Is there another frog in your area that looks similar to your backyard frog? Compare your picture with the pictures of the other frogs in your RDG. Don't limit yourself to just the frogs that are on pages 194 and 195—they aren't the only frogs in the book that might be in your area! If there are any frogs that look similar to your backyard frog, take a moment to figure out what makes them different. Is it just a matter of size? Does one have larger dark spots on it that another? Write the name of any similar types of frogs (or toads for that matter!) in the space below with some brief notes about how to tell each of them apart from your frog.

Get to know your reptiles and amphibians—for your neighborhood's sake. You may be the only one who knows. Interestingly, while there are many people out there in the world who are good at identifying bird songs, there are few people who recognize frog calls. In my opinion, though, the calls of the frog chorus is one of the most beautiful sounds that there is and they often inspire me to fall asleep with my window open (much to the chagrin of my house mates who then have to pay a higher heating bill!). With the knowledge of mammals, and frogs (and soon birds, too) that you are cultivating here, you could even go on to become a triathlete in nature observation! You can bet that since there have been frogs for millions of years now upon this Earth that it is a skill that our ancestors once had, and it is one that we can easily reclaim as we continue to learn to see through native eyes.

AFTER LISTENING TO DISC FIVE AND COMPLETING CHAPTER SIX

1. What is the attribute of the West?

2. Why is community so essential in nature connection mentoring? How can community help to build connections in nature?

3. Why are Peace and Unity such important foundations for community process?

4. What can you do to support nature mentoring in your community?

5. What are some examples of "indicator species"? What can they tell you about an environment?

Jon Young's Kamana Certification Program

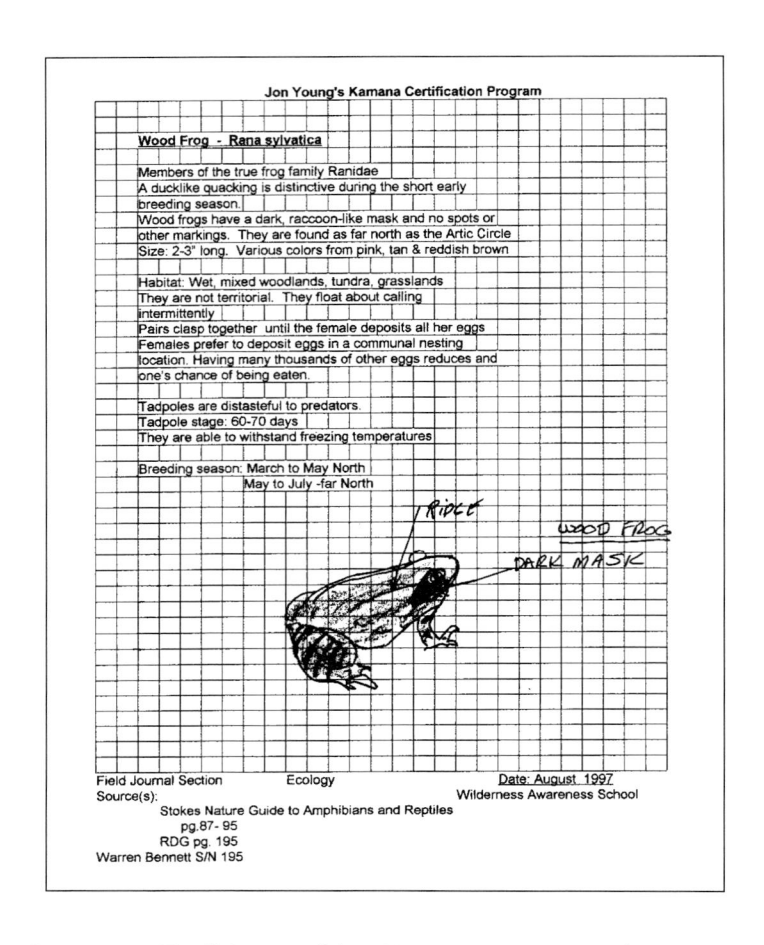

Wood Frog - Rana sylvatica

Members of the true frog family Ranidae
A ducklike quacking is distinctive during the short early breeding season.
Wood frogs have a dark, raccoon-like mask and no spots or other markings. They are found as far north as the Artic Circle
Size: 2-3" long. Various colors from pink, tan & reddish brown

Habitat: Wet, mixed woodlands, tundra, grasslands
They are not territorial. They float about calling intermittently
Pairs clasp together until the female deposits all her eggs
Females prefer to deposit eggs in a communal nesting location. Having many thousands of other eggs reduces and one's chance of being eaten.

Tadpoles are distasteful to predators.
Tadpole stage: 60-70 days
They are able to withstand freezing temperatures

Breeding season: March to May North
May to July -far North

RIDGE — WOOD FROG — DARK MASK

Field Journal Section — Ecology — Date: August 1997
Wilderness Awareness School

Source(s):
Stokes Nature Guide to Amphibians and Reptiles pg. 87-95
RDG pg. 195
Warren Bennett S/N 195

Kamana Resource Trail Journal by Kamana Four graduate Warren Bennett

Create a Reptile or Amphibian journal page.
Please take no more than 20 minutes to complete.

Name:

Date:

Species Name:

Scientific name:

Source(s):
Reader's Digest:
North American Wildlife

Sketch and color the species

Range Map

Important facts:

KAMANA
Naturalist Training Program

Chapter Seven

The History of Your Landscape

Listen to Disc Six of the *Seeing Through Native Eyes* disc series before or while you are completing this chapter.

She awakes before first light. There are still embers from last night's fire, but the air is cold. The light in her family's home is dim. There is no electricity in this Western red cedar longhouse.

She moves quietly, so as to not awake the others. She foxwalks to her bentwood box and grabs her woven cedar hat, some salmon jerky, and her cedar bark travel basket. She is almost out of the door when she thinks, "My paddle!" She can't believe she almost forgot her beloved paddle.

The sun is cresting the horizon as she retrieves her canoe. Her Uncle made her that canoe. She remembers the cedar tree that it came from and watching him dig out the wood with an adze. It took months to complete. She loves this beautiful boat.

The canoe slides smoothly into the large lake; the water is still as glass. Her paddle dips into the water, and it feels good to tap into her strength. As she paddles along the lakeshore, the trees stand out to her. She couldn't imagine life without trees, especially the cedar tree. Her people call it the Tree of Life.

The name is not an exaggeration. The cedar tree provides wood for their homes, bentwood box containers, fire-making tools, heat, bowls, and so much more. The bark of the tree is used for baskets, hats, capes, diapers, mats, nets, and decorations. The roots and branches, or withes, are used for incredibly strong woven rope, lashings, and baskets.

She returns to the shore from her morning paddle. The village is awake now. People are gathering and starting their morning routines of fishing and gathering food. Today will be a good day…

Heritage Species

This short story captures the essence of the cedar tree and its importance to native people of the Pacific Northwest coast. The cedar tree was literally used from cradle to grave, and all points in between. There are many species that humans rely on, but there are some that were exceptionally vital to their existence. We call these heritage species.

A heritage species is typically a plant or animal that was used extensively by people in their daily lives. Some of these species were cultivated over many generations. The Hawaiians migrated from Polynesia, traveling thousands of miles by canoe. On their voyage, they brought with them several plants that allowed them to survive the journey and to survive on the new land that they were moving to. These were known as the "Canoe Plants" and they provided almost all of their food, medicine, clothing, and tools.

A heritage species is something that is vital to humans surviving and thriving in their local area. It's an organism that provides so much sustenance, that life without it would be much harder. Some of these species provide everything as they are, while others have been tended and cultivated over time. An example of a cultivated heritage species is the valley oak of California.

When European settlers arrived in California they assumed they had found a paradise of natural abundance. Wildlife and food were overflowing in the landscape. What they didn't realize was that this land had been cultivated into a large-scale garden by "primitive" people. Over generations, the natives had been pruning, cultivating, transplanting, weeding, and performing controlled burning. One of the key species that was cultivated over time was the valley oak. The acorns provided a food rich in protein and fat. This not only fed the people, but also the elk, deer, bears, and turkey. Some of these animals, in turn, fed the people as well. You can read further about the valley oak and other heritage species in the book Tending the Wild by Kat Anderson.

The ultimate example of a cluster of heritage species plants that were cultivated over time are the three sisters: corn, beans, and squash.

This was a vital food source for many Native American farming societies. These plants were all planted together for the benefit of the whole. The corn is planted and used by the beans as a trellis to climb. The beans are nitrogen-fixers, providing an essential nutrient for the plant growth. The squash provides a live "mulch" to help provide shade for the roots of each plant, helping the plants survive through times of drought. Once all of these plants die back in the winter they provide organic matter to help rebuild the soil. The three sisters supplied lots of delicious food.

How do you identify a heritage species?

Wherever you are in North America, or the world for that matter, the best way to identify the heritage species of your area is to do a little research. For some of you this is going to be obvious. For others it will probably take a little more digging. This information is not likely to be found in your Reader's Digest field guide, so we are going to turn to the internet for some help. Take out a scrap piece of paper, and let's take some notes.

I want you to start by answering two questions:

1) Who are the native peoples of your area?
2) What plants and animals did they rely on the most to survive?

You can start with a simple internet search like "Native Americans in California". Once you identify a tribe that is in your area, you can then list that tribe and then add "food" to the search. For example, try "Chumash food". You can also add "diet", "medicine", "tools". Be creative and jot down notes of any plants (trees and shrubs included!) or animals that you see. If you are able to find a few different websites, you can cross-reference any information that you find. Your goal here is to come up with a list of 5-7 different species. From that list you can narrow it down to one plant and one animal. Do your best and realize that you don't have to get it "right". Make sense?

If you don't have access to the internet, or if you want to do some in-person research, you can go to a library, a natural history museum, or talk with people that are familiar with the subject. As you do your research, keep in mind that heritage species will often be related to food, though they do not have to be. As with the cedar tree, this can also be an organism that provides shelter, clothing, transportation, or any number of other uses. Look for things that were used for the basic needs and beyond - fire, shelter, food, water, tools, and clothing.

Since heritage species span across many different sectors of life - ranging from plants, animals, fungi, bacteria (yogurt), and even algae - you will notice overlap between your research here with that from other sections of the Kamana Resource Trail. Think of the "heritage species" concept as another layer to your research, that allows you to build even deeper connections with your local ecosystem.

I have my two heritage species! Now what?

Now that you have one plant species and one animal species, it's time to further your research. You can start with your Reader's Digest guide. Again, you will likely need to expand your research efforts to the internet or other resources.

For each species, I want you to:

- draw a detailed picture (include some basic information on identification)
- create a list of how humans used this species
- make a drawing of humans interacting with this plant or animal

With many parts of the Kamana program, we want you to balance the scientific observer with the creative naturalist. Be efficient, and have fun. Okay?

Create your two journals using the provided templates at the end of this chapter.

After you have completed your journals, I encourage you to find one of these heritage species in the real world. If you are inspired to test out something that you just learned, please do so.

Getting to know these heritage species can be a powerful experience. As we have become less dependent on our knowledge of the natural world for our survival, our awareness of these heritage species has declined. With some research and practice, who's to say we can't revive that powerful connection? Maybe you will help to bring this knowledge to your peers and the future generations.

AFTER LISTENING TO DISC SIX AND COMPLETING CHAPTER SEVEN

1. What is the attribute of the Northwest shield? How does its manifestation in our lives relate to cultural patterns moving through time?

2. What are some cultural elements that relate to the passage of wisdom between generations?

3. What is culture? What does it do? How does it relate to health and nature connection?

4. What are some simple practices that can be used on a daily basis to restore and nourish connection in a household?

5. When have you felt the most connected? What and who do you feel the most connected to and why? What led to that connection?

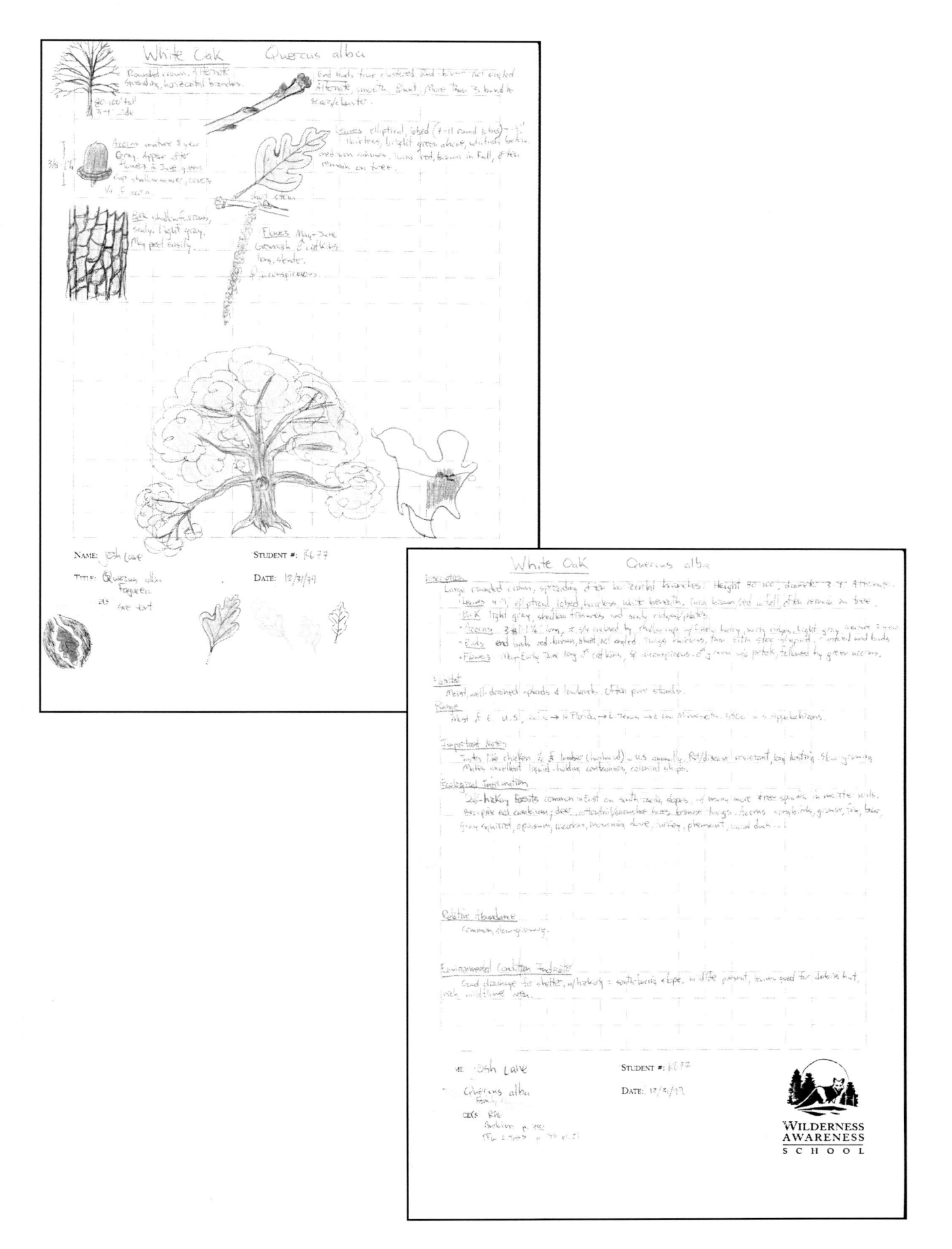

Kamana Resource Trail Journal by Kamana Four graduate Josh Lane

Create a Heritage Plant journal page.
Please take no more than 20 minutes to complete.

Name:

Date:

Species Name:

Scientific name:

Source(s):
Reader's Digest:
North American Wildlife

Sketch and color the species

Range Map

Important facts:

KAMANA
NATURALIST TRAINING PROGRAM

Create a Heritage Animal journal page.
Please take no more than 20 minutes to complete.

Name:

Date:

Species Name:

Scientific name:

Source(s):
Reader's Digest:
North American Wildlife

Sketch and color the species

Range Map

Important facts:

KAMANA
Naturalist Training Program

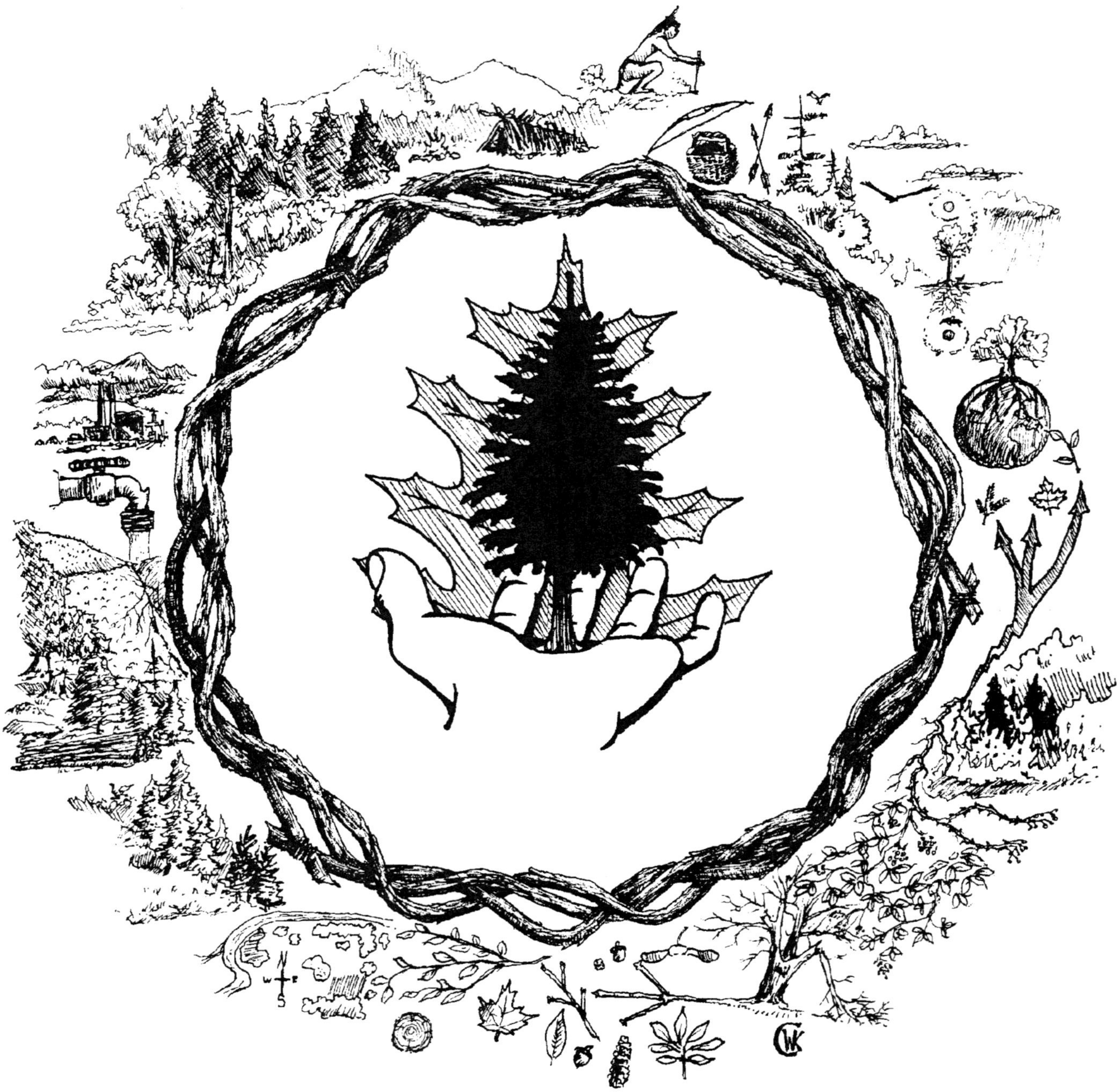

Chapter Eight

Learning To See the Forest and the Trees

Listen to Disc Seven of the *Seeing Through Native Eyes* disc series before or while you are completing this chapter.

It was a cold and wet morning out on the sandbar and the sun hadn't fully risen yet. I was out tracking early in the morning and having fun hopping over streams and puddles and listening to the soft sound of the rain falling on the water. I came to one place known as "Wolf Crossing," and, through poor judgment of my jumping ability, landed with both feet squarely in the frigid water. It wasn't so bad. I quickly pulled my shoes off and squeezed the water out of them and then kept walking along barefoot. A few minutes later, though, I began to notice that I was beginning to act strange. My thoughts and speech were beginning to slur and slow down. I was staring at seemingly nothing for a long time and just "spacing out." I was tripping over my own feet.

It may seem strange, but since my thinking was slowed, it took me a few minutes to realize what was happening and to recognize that these things were symptoms of hypothermia. Hypothermia is a dangerous condition where the body becomes so chilled that it starts to restrict the flow of blood to the arms, legs, and head as a last-ditch effort to keep the body's vital organs warm. Whenever it happens, it is certainly not a good sign and is an indication that you need to get warm as soon as possible. Complicating the matter was that fact that, beyond my cold and wet shoes, I was only wearing a T-shirt, flannel shirt and a pair of jeans, all of which were rain-soaked and offered me little warmth. I ran around for awhile to get my blood pumping, but began to tire quickly. What was I going to do? I was wet and cold with no place to go!

Trying not to trip over myself, I ran into the cedar forest nearby. I stood and looked around for a moment at the trees that were all around me. They were all glistening with tiny droplets of water. Where was I going to find dry twigs to start my fire? I ran up to a fir tree, and the lowest branches were twenty feet off the ground. I ran over to a cedar tree, and it was the same story. The twigs on the maples were still alive and green. The sticks on the ground were all spongy and soft with moisture and covered with moss. I went over to a hemlock tree, though, and found that there were a few thin, dead twigs at a height where I could reach them that had remained sheltered from the rain. I grabbed as many of the dry ones as I could off each hemlock tree until in just a couple of minutes I had two handfuls of dry twigs. I still had to get my fire lit, though.

In a situation like this, starting my fire with a hand drill or other primitive tool wasn't what I wanted to do. Don't get me wrong—I have a lot of respect for those tools. I was shivering so badly at that point, though, that I had a hard time pressing the flint of my lighter to get it to light. After some frustrating failed attempts to light my lighter with my numbed fingers, I got it going and soon had a nice fire to dry my shirt by while I ran around to keep my blood flowing.

That was a frightening experience for me. Truth-be-told, my car was only about half-a-mile away and I could have made it there and been safe. Had the situation become any more dire, I would have run there right away rather than continue to take my chances with a fire. I learned an interesting thing about hemlock trees that day, though—they produce good twigs for starting fires, even in the rain. Later on when I was back at home, I noticed that when it rained, the deer around my home rested under the cover of a dense hemlock tree. Many times since then I've sought my own shelter from the rain under the boughs of a hemlock tree, and even now as my eyes grow weary from typing the chapters of this book, I spend my breaks sitting under the shelter of the old hemlock that lives right outside my front door.

The Giving Tree

Humankind has always had a great fascination and respect for trees. Stand next to a tree and it is easy to realize why, for they stand tall and silent, and their roots reach deep into the ground and hold it together. Trees are sources of food, shelter, and water. These things are the staples of life for not only humans and deer, but for all living things.

Be it a person who lives off of the land in a small shelter or a person living in a home made of two-by-fours, people the world-over depend on trees for many aspects of their survival. We take the materials that we use to build our shelters and homes from the body of the tree. Many of our tools are made from the tree's limbs. Their bodies also serve to heat our homes and our bodies through fire. To the survivalist, the tree is essential as a source for making friction fires and as an indicator of where to find water. In fact, without knowledge of the trees, the survivalist's chances of survival are poor, at best. We are all indebted to the trees, for beyond these many things that they provide, they also purify the very air that we all breathe.

Beyond these physical needs, the trees also inspire our creativity. Any person who has spent time in the Northeast during autumn will be able to tell of the majestic tapestry of color that the trees reveal. Here in the rainy Pacific Northwest where the trees grow so very tall, the art of woodcarving has been refined to one of its highest expressions by the local Native peoples, whose stories and culture are passed from generation to generation through their totem poles. For the individual, the family, and the community, trees are not only vital life-supporting resources—they are generous friends.

The gifts of the trees are not just enjoyed by people. The Mohawk people of the Iroquois Confederacy give credit to the trees for creating a suitable and beautiful place for all things to live, saying that the trees "alter their environment so that all living things may enjoy a better life." When we look into the lives of the animals, we can begin to see why this is so. Just like you or me, animals develop routines around their basic needs for survival. Just as repeated traffic on your rug or floor will wear thin spots that connect the front door to the kitchen and the refrigerator to the sink, an animal's trails connect its home to its favorite feeding areas—areas which are frequently related to trees. Think of a park with mostly grass and one tree in the middle of it. If we were to visit that park and record the comings and goings of wildlife, we would find that the tree is the center of most of the activity of the birds and animals there. We would find many well-worn trails leading to that tree during the time of year when there is fruit on its branches. By the same token, however, just as you would stop walking to your sink when it is broken, we would see those same trails fading away in the spring when there is no fruit on the tree to attract the animals. Beyond the attraction of the tree's fruits, though, what if the park's caretakers allowed the leaves to accumulate beneath the tree after they fell off? The tree would become even livelier with activity! Shrews would voraciously hunt for insects. Foxes would visit the tree to feed on the shrews, and hawks would wait in the tree's branches for the shrews as well. Considering this, imagine what sort of activity there must be in a forest! The trees do enhance their environment—giving everything a better chance for survival—both through what they offer and what they "leaf" behind.

—Jon Young

Let's take a walk now through an imaginary pine forest. As we enter the forest, we notice that, with the exception of a few oddballs here and there, most of the trees in this place are pines. On our walk together through this forest, we come upon a pile made of small pieces of pinecones all around the base of a tall pine. The pile is *huge*! Not knowing exactly what it is and unable to shake our curiosity, when we return home we consult our field guides together and learn that there are certain squirrels that build their homes only in pine trees. They do this, it turns out, because their favorite food is the seeds that are contained inside the tree's cones, which would account for the size of the pile.

On our next trek through that same forest, we see from the footprints we have been following in the snow that the bobcat went out of its way to see if our friend the squirrel was available for lunch. Our next time out together, we find the bones of squirrels scattered around the base of a nearby tree. Looking up to where these bones have come from, we see there is the nest of a hawk high above with many hungry young ones in it. When we talk about this, we begin to realize the importance of the trees to all of this—they feed the squirrel, who in turn is food for the bobcat and the hawk. In talking, too, we come to see from their nests high above that the hawks understand the importance of trees, too, for they provide them with food and a safe place to raise their young.

Remember now that we have been walking in a forest that is made primarily of pine trees. Different types of trees make their own unique contributions, and all trees have their own unique combinations of plants and animals that they attract and support. When there is a forest of varied trees, there is an intricate web of life woven on a non-ending loom of ever-changing diversity—all made possible by the trees!

For a moment, now, let's look at a single tree. A single tree can even be an entire environment all by itself. A bend in the trunk or branch may collect the rain to form a small puddle where mosquitoes and frogs may breed. Innumerable plants—algae, lichens, and mosses—may grow on the tree's bark. There are vines and other plants that cling to and send their roots into the tree for their support. Animals and birds seek the hollow holes and forked branches of the trees for their nests, and they also feed on the many nuts, seeds, and fruits that the trees produce. Insects feed and forage on nearly all parts of trees, too, from the leaves and wood to the roots deep in the ground. All these things may be happening at the same time on just one single tree, which helps us to see that a tree can be a veritable world all its own!

The Green Magnet

When I was in college, I took a field trip into the desert of eastern Oregon to a national bird refuge. The place was very open and one could see out ahead for miles in all directions. The landscape was dotted with lots of small brush and grassy wetlands, but there were no trees to be found except in one small location clustered around the refuge's main office building. My best guess is that they had been planted there many decades ago to offer shady relief to the rangers who worked there in the hot sun. Of the entire trip, the most amazing day was the one we spent outside of that main office. In the trees around there I noticed more birds congregated in one place than I've ever seen before. Those trees were literally a magnet that drew in birds from all over the landscape. Owls, hawks, warblers, nighthawks, magpies, orioles, quail, and too many others to mention were all attracted to that small clump of trees.

Recently, I had an interesting conversation with a fellow nature-enthusiast who described a similar experience in a different type of desert. He said that in the middle of the city he noticed that an amazing variety of birds and animals were drawn to living in a small cluster of trees that were nestled in between a shopping mall, car dealership, and office buildings. He said they seemed to be drawn there from far and wide, and that they were more dense in those trees than anywhere else around there—even in the countryside! That's saying something about the magnetism of trees to wildlife. If you live in the city yourself, take a look in the trees that line the sidewalks or the bushes in the parking lot at the grocery store. I'll bet that in most cases you'll find birds or animals inside of them. On a recent trip to Brooklyn, New York, I came across a squirrel that lived in a streetside tree. *A squirrel*! It lived its life feeding out of the trash and lived in the trees along the street. Given the fact that the only bare patch of ground was the small square of dirt around the tree where it grew through the sidewalk, that really amazed me! What do trees do for the wildlife and people in your area?

And Now, the Main Event!

Where do we look to begin understanding the trees? Perhaps the best place to start is to understand what a tree is. "Come on. You have to be kidding me," you might be saying. "Everyone knows what a tree is." Okay, fair enough. Since we aren't together to go out for that walk through our pine forest together, though, let's use the illustrations below. Now, I understand that this is a simple exercise, so please bear with me. Study the pictures below for a brief moment, and then put a light "X" through the one that is not a tree.

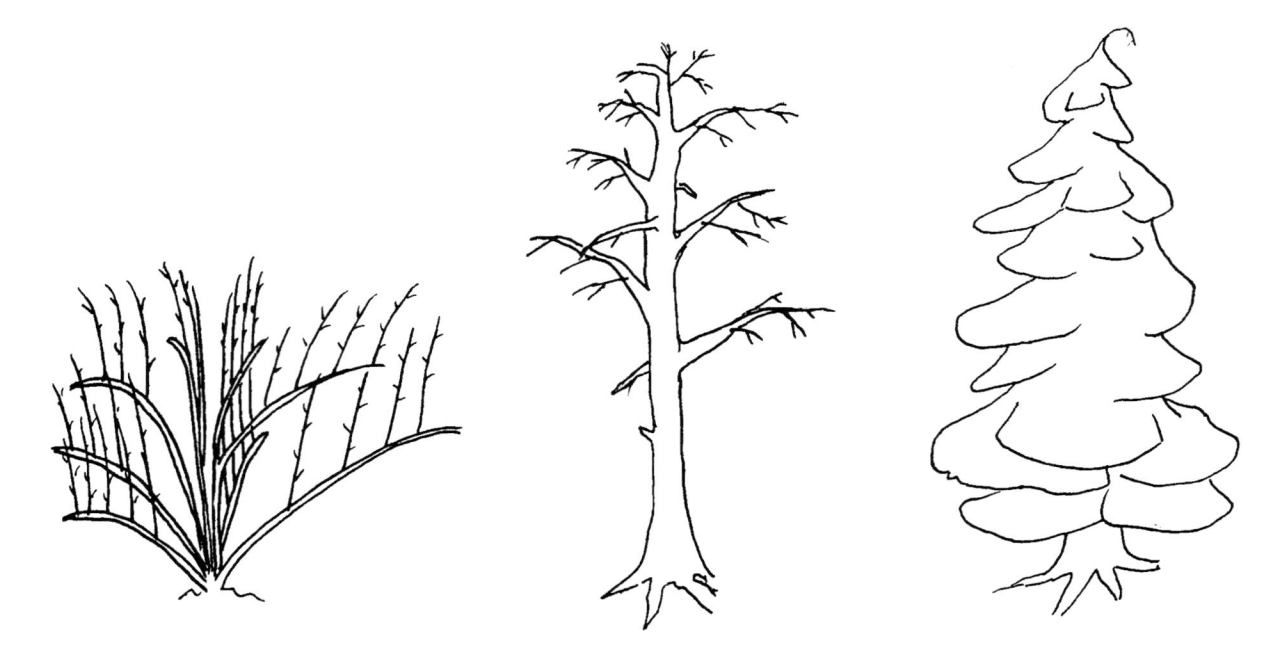

Okay, that was fairly simple—it was the one on the left, which was a shrub. Now that you've got that one, though, I'm going to up the ante a little bit. Do you remember from Chapter Four that there were certain features of the plant that clued you in to whether the plant was a dandelion? The same reasoning can be applied here. Forget the technical jargon that you may have learned and just compare the three illustrations above. What makes the two trees alike? How is the picture of the shrub on the left different from the other two? Use the space below to make some brief notes to answer these questions.

Now that you've done this, turn to pages 286 and 287 in your RDG and read about trees. In there, the question of "What makes a tree a tree?" will be answered. There is a lot of good information about trees given there. Read through those two pages now.

Let's use what you just read to examine the tree illustrations again. We've already hammered the "shrub vs. tree" question pretty well. The two trees that were pictured earlier are pictured in the space below. Obviously, these two aren't the same type of tree. What types of tree are they? Don't think in terms of the specific type of tree so much as the general category that the tree might be placed in. Refer back to pages 286 and 287 of your RDG, this time focusing on the questions, "What are the two general types of trees?" and "What distinguishes one type of tree from the other?" Skim those pages from your RDG again and then label each of the pictures below according to which category it falls into. Make some brief notes next to each picture, too, that describe the features that distinguish one from the other. Do these things now.

That last bit may have been a bit of a curve ball since there were no pictures of what a conifer or broad-leafed tree looks like on those pages that you read. If it gave you any difficulty, I hope you

PART THREE: THE RESOURCE TRAILHEAD   212

were able to puzzle it out. As it stands, the tree on the top is the broad-leaf, while the one on the bottom is the conifer. Good job, though! It's been a lot of work to get to this point—and there is a lot more to go. I'm feeling like I need to get outside now and take a quiet break to look at some *real* trees. Why don't you take a moment now and do the same and we'll come back together to continue our walk through the forest of information on trees.

Intermission. (Please stretch, buy popcor   n, soft drinks,   candy, and return to your seat. Really—go and take a break!)

Now that we've come back together, let's gather our stuff and head out for another imaginary walk through our local pine forest. We need to be sure to take a water bottle, lunch, notebook. Wait a minute! There is something wrong with taking that walk through our "local" pine forest. In looking at the map of forests on page 286 of my Reader's Digest Guide, it seems that there aren't pine forests everywhere. In fact, right here in the Pacific Northwest—my own backyard—pine trees are very rare. I don't doubt that there are others of you across the country who will encounter the same predicament, and what is the point right now of learning about a tree that you won't see every day? Looking again at that map, it seems there aren't any trees that all of us scattered around the country will certainly have in common. That's kind of a bummer, because there are some mammals, plants, and birds that are common to us all that we will be able to see wherever we go in the United States. Since there are no trees that we all have in common, though, I guess we will have to take a different approach to trees.

For those of you who live in an area that the map says has no trees, just flip through the pages of your RDG that describe trees and find one conifer and one broad-leaf that have range maps that cover the area in which you live. Write each of their names in the space here and then continue with the reading.

The first step to figuring out this puzzle is to find out what trees are in your area. Take a look at the map on page 286 of your RDG. Where is your home on that map? What type of forest does the map say your home is in? What this map is telling you is that certain types of trees will be the most common in a particular area. For instance, in the Pacific Coast Forest, the western hemlock, redwood, douglas-fir, and western redcedar are the most common trees. That's a great place to start. Write the name of the type of forest that is found in your area and the types of trees that are listed as being the most common. Do this now in the space below.

In looking at the map myself, I'm noticing that many sections of the map don't list any trees at all. Hmmm. If you live in one of those areas, follow the directions in the sidebar on the previous page. There have to be some trees living in your area!

In looking again at the Pacific Coast Forest, I know that redwoods are not found in the area of the Pacific Northwest where I live. They live further south. The map next to the picture of the redwood on page 295 supports my belief, showing that their range is far from where I live in Seattle. Where the redwoods live, though, is still considered to be a part of the Pacific Northwest Forest.

Look now at the list you created above. Are all the trees on your list found in your area? Use your RDG now and look up the description of each tree on your list. Check the map for each and see if that tree is found in your area. If it is, put a check mark next to it on your list. If the range map says that the tree is not found in your area, then just put a line through the name. While doing this, also pay attention to whether the tree is a conifer or a broad-leaf. Write a "C" next to the conifers on your list, and, you guessed it, a "B" next to each of the broad-leaves. This will come in handy in just a moment.

You now have a list of trees that are found in your area. All right! It can be a lot of work to sort through the wide world of trees. Thank goodness we're only going to focus on two trees here, and thank goodness that most of us don't live in the tropical rain forest! We'd be here listing trees all week!

Let's focus on our two trees now. It is here that the "C's" and "B's" you wrote next to your trees will come in handy. Choose one conifer and one broad-leaf from your list. It doesn't matter what tree it is, as long as it is found in your area. If you are missing one type of tree from your list (either conifer or broad-leaf), skim through the pages on trees in your RDG and check the range maps for each tree until you find the type you are missing. When you have chosen both of your trees, write their names in the appropriate space below. Do this now.

It seems that we are just now getting down to business. Could this have been easier if we had just gone outside with our book, picked two different trees, and figured out what they were? Maybe it would have. It would have meant a lot of flipping through pages to find the right match, though, with no guarantee that the tree you were looking at would be in the book. I was taught that field guides are not meant to be used outside. Whenever I do use them outside, I inevitably miss something cool like a pretty bird or a breeze rattling the grass while my nose is buried in the book. Also, when I can't picture the tree in my mind, I know that I don't really know that tree.

You now have your two trees. Good job. Let's get down to business again! Mark the pages in your Reader's Digest Guide that describe your two trees so you don't lose them. Now I'll let your RDG take you through the process of getting to know your trees. Having marked your pages, turn to page 287. Using your mind's eye, read the section titled "Tips on Identifying Trees." This is the nitty-gritty of learning how to tell one tree from another. Each tree description in your RDG does not include all of the details that are given for you on page 287. Some of them include a picture that shows you the shape of the whole tree, while others do not. Other descriptions include a picture of the tree's bark. Below you will see two columns, one labeled "Conifer" and the other labeled "Broad-leaf." Under the heading for each column, write the name of the tree you have chosen. Along the left-hand side of the page are labels that say things like "Leaves," "Flowers," and "Bark." Go down the column and for each label along the left-hand side, study the picture and written description for your tree. If you find no picture for bark, just skip it. Once you have studied the picture and description of your trees, use your mind's eye and draw a simple sketch and write a brief note to describe what is unique about the part of the tree you have drawn. By now you've practiced using your mind's eye through the chapters on hazards, mammals, plants, and indicators, so this should take no more than a couple of minutes to do. So start by reading page 287 and get cracking!

<u>**Conifer**</u>   <u>**Broad-leaf**</u>

Name of tree:

Leaves:

Flowers:

Fruits:

Bark:

Shape:

Take a moment and flip back through the pages that you've just filled out on trees. It is really quite impressive. What is more impressive is that all of that is now in your head, readily available for you to recall whenever it is needed!

One final thing to look at is whether your trees serve any value as a resource, either in the contemporary sense as lumber or furniture, or to the Natives of your area for making tools or as a source of medicine or food? Did the written description for your tree talk at all about such uses? If so, write some of them in the space below.

To me, it is the things that trees do for all of us that make trees really cool. They provide air for us to breathe, bind the soil together, provide homes for people and animals, and give us many useful tools. It was knowledge about hemlock trees that prevented my coming down with hypothermia, and I'm sure that, with people playing and living in the woods for thousands of years, hemlocks have saved others, too.

In closing, I'll just add that some kinds of trees have been so important to the survival of some Native peoples that the tree was central to much of their way of life. The western redcedar of the Pacific Northwest is a great example of this, so much so that this trait is recognized by another one of its modern names: "giant arborvitae," which means "giant tree of life."

I'd encourage you to take what you have learned today about these two trees of your area and take a real-life walk to your local library. Spend some time consulting the books that describe the traditional uses for your trees by the Native people who inhabit your area. If you have the opportunity, talk to the Natives yourself, or go to an expert on the ways that the trees and plants of your area have been traditionally used. The information is rich, and often accompanied by rich and ancient stories. Combining these things together with what you have learned here about your trees, you will have gained yet another important part of what it means to see through native eyes.

AFTER LISTENING TO DISC SEVEN AND COMPLETING CHAPTER EIGHT

1. What is the North Shield attribute?

2. What's the difference between survival and "thrival"?

3. What's the difference between hard skills and soft skills? Why are they important to do together?

4. Why is accidental nature connection not enough?

5. How does learning primitive skills lead to you feeling like you belong to the earth?

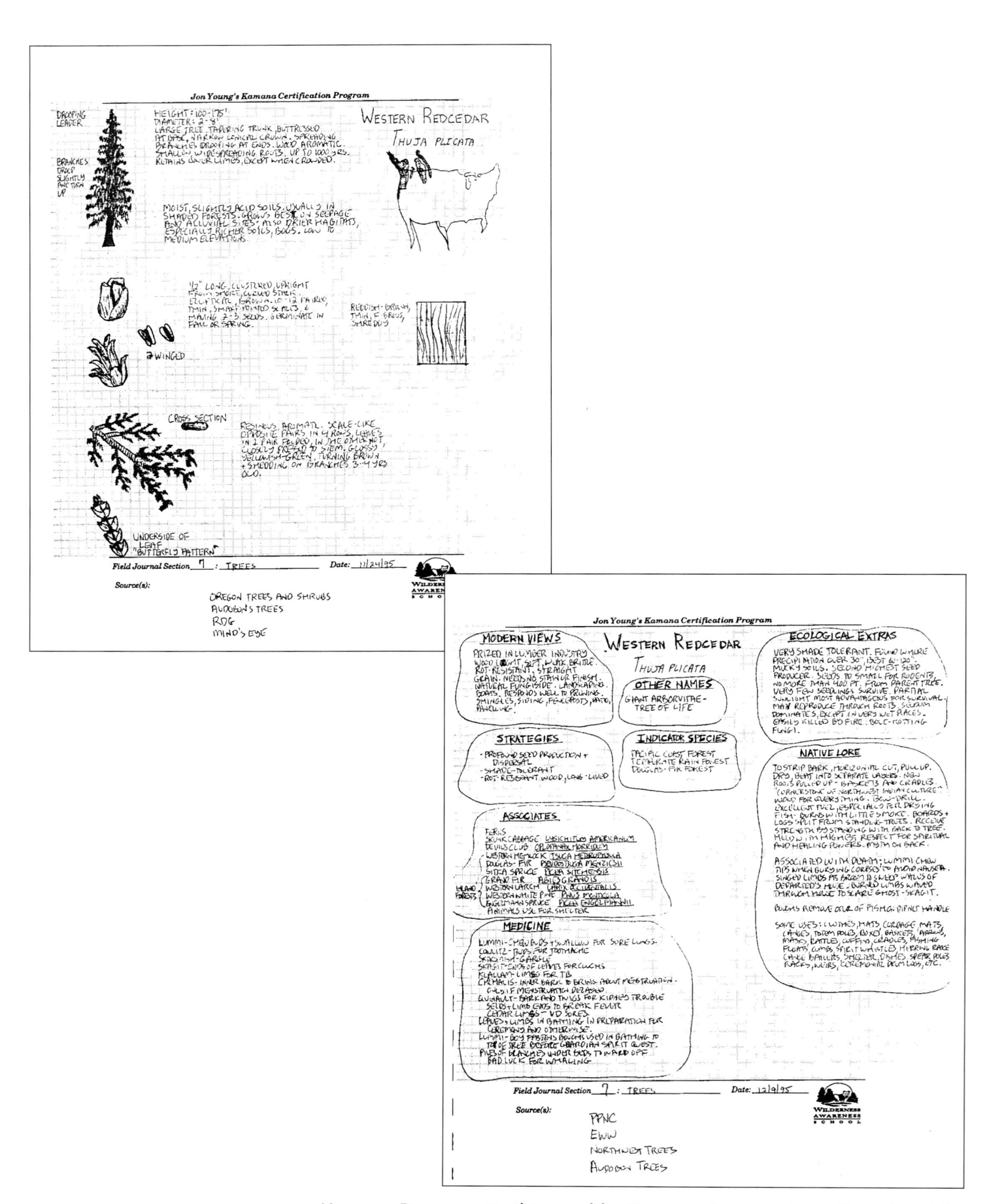

Kamana Resource Trail Journal by Kamana Four graduate Dave Franklin

Create a Trees journal page.
Please take no more than 20 minutes to complete.

Name:

Date:

Species Name:

Scientific name:

Source(s):
Reader's Digest:
North American Wildlife

Sketch and color the species

Range Map

Important facts:

KAMANA
NATURALIST TRAINING PROGRAM

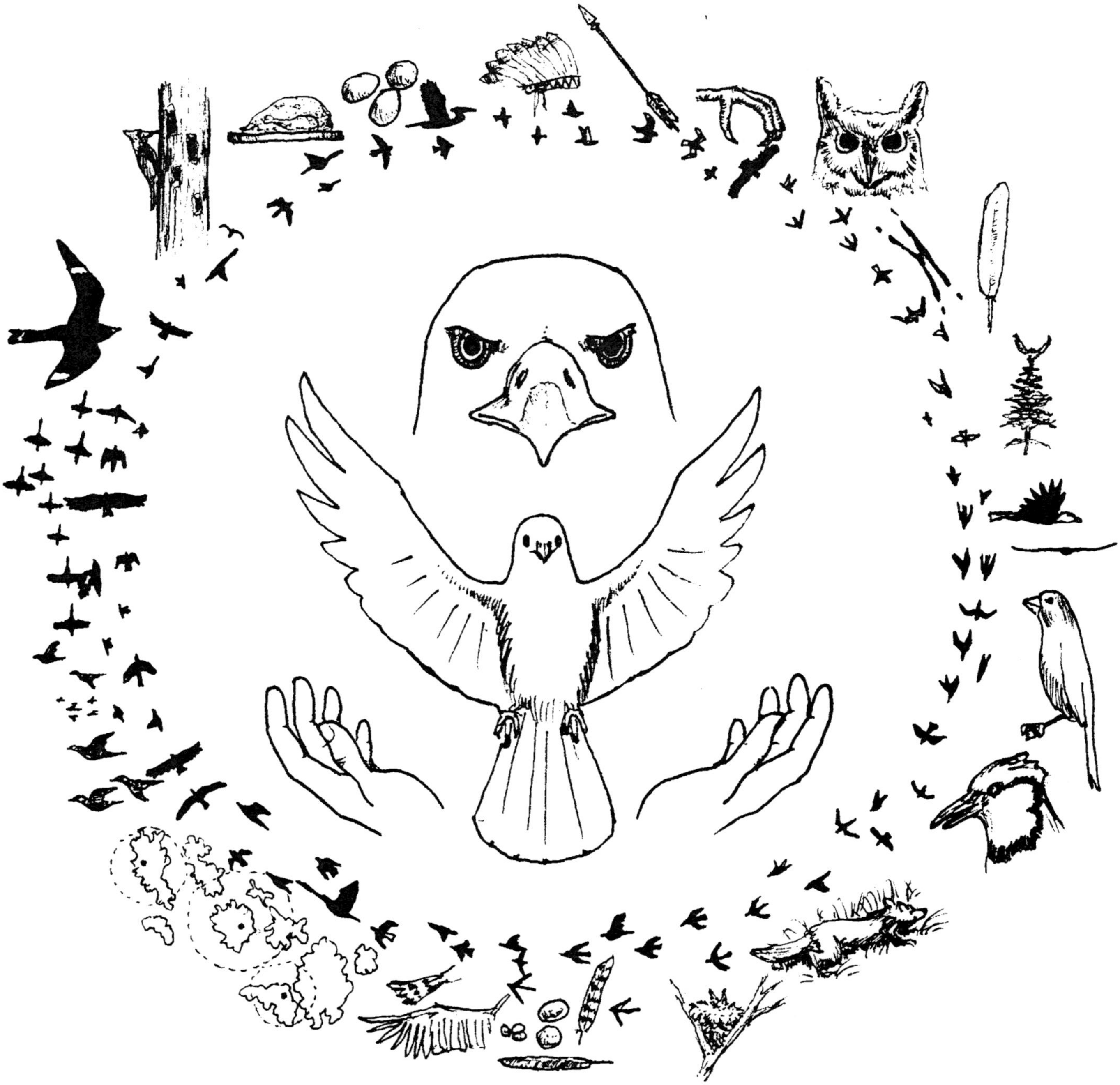

Chapter Nine

A Universal Language

Listen to Disc Eight of the *Seeing Through Native Eyes* disc series before or while you are completing this chapter.

The sun had just broken the horizon. My friend Chase and I were both squatting down on either side of a fire that we had been poking at and tending outside of my house since the early morning hours. The songs of the birds could be heard all around us welcoming in the new day, and we were talking in a half voice/half whisper.

When we had started our fire earlier in the night, it was raining out. Needless to say, we were thankful to see the sun coming over a cloudless horizon as we listened to the bird song that was all around us. The raspy squawk of a steller's jay broke the calm of the morning. If you've ever heard the call of a jay, you'll probably agree with me that jay's call—while beautiful in its own way—is sort of the "black sheep" of bird noises when compared with the songs of many other birds. At first, the squawk of the jay didn't grab our attention too much. We noticed it but kept on talking. Then another jay came and began making that same noise in the same place—and together they were making a lot of noise and being very persistent at it. That seemed a little bit unusual. In the blue haze of the dawn, I looked over toward the thicket about one hundred feet away from where Chase and I were. I could see the jays making their racket on the top of the thicket, sitting a few feet away from each other, but they were both looking at the same spot below them. Their long beaks were like a pointer that showed where they were looking. Because there was a thick cover of leaves on the bushes, though, we couldn't see into the thicket to tell what they were pointing at.

The jays were moving slowly along the tops of the bushes and soon moved out of sight, continuing to make a racket as they moved. Even though we could no longer see them, since we could still hear the jays, we could follow where they were going. It seemed like they were following something and heckling it as it moved through the thicket. A song sparrow began to call out "cheet, cheet," as the jays passed by it and other birds would join in on occasion as the jays moved by. What was going on?

Since I knew the area they were in (this entire episode had started right next to the front door of my house, so it was an area that I walked past every day), I knew that they were heading for the other side of the thicket. I got up and left Chase by the fire and went down to the corner and waited behind a tree to see if I could see what they were following. I had an idea, but I wanted to see it for myself to make sure. I waited, but I didn't see it. Soon the sound of the jays died off and things returned to normal. The whole episode had lasted only about ten minutes.

A little while later, the clouds returned and it began to sprinkle on us a little bit. We'd been up for several hours by then, so we went for a short walk before we were going to head into town. Our walk brought us down a trail that formed the other side of that thicket where we had heard the birds earlier. There, in the dark soft mud on that trail, was the fresh track of a *bobcat*! Since it had rained earlier, it could have been made no more than a couple of hours earlier, which would have put it at just the time that we had been listening to those jays. That was *exactly* what I had thought that it might be when I had gone down to the corner earlier and waited by the tree! I was so happy. I drew pictures of the track and the area around it and wrote the whole story of the birds down in my journals.

A Language without Words

What does this event say about birds? In many ways, it says to me that the birds are the scouts of the forests. When I say "scout," I'm not talking about a Boy Scout. What I'm referring to is the scout who goes out in search of information for a group. In his books, Tom Brown, Jr. writes a lot about the Apache scouts and the amazing skills of tracking and awareness that they developed from going out in search of places for their people to live and find game. They were always on the lookout for the threat of enemies who might be moving in on their people, too. Geronimo, who you read about in Chapter Four, was a scout. One place where the idea of the scout is still employed these days is in the area of professional sports. Sports teams and many colleges employ scouts to go out and seek out the best young talents to ensure the survival or growth of their teams. Is that any different? In many ways, the birds seem to be the scouts of the forest. I'll explain that one in a little while.

Understanding what the birds are saying is not a magical skill. More than anything else at first, it is the process of elimination. Just as with tracking, there are many mysteries that remain unsolved, which is why I was so excited about the jays Chase and I heard that morning and the bobcat track—the mystery had been solved!

There are a few keys to learning to interpret what the birds are saying. Of course, knowing the birds and their calls is one of those things. Another key, though, that you can practice anywhere with anything is studying body language. Say, for instance, that after Chase and I left the bobcat track and went into town, we went over to my parent's house (true, my folks live in New York, but let's pretend for now that they live just down the road here in Duvall). As we walk in the door, I forget to take off my shoes and track mud from the front door straight through the living room and right to the refrigerator in the kitchen (usually that line is straight as an arrow). My mom comes in to see who has come into her home. Upon seeing the spots of mud all over her floor, however, her greeting changes. What she does is: 1) leans forward a little, 2) puts her hands on her hips, 3) cocks her head a little bit to the side, and 4) asks me some very pointed questions about my behavior with a very annoyed tone to her voice. The only thing that will atone for my boldness is if I get out a mop and clean up the floor. Can you relate to an example like that? I've seen the mothers of friends do that, too. Now, I don't intend to limit this to just mothers—people in general do it all of the time. There are common expressions that are unspoken but that communicate our thoughts and intentions very clearly, and that is what we all refer to as "body language."

If body language is common from person to person, could it not be common from animal to animal? Bird to bird? Person to bird? A good example to look at is geese because they move very slowly. Walk up on a flock of geese and watch what happens. As you first begin to move toward them, they might not notice at all. At some point, though, you will cross an invisible wall and begin to violate their "comfort zone." At this point, one or two of them might pick up their heads from feeding and look right at you, as if to say, "Yes, we see you. What do you want?" If you take another step, those two may make a quiet noise to the others and suddenly there won't be two geese looking at you, there will be fifty. A few of them might start to get nervous and fidgety, too, and will start to move away from you. If you take another step or two, they will start to get a little bit louder and more will begin to move away until suddenly one of them can't stand the pressure any more, freaks out, and takes flight, causing every other goose to panic and fly away.

People might act that same way. If you go up to a strange house and knock on the door during dinner time, someone will come to the door to see who it is. When they see that you are not someone familiar to them, they'll probably keep the screen door closed between you and them and talk to you through the screen, or if there is no screen door, the door will stay only cracked so that it can be easily closed. The door is a visible version of that same "invisible barrier." Standing with that door between you, they'll give you a chance to say what you have to say. Chances are, though, that since it is dinner time and you have interrupted the family's meal, unless you have something interesting to say, the person answering the door will tell you to go away and leave them alone. When that person goes back to their dinner table, everyone will want to know who was there and they might talk about it for a moment before resuming their conversation. Knock on the door again. This time dad will come to the door, and he will be visibly annoyed. "Hey, we told you to go away. You're interrupting my family's meal, and no thank you, we don't want any of what you are selling." This time he will close the door harder, shaking the house a bit. When dad returns to the table, the family might get a little worried that there is some wacko at the door who might want to hurt them. Someone might start to fidget in their chair or poke nervously at their food. You knock on their door again. This time, out of a mixture of anger and fear for his family, dad gets up and flings the door open and steps outside boldly to chase you away. Big brother goes to the door, too. Mom gets on the phone and calls the police while the smaller brothers and sisters get in the car in case they'll have to leave. Chaos ensues, and you end up in jail having made enemies and not friends.

Does this show the parallels in body language? A strange dog will do that, too. If you go up to it and poke it once, it might just move away and look at you as if you were weird. Go up to it and poke it again and it might move away and growl. Go and poke it again and you might be bitten before it runs away to get as far away from you as possible.

Besides body language, a common theme through this is that you are a stranger who is acting very boldly. Birds in the forest will act the same way when something comes through their home that they are not familiar with. If they are familiar with it, then they will react according to their experience with it. To illustrate, let's go up to a house again and knock on the door (I'll wait in the car with the engine running while you knock, okay?). Instead of it being a stranger's house, though, now go to a friend's house. Once they see who you are, they will let you in right away and you will be welcomed. That is because they know you and enjoy your company. If you were to go back to the same house that you visited in the first example, though, upon seeing who you are, the dad would immediately come out into the yard to chase you off and mom might get on the phone again to call the police. Again, birds are the same way. If you always act respectful of their presence and watch what they are saying to you through their body language, in time the flock will welcome you into their home like a friend would. You'll even be able to walk right up to them without them being bothered by your presence. Conversely, if every time you see the geese you act boldly and don't listen to what their body language is saying to you, you will develop a "bad reputation" and in the future they'll fly away from just seeing you.

Ask yourself now: What type of reputation would a bobcat have to a jay? Most likely, the bobcat would try to kill and eat the jay, so the bobcat would not have a very good reputation with the jay. The jay would yell and shout every time it saw the bobcat. What would the jay think of a deer? Since deer don't eat jays, most likely the jay's opinion of the deer would be something like, "Hey, the deer has never done anything to bother me. Why should I care if it comes by?" True, it isn't exactly this cut-and-dried, but you can probably see now that by understanding which birds might be bothered by what animals, understanding what is happening around you in the forest then becomes—you guessed it—a process of elimination.

Now, I had a hunch that it was a bobcat moving through the thicket because I knew the jay's distaste for bobcats. Before I knew who it was, though, the body language of the jay informed me that something was happening. It reminded me of my mom whenever she would get annoyed with me. Her habit of placing her hands on her hips, leaning slightly forward, cocking her head, and using a stern voice was mirrored in the jay's own body language: leaning forward, its wings and tail twitching slightly, its head cocked to the side, and a stern voice.

I hope this is enough for you to get a broad picture of how bird language works. Go out and try some of these things for yourself. No, don't knock on stranger's doors. I don't want to be called to testify at your trial and be responsible for your resulting jail term. Find a park, though, and practice with the geese. Also, follow Jon's advice from Tape Six of the *Seeing Through Native Eyes* series and find one place to visit regularly. Get to know each individual bird in that place as you would a friend. Get to know their individual likes and dislikes and how they would like to be treated, and in time they will welcome you into their home.

A Bird in the Hand

The first step in getting to know the likes and dislikes of the different types of birds is to learn how to tell those different types of birds apart from one another. My first introduction to studying nature came during my second year in college through studying birds. I was fortunate enough to have learned about the science of studying birds from a professor whose life-long love of birds helped me to develop a real appreciation for the remarkable animals that birds are. The way that I was taught to recognize a bird was to watch the bird for as long as it was in front of me, and to then—after it was gone—get out my field guide and look it up. When I was first beginning, there were so many times I would want to know the name of the bird right away. I would stop watching the bird and start flipping through my field guide—even while the bird was still in front of me. It was at those times when I'd hear my professor's voice call out to me, "The bird is over there, Paul, not in the book." It was only after the bird had gone that I was encouraged to get out my field guide and recall from my memory what the bird had looked like. That helped me to build my powers of observation quite a lot, and I learned how to identify birds very quickly.

Your RDG is a good source for pictures, so we'll just have to use this exercise to make the pictures come to life for us. Before we do this, though, let's take a brief step back and look at birds in general. Turn to page 76 in your *Reader's Digest: North American Wildlife*. Read the introduction to birds that ends on page 77. There are many good tips and ideas. After you have read this, make notes in the space below about five tips that will help you to learn birds.

Now that you've read the section on how to approach learning about birds, use your mind's eye and read the section titled "Tips on Identifying Birds" on page 77. Read this section a couple of times, because the information there is very important for you to understand. Once you have done this, mark your page and close the book. In the space below, make a brief list of three or four key features to pay attention to when identifying a bird.

1)

2)

3)

4)

Now it's time to go "watch" some birds! Turn to page 134 in your RDG. On the top of the page is a sight that may be familiar to you looking out your back window—a bird pulling a worm out of the ground. We already know what the bird is because next to the picture it says "American Robin." Pause for a moment, though. Would you be able to recognize this bird if you saw it outside on your own? Turn and look at the picture of the black-headed grosbeak on page 149 and the picture of the rufous-sided towhee on page 151. Study those pictures for a moment, then mark the page and close your book. The robin, grosbeak, and towhee have some features in common that might throw you off if you are just beginning. What are three features of their coloring that these birds have in common? Write those three now in the space below.

1)

2)

3)

Thanks for taking the time to do that. As I said before, what I wanted you to see was that there are certain birds that can easily look alike to you when you are first starting out. Below the robin in your RDG there is a picture of the varied thrush, which is another bird that can easily be confused with a robin if one doesn't take the time to really pay attention to what the bird looks like. That doesn't mean staring at the bird. Birds don't like being stared at any more than you or I would. After all, you want to make a good impression with the birds so they'll welcome you into their home, right? Plus, didn't your mother tell you that it's rude to stare?

Instead of staring at a bird, what you want to do is know what key features to watch for that will help you to identify the bird quickly. In the space below you will see the outlines of two different-looking birds. One of them is the silhouette of a robin, while the other is the silhouette of another type of bird. Is it *possible* to identify a bird from just a silhouette? How can you tell which bird is the robin? After all, there are no field marks on the picture. Look over the silhouette and then write some brief notes in the blanks next to each picture that correspond to the following features: 1) the shape of the body, 2) the body's posture, 3) the beak, and 4) the tail. Just write a brief note next to each number that compares the two silhouettes. Consult the picture of the robin in your RDG, too—it will help you a great deal. Do this now.

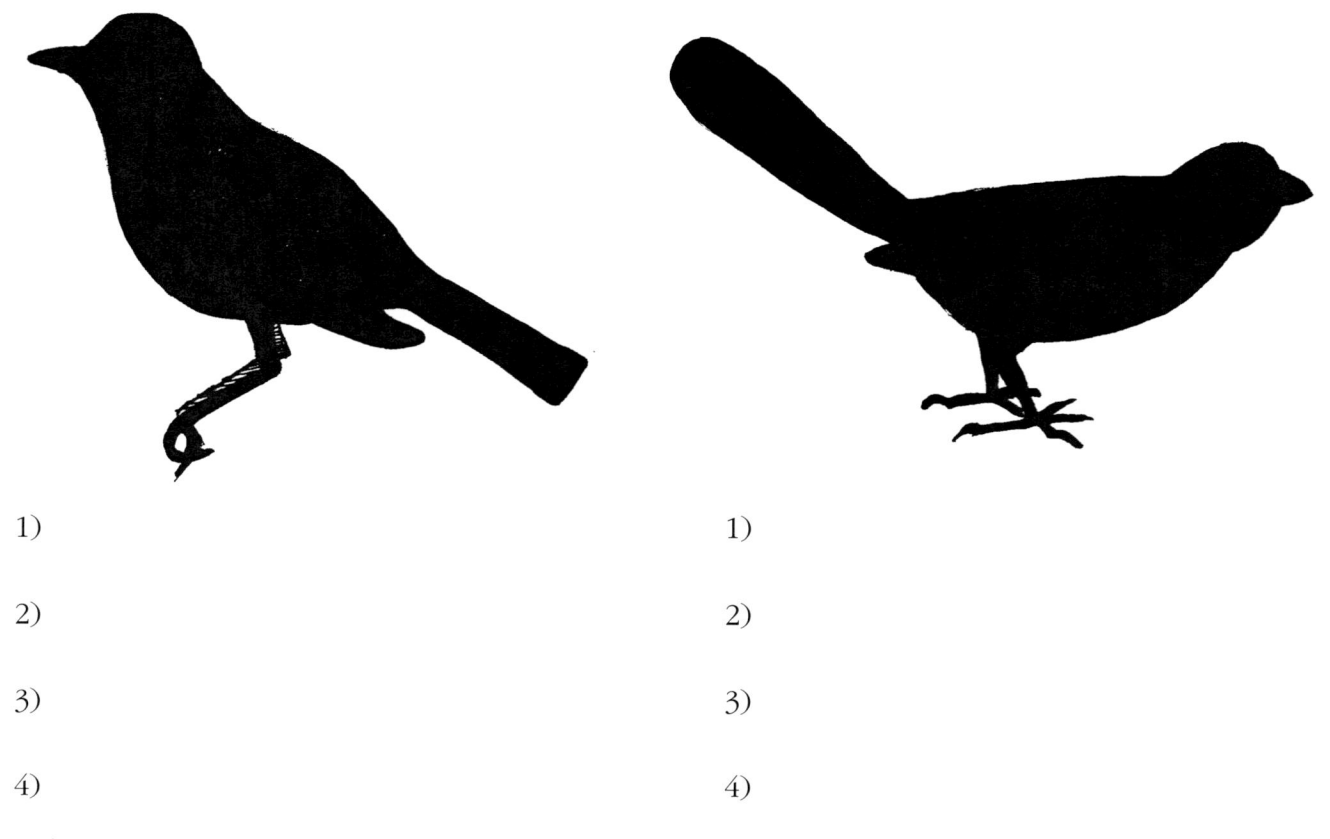

1)   1)

2)   2)

3)   3)

4)   4)

If you chose the outline of the bird on the left, you chose the correct bird. Turn to page 134 of your RDG again. Use your mind's eye to study the picture of the robin. Pay attention to the lines and check marks that are pointing to certain features of the bird. The colors and features that these are pointing to are known as "field marks," and these are really what you need to pay attention to if you want to learn how to identify a bird. Below is another outline of a robin. Use your mind's eye now to color or shade it in based on the field marks that you can recall from studying the picture. Do this now.

Turn back to page 134 again and now read the description of the robin titled "What to look for" using your mind's eye. Compare what you've read with the picture that you colored in above. Are there any features that you've missed? Did you remember to draw in the black and white stripes on its throat? What about the patch of white under its tail? If you missed these, or anything from the list that you read from the book, color or shade them in now. Take a moment to also to label your drawing based on what you have just read, with arrows pointing to the markings of the bird that you are describing. Do these now.

So, now that we've done all of this studying, what does a robin have to do with understanding what birds are saying? Rather than give an explanation, I'm going to let you answer this one for your-

One of the most helpful books that I can recommend for identifying birds is one of the Peterson Field Guides to Birds (Eastern, Western, or Texas depending on where you live). The author, Roger Tory Peterson, created a fantastic tool for you to use when he created these books, which are a blending of his two loves—nature and art. Up until Peterson, identification was thought to be something that one couldn't be certain about unless the bird was "in hand," which in those days often meant "dead." Once the bird was "in hand," there was a long series of very fine details that were looked over in the lab to confirm the bird's identity. Peterson created his field guide system to highlight what have come to be known as "field marks," which are colors, shapes, postures or other features that are unique to that bird only. They allow someone to identify a bird "in the field," or "outdoors" and from a distance without having to have the bird in hand. In the

Peterson system, these markings are indicated with arrows that point to the distinctive features that you should pay attention to. Because of the easy system—which is used also for plants, mammals, weather, and many other aspects of nature—Roger Tory Peterson can be credited with almost single-handedly igniting a passion for learning about nature that has touched millions of people around the world.

Your RDG has a version of the Peterson system that you have been using, with lines and check marks that point to different features of the bird that you should know.

self. Have you ever seen a robin? If you have, you've probably seen them most often in one of two places: on a lower branch of a tree, or on the ground in an open area like the park, your lawn, or along a trail in the forest. What are they doing there on the ground? If they can fly, why don't all birds just spend all of their time in the trees? Heck, some birds do spend all of their time in trees—but not robins. Why? What would cause a robin to come down to the ground—down near the jaws of dangerous predators? Think like a robin yourself—what would attract *you* to spend time on the ground even though it is a dangerous place to be? Your RDG has an excellent section about robins next to the picture on page 134 that can help you. Read that now and, as you read, ask yourself, "Why would a robin come down to the ground?" In the space below, write your best guess based on what you have just read.

If you wrote "to feed," you're right on target. Robins typically feed on the ground and spend time in the trees either when they aren't feeding or when they are afraid of something that is on the ground. What do they eat, though? Write what you can remember in the space below, and then check with your RDG to be certain (because, if your mind's eye is like mine, it probably adds a few things in here and there that the book didn't really say). Add anything to your list that you didn't remember the first time.

If you flip back over the previous few pages, you'll find that you've actually learned a lot about recognizing robins and a little bit about their needs and behavior. That is a great starting place, and there really isn't much to it. All you need to do now is go out and start watching them. If there are no robins near you (check the map in your RDG to be sure), you can go through this same process for another bird of your area. If you decide to choose another bird, though, remember this: The birds that will teach you the most are the birds that feed on the ground. Read in your RDG about what each bird eats, and look at its color, too. Is it a bright yellow bird? If it is, it probably does not come down to the ground at all! After all, what would stand out better on a green grassy lawn than a bright yellow bird? No, you'll typically find those birds high in the trees. What you will want to find to continue your studies are the birds that feed on the ground and that are brownish in color. They are brown because the ground is brown, too, and what could be harder to find on the ground than a brown bird? It is interesting that the birds that tend to be your greatest teachers are also, generally, the birds that are most frequently overlooked because they are brown and, usually, also common.

Now, list three birds from your area that are good for learning bird language. Write the names of those birds in the spaces below that are numbered 1 through 3. If you included the robin on your list, choose another bird that is useful for learning bird language. Look each of the birds up in your RDG and make some brief notes next to each name below that describe why this bird might be good for learning how to understand the birds. Do this now.

1)

2)

3)

As a bird watcher myself, I'll say that my drive when I was first beginning was to find the most majestic bird that I could, which often meant that it needed to be either large, a predator (like a hawk or an owl), brightly colored, or rare to get my attention. The birds that we want to study here, though, are often none of the above. Get to know them. Learn to tell them apart and what they need as we have done here, and then follow Jon's advice from Tape Six, "Seeing Through the Eyes of the Forest." Understanding the language of the birds is an important art in learning the language of nature. Learning to hear what the birds are saying will open up an ability to know things that are happening around you in the forest without seeing them. It is a skill that all of our ancestors from all parts of the world once possessed, and it is a skill that we can teach ourselves again. It's another part of learning to see with native eyes.

AFTER LISTENING TO DISC EIGHT AND COMPLETING CHAPTER NINE:

1. What is the attribute of the NorthEast shield? Why does a foundation in this attribute help all of the other attributes of connection to emerge more quickly?

2. How can listening for bird language help a person to develop a quiet mind and deep presence in the moment?

3. Where is a good place to practice listening for bird language?

4. How does intention relate to bird language?

5. What are the "five voices" of the birds?

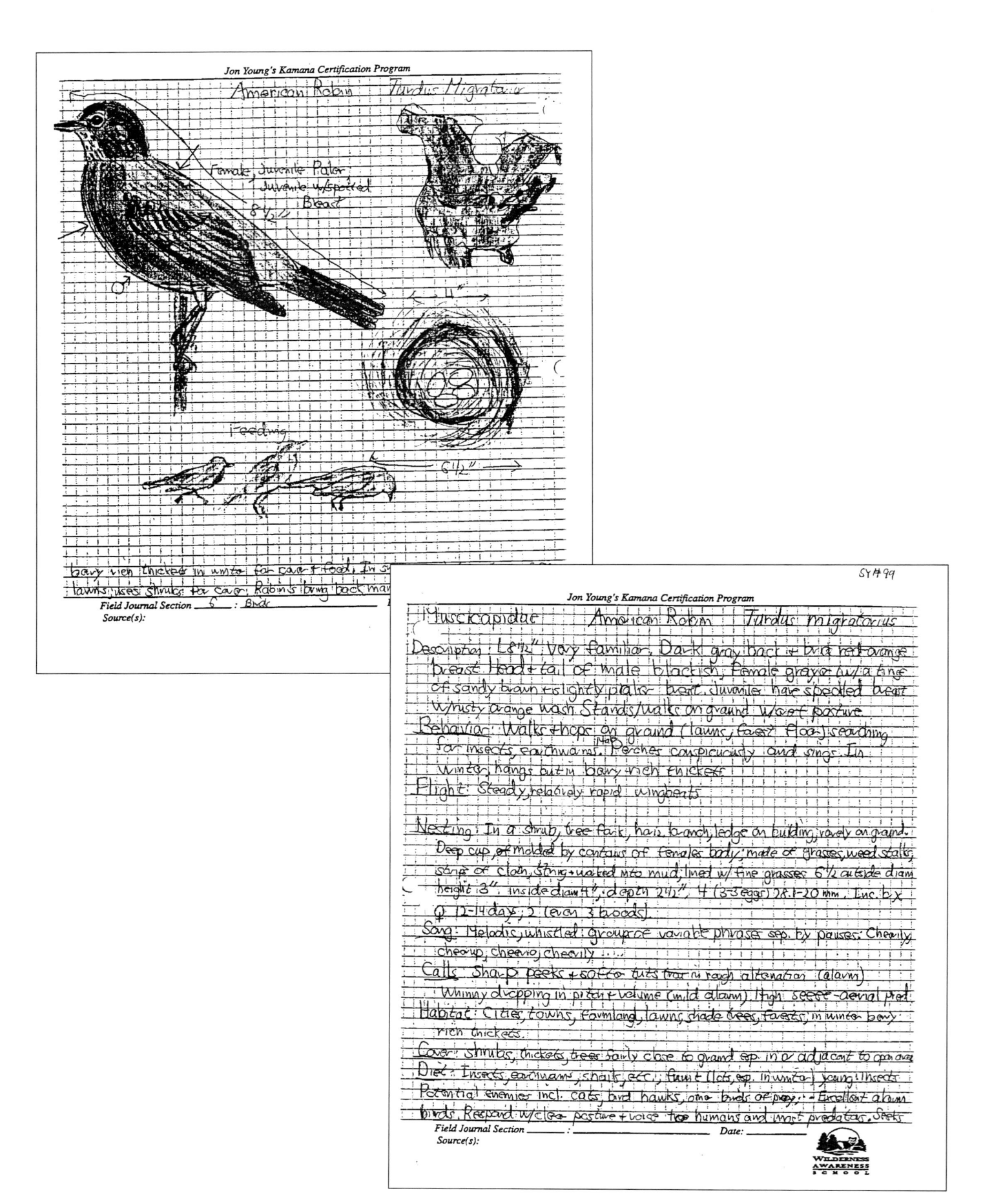

Kamana Resource Trail Journal by Kamana Four graduate Steve Young

Create a Birds journal page.
Please take no more than 20 minutes to complete.

Name:

Date:

Species Name:

Scientific name:

Source(s):
Reader's Digest:
North American Wildlife

Sketch and color the species

Range Map

Important facts:

KAMANA
Naturalist Training Program

Chapter Ten

Wrapping The Bundle

To wrap up what you have experienced in *Kamana One*, we'd like you to take the Tourist Test and to fill out the Questionnaire to tell us about what you think of this course. You'll find both of these in the Appendix.

The Tourist Test

Remember the Pop Quiz at the beginning of the Nature Awareness Trail? That was a little set of questions. Now we give you the Big Set, from the original "Test That Made a School." Remember the story – nearly no one passes this test! So, don't feel bad if you find it more complicated than you're ready for. But do take it. It's challenging, intriguing, and stimulating. Just sit down for an hour or so and go at it. See what you know. Should you decide to go on to our *Kamana Two* course, this test will be put on record as your beginning point. Find the test as Appendix A , and enjoy!

The Questionnaire

We ask you please to answer four questions. The first two ask you to reflect on what you learned and the others help us make this course better. We really appreciate your help. Find the questionnaire as Appendix B.

Wrapping the Bundle

What you have been reading here are stories from my own experience as a student of nature and the world around me, along with stories and exercises from Jon Young. Though I have been studying in this way for a few years now, I feel that I am just a beginner. I know that Jon himself still feels this way, even though his experiences in the outdoors cover nearly thirty years more than mine do. In fact, for me, writing this book has been a great reflection of where I can still grow as a naturalist and tracker. No matter how many years of experience in the outdoors we have accumulated, there are always more questions that can be answered and more mysteries that can be followed.

The exercises you have been practicing in this book are one piece of a whole way to approach the study of nature.

The other piece is the book that Matt wrote, the Nature Awareness Trail Head. Together, these routines and ways of approaching the study of nature are a way of observing—observing your surroundings, observing plants and animals, and observing yourself.

This way of seeing is not the sole property of Wilderness Awareness School. Rather, it is the shared lineage of all of the people of the world, for at some point in each of our own ancestries, we all lived close to the land. Wilderness Awareness School has played the role of the "bundle wrappers," so to say—the ones who, through the contributions of Native people from around the world, have sought out and explored the common threads to share them again with you. This way of seeing is a natural part of who we all are. For every generation since the beginning of time, people have lived off the land with rich cultures that supported our understanding of our place in the world.

The cultures of people who live close to the land focus much of their attention on being aware and learning about nature because it is a part of their daily survival experience. In these cultures, everyone has a general knowledge of the world around them, and it is the elders, those who have gained the greatest knowledge and wisdom, who guide the direction of the culture. Where is that in modern society? If you go to an elder businessman and ask him a question about a work situation, chances are that he will be able to steer you in the right direction. He may even give you some things to try that will help you to improve your own business skills. What if you had a question about something in nature— who would you turn to for guidance? Over the course of a typical day, many of us don't even set foot on bare earth or grass. It is very easy for us to go all day driving in our cars on smooth asphalt roads and walking on concrete and floors. Nature is just not a part of our everyday experience, and as such has simply been shed as something that is not worth paying attention to.

Ask yourself this now: Who has been your elder throughout this course? Has it been me? No. Jon Young? No. Your elder has been your *Reader's Digest Guide.* Remember, field guides are a compilation of the observations and experiences of many hundreds, if not thousands, of naturalists that have been condensed into a format that is easy for you to use. Does that not sound like an elder, whose lifetime of experience and reflection carries a great deal of wisdom and knowledge? Like an elder, too, you need only to identify your question and know which elder to go to for assistance. Our role here has been to help you learn what questions to ask. That is all. Your questions will give you a focus for your attention. Likewise, your observations and reflections will guide your questions, so in that way questioning and observing are both one and the same.

This book is just a first step in learning to see through native eyes. Once you have finished these final pages, please take a moment to go outside and reflect on what you have learned. Consider this: Do you notice more of the landscape and what is happening around you? Imagine the strength of your skills after practicing these routines not just for two weeks, but for two years! Twenty years! You have the basics right now. Someone once said, "Practice doesn't make perfect. Practice makes permanence." There's a lot of truth to that, for it applies to developing good habits as well as to forming bad habits. Here in this course, you've received the basics of good naturalist habits.

As you know, though, *Kamana One* is just the first of four levels of training in nature observation. With each successive level of study, your skills will become increasingly refined and honed until they are razor-sharp. Your knowledge of the hazards, mammals, plants, indicators, trees, and birds of your area will grow tremendously to include knowledge of not just one of each, but dozens. Your experience with them will grow, too, one step at a time through your completion of the program. It is all at your own pace and designed to give you the routines to practice and add upon so that your skills will grow with confidence.

In the next level of study, we will branch out to use several different field guides. In the next level of study, too, you will learn new techniques to help you mine each one of those field guides for every bit of information they will yield. The awareness exercises that you've practiced here will also be intensified to advance your learning efficiently. Instructors from our Office of Independent Studies will work with you to streamline your growth to propel you to higher levels of understanding about nature as quickly as possible. (See Appendix C and the registration form at the end of the book.)

In closing, I'd like to send you my heartfelt thanks for taking this first step on the path to fostering a greater awareness of the world around us. Your hard work in this book is worthy of congratulations. Take what you have learned to heart, for it is the things we understand that we will take care of. The choices that we make now will impact the knowledge and state of the world that we pass on to our children. Tell a friend, and share what you have learned here with them, for the knowledge and understanding that you possess is a rare gem these days. You now own a piece of what it means to see through native eyes.

We hope to see you again...

Jon Young, Matt Wild & Paul Houghtaling

KAMANA
NATURALIST TRAINING PROGRAM™

PATH OF THE NATURALIST
KAMANA TWO

Final Reflection

Name: _____

Date: _____

Final Reflection

APPENDIX A: THE TOURIST TEST

The "official" title of the test you are about to take has changed several times. "Alien Test," "Tourist Test," and "Tracker's Backyard Journey" are some of the names we have used to describe this experience. On some fronts, "Alien Test" has seemed harsh, while "Tracker's Backyard Journey" hasn't adequately captured the essence of what the test is creating for the person taking it. Perhaps "Tourist Test" is the best option, and recently it was decided to stick with that title for this experience.

If you don't know the answer right off, just move on to the next question. It shouldn't take you that long, maybe an hour. Enjoy the test and regardless of whether you feel you were able to answer many of the questions or not, take time to reflect upon this once you have finished. Have fun and enjoy taking...

THE TOURIST TEST

Name:

Today's date:

Name of nearest town:

Simple description of the area:

INSTRUCTIONS: The first thing you should remember when taking this test is that honesty is the best policy. The object is not to prove anything, but simply to find out what you know and what you do not know. The test will illuminate for you what Wilderness Awareness School is all about. If you find yourself interested in knowing the kinds of things that are on this test, then this school is for you.

Find a quiet place where you will be able to concentrate. Answer the questions in short, succinct phrases or with single word answers. If you do not know the answer, leave a blank. Quick guesses are fine. If you were asked, "What is 2+2?", in a second you would write "4." This is how we want you to treat this test.

When answering the questions on the following pages be sure to think of plants and animals that are specifically located in the area described above (only name animals and plants from the bioregion that you have chosen).

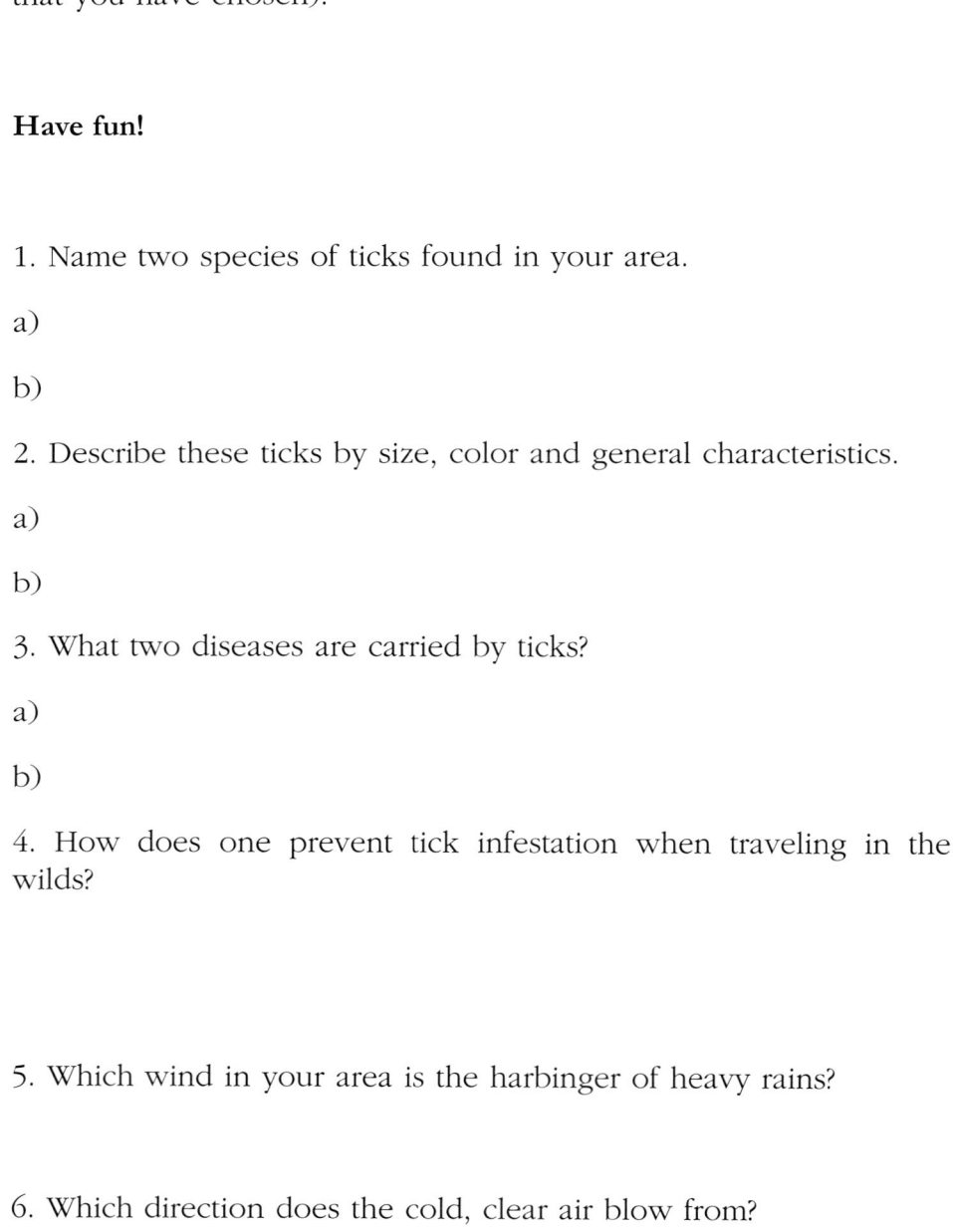

Have fun!

1. Name two species of ticks found in your area.

a)

b)

2. Describe these ticks by size, color and general characteristics.

a)

b)

3. What two diseases are carried by ticks?

a)

b)

4. How does one prevent tick infestation when traveling in the wilds?

5. Which wind in your area is the harbinger of heavy rains?

6. Which direction does the cold, clear air blow from?

7. What type of tree is lightning most likely to strike in your area?

8. What five plants in your area are most poisonous to eat?

a)

b)

c)

d)

e)

9. Name one poisonous snake in your area. (If none, write "none")

10. What is a sign in your area of a particularly cold winter to come?

11. Which plant growing locally is known to natives of the region for its effectiveness in cases of fever, colds or respiratory ailments?

12. Which plant growing locally is known to natives of the region for its effectiveness in aiding insect bites or stings?

13. How are they used?

a)

b)

14. When is the best time of year or in their life cycles to gather these plants?

a)

b)

15. Name two plants which are edible that have poisonous look-alikes growing in the same bioregion.

a)

b)

16. When people encounter bears in the wild, they sometimes do things which cause bears to become aggressive. Name two of the most dangerous and common situations where bears are known to attack people.

a)

b)

17. What time of day (during daylight hours) is least active for birdsong and calls?

18. When a mountain lion makes a kill, what does it do with the carcass after it has had its fill?

19. What are the symptoms of rabies in a wild animal?

20. Which mammal in your area does not have the potential to carry rabies?

21. What are the symptoms of distemper?

22. Name an animal in your area which commonly carries distemper.

23. Which trees are most dangerous in a wind storm? Name two species and explain why they are dangerous.

a)

b)

24. Name a tree that is good to hunker down by during a severe wind storm.

25. Which trees make the best products for use as insulation in a survival situation for building a temporary shelter.

26. Which trees in your area indicate an area of low sunlight, cold or wet situations which should be avoided in a cold emergency situation?

27. When a twig is ready to be harvested for burning there are ways to tell. How does one recognize twigs which are perfect for kindling?

A
3.5"

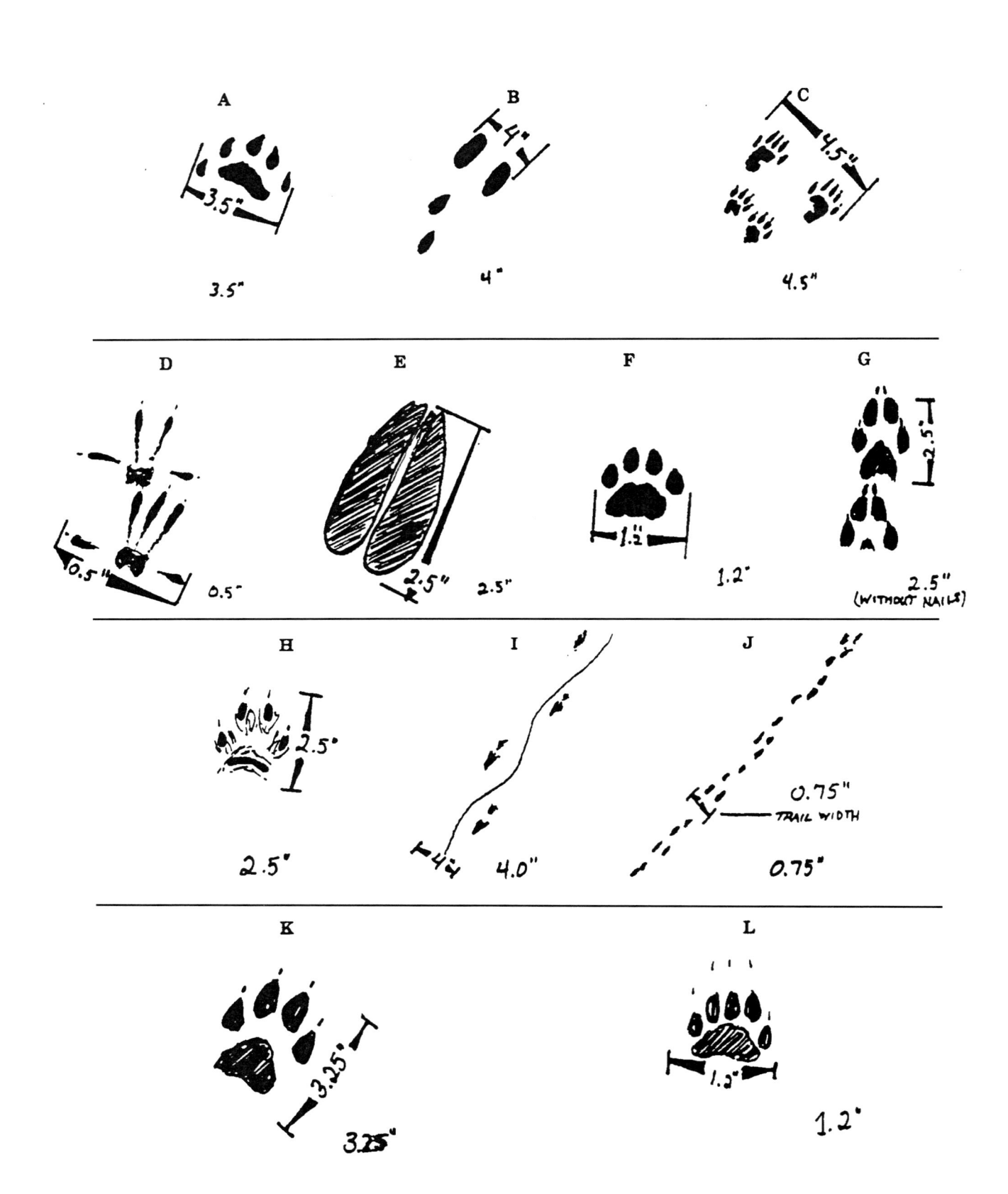

B
4"

C
4.5"

D
0.5"

E
2.5"

F
1.2"

G
2.5"
(WITHOUT NAILS)

H
2.5"

I
4.0"

J
0.75"
TRAIL WIDTH

K
3.25"

L
1.2"

251 Kamana One: Exploring Natural Mystery

Track Identification

Use the illustrations A through L to answer question 28.

28. Pick 10 of the 12 tracks from the previous page and identify the animal, or a close relative that lives near to you (non-human that is). Identify the species (or at least family) of animal for each of the 10 that you have chosen. Place the letter of each track next the name.

1)

2)

3)

4)

5)

6)

7)

8)

9)

10)

Trail Interpretation for Gaits and Body Mechanics

Use the illustrations/questions A through L to answer question 29.

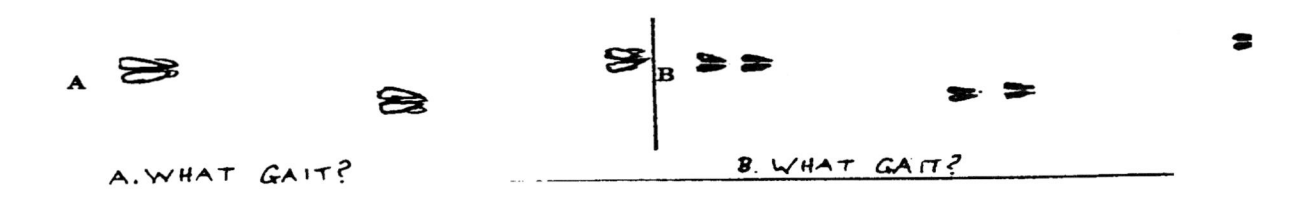

A. WHAT GAIT?

B. WHAT GAIT?

C. WHAT GAIT?

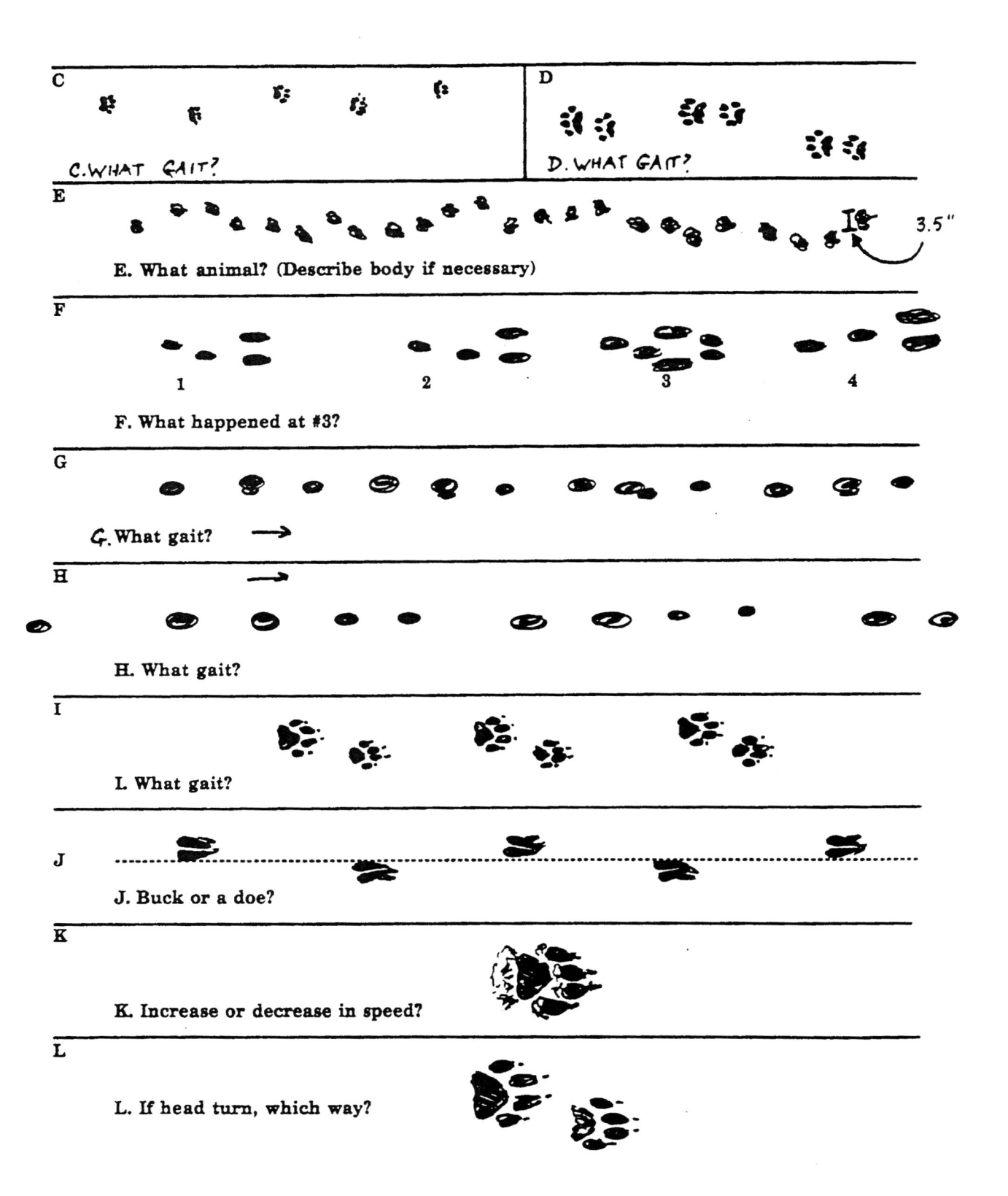

D. WHAT GAIT?

E. What animal? (Describe body if necessary)

F. What happened at #3?

G. What gait? →

H. What gait?

I. What gait?

J. Buck or a doe?

K. Increase or decrease in speed?

L. If head turn, which way?

29. Look at the track and trail patterns on the previous two pages and choose 10 which you can interpret. Place the letter of the track pattern next to your brief interpretation.

1)

2)

3)

4)

5)

6)

7)

8)

9)

10)

30. What is the relationship between the rate at which a track ages and sunshine?

31. What is the relationship between the rate at which a track ages and:

a) sand content?

b) clay content?

32. When a bird is singing from a low perch, how will a feeding deer respond?

33. What predator leaves its droppings at the base of large trees or on logs?

34. What predator leaves its droppings concisely at the intersection of two trails but only in places in open country or with open sky above?

35. What predator marks its droppings, or those of another of the same species, with urine?

36. What animal sometimes fills hollow trees or caves with its bean-shaped droppings?

37. What is a deer's most likely response to approaching humans?

38. Why do deer respond to approaching humans in this fashion?

39. Think of a deer's most common response to approaching humans. How do jays respond to the deer's actions?

40. Describe the odor of red fox urine.

41. What predator will eat a bird and leave feathers which are cut neatly at the base—especially of the larger feathers?

42. What predator will eat a bird and leave the feathers mangled and matted with saliva?

43. There is a large tree on the edge of a dense thicket bordering a field. There is a slight breeze blowing from the southwest to the northeast. There are many intact dove feathers in a northeast-southwest line with the smallest the furthest out into the field, the largest right beneath the tree. It is afternoon. That morning at dawn there was no wind, last night a south breeze blew. What is the predator most likely to be?

44. At the base of a pine tree there are several egg-shaped gray masses of fur, skulls and feathers littered about that are of varying ages. The masses are about golf-ball-sized in diameter. What are these most likely to be?

45. Name an insect that becomes very abundant during late summer and early fall in the grasslands and meadows and that provides an important staple food for many ground feeding mammals and birds.

46. What do green, shiny flies in large concentrations indicate?

47. What type of caterpillar feeds on cherry and makes visible webs that are commonly seen in spring?

48. What is one of the most dangerous spiders of your area and what markings identify it?

49. What four-legged animal has five toes on the rear foot, four on the front, and leaves footprints in the snow around the base of berry or seed sources in the snow showing a predominately hopping gait, with tail mark in the powder and a trail width of 1.5"?

50. What animal is so strong that it can hardly contain its energy when it moves across the level ground and must jump extra far every so many bounds just to use up that extra energy? Hint: It is quite dense in body mass, it has bark colored fur and speaks with its tail.

51. The tracks of this animal are in a pattern often confused with the animal in #50, as they are similar in width and in the number of tracks together. But it is almost its opposite in body density: light, almost bird-like in its build, especially its bones and skull. It uses its tail in a different way. It is colored like the ground it lives next to and uses almost no trails in its usual forays for food—that is, unless one considers the whole of its environment a trail.

52. Where would one most likely encounter a network of vole trails (Describe the environment especially concerning the relative height and species make-up of the vegetation)?

53. What is a small mammal that feeds beneath the leaves and litter but above the soil, either moving incessantly in its search for insects and other invertebrates, or going into a state of torpid rest? Its remains are often found in the pellets of owls.

54. What small mammal feeds on insects, insect larvae, and other invertebrates by wedging the root mass of surface vegetation into a continuous trap for its prey?

55. Deer trails in the wilderness (away from the influences of the modern world) appear and disappear as one follows them through the forest. What is the reason for this?

56. What are two common rocks of your area (by name or description)?

a)

b)

57. What are three basic soils of your area?

a)

b)

c)

58. What can you predict about the whereabouts and/or exposure of deer regarding their winter daytime bedding areas in relation to the four directions, weather, and position of the sun?

59. How do squirrels and birds behave before a cold weather pattern arrives in the winter or fall?

60. What did the settlers of the region do to the area that created a major impact on the life of the area?

61. How did this change in the land effect the rivers, lakes and/or bays of the area?

62. What is the single most important factor affecting a deer herd's choice of trails in a suburban setting?

63. What animal leaves a dropping, or series of droppings, in one location composed entirely of one food type including all yellow jackets, all berries, all animal products or all acorns?

64. List two mast (nut producing) trees of your area.

a)

b)

65. List four types of edible berries of your area.

a)

b)

c)

d)

66. If there were no sun shining (cloudy sky) and you needed to walk in a straight line for several hundred yards through a thicket, how would you do it? List three ways.

a)

b)

c)

67. Describe three methods that you can use to find your way back through trackless wilderness in a situation where there is no snow or sand and where tracking is difficult (such as through a forest)—in other words, back tracking is not an option.

a)

b)

c)

68. Where in the sky is the sun at noon?

69. In the summer, the sun rises _____ (North, East, South, or West) of _____ (North, East, South, or West).

70. The most reliable part of an herb to be studied as far as identification is concerned is which structure or part?

71. What is a compound leaf? (Draw one.)

72. What is an irregular flower? (Draw one.)

73. Name two ways you can be sure you are looking at a leaf on a tree and not a leaflet.

a)

b)

74. Draw a simple map below and simply place a check mark next to the letter if you have completed that task as indicated by the instructions and letters below.

If you were flying above your neighborhood at the altitude of a high-flying hawk, could you easily map out the waterways (a.), the forests (b.), the thickets (c.) and the other features of your neighborhood for a one mile radius (d. indicate the four directions)?

a)

b)

c)

d)

75. Name five plants that are extremely common in your area:

a)

b)

c)

d)

e)

76. How did the native people ensure that there would be enough plants for medicines, crafts and other uses of herbs, in their area?

77. Why did the forests flourish as result of the interaction of the people and the land?

78. Name four non-flowering more primitive plants of your area.

a)

b)

c)

d)

79. What was the indigenous culture of your area?

80. What was their primary staple food in winter?

81. What was their primary staple food in the autumn?

81. What was the most important food in the summer?

82. Did they migrate?

82. From where to where?

83. What time of year is the time of most rapid plant growth?

84. What is the time of year where plants add wood to their structures?

85. What key animal and/or plant species are missing today from your local forests (name three)?

a)

b)

c)

86. Describe second growth forest.

87. What in an aquifer is the recharge zone? Describe it.

88. What does an established river otter population indicate about an ecosystem?

89. What does the presence of many frogs indicate about an ecosystem?

90. What does the presence of many kinds of vines and thorns indicate in a forest?

91. Name local ecosystems of at least six types.

a)

b)

c)

d)

e)

f)

92. Where in your area can you:

a) find sand?

b) clay soil?

c) really rich soil?

93. What is the first type of tree to move into a newly cleared area (name two)?

a)

b)

94. What is the most common soaring hawk of your area?

All animals have certain strategies which they follow. Their bodies and behaviors are a reflection of this. For instance, a house cat has large eyes, as that is the dominant sense, and therefore its strategy is to walk slowly, and to look around often during a short pause. Considering that, answer the following questions:

95. Coyote:

a) What is the dominant sense of a coyote?

b) What is its *hunting* strategy?

c) How does this strategy influence a coyote's choice of trails?

96. Weasel:

a) What is the dominant sense of a weasel?

b) What is its *hunting* strategy?

c) A weasel has a concern that a coyote does not, which greatly affects its behavior. What is this concern?

d) How does this affect a weasel's behavior?

97. Deer:

a) What is the dominant sense of a deer?

b) What is its *feeding* strategy?

98. What is the *activity* strategy of a typical, suburban house dog?

99. Where are the descendants of the native people who once inhabited the area located today (What states or reservations primarily)?

100. Describe the difference in forest cover between a North slope and a South slope in natural-timbered areas. What species really gets more numerous on the north side?

101. What herbs grow in the winter on southern exposures in local parks, yards and roadsides (name three)?

a)

b)

c)

102. Draw a fast and effective shelter for emergencies (label materials in a cut away view showing some detail of structure, insulation and other important aspects of practical shelter building).

103. What tinder works fastest in your area under:

a) dry conditions?

b) wet conditions?

104. What trees in your area have opposite branching with compound leaves (name two)?

a)

b)

105. What are the most common native trees in your area growing in wetlands (name two)?

a)

b)

106. Name three more shrubs not mentioned in the previous questions that are common in your area.

a)

b)

c)

107. What is a common creekside plant in your area?

108. What are three native grasses of the area?

a)

b)

c)

109. Name four plants which are used for making baskets in the area.

a)

b)

c)

d)

110. Name three plants good for making cordage in the area.

a)

b)

c)

111. What wood in the area makes good bows (name two)?

a)

b)

112. What wood in the area is good for arrows?

113. What wood is really hard in your area (name two)?

a)

b)

114. Which are the hottest burning woods (name two)?

a)

b)

115. Which tree grows really fast?

116. Which tree grows really slow?

117. Name five animals that can be physically or strategically imitated in your area which would help you in a survival situation. Give the behavior you would mimic from each next to the animal's name.

a)

b)

c)

d)

e)

118. Name one type of call (a sound emitted by wildlife) that affects many species of birds or animals.

119. Name two kinds of insects which call in your area.

a)

b)

120. What common bird in your area has a crest on its head?

121. What common bird of your area has a white eye-ring?

122. What common bird of your area has white wing bars?

123. What common bird of your area feeds on the ground and has white in its tail feathers?

124. What common bird of your area lives in thickets and will not usually be seen in tree tops?

125. What common bird of your area loves the tree tops?

126. What are five really common birds in your area that you haven't named yet?

a)

b)

c)

d)

e)

127. Name two kinds of common woodpeckers in your area.

a)

b)

128. Name two birds that will tell on a stalking hunter or animal in your area.

a)

b)

129. Name a bird that will tell of the presence of a large soaring hawk or owl by mobbing the predatory bird.

130. What is the most common snake in your area?

131. What is a common turtle of the water in your area?

132. What is the first frog, toad or treefrog chorus to sing in your area in spring?

133. What is a common salamander in your area?

TOURIST TEST REFLECTION

After you finish all four levels of the Kamana program, we will ask you to go back and take the test again so you can compare the differences. Take a few minutes to reflect on your experience before writing.

Name: _____

Date: _____

APPENDIX B:
INVITATION TO CONTINUE WITH KAMANA

To sign up for Kamana Two, please fill out the registration form at the end of this book.

Have you read Tolkien's Lord of the Rings? If so, *Kamana One* was kind of like The Hobbit, and *Kamana Two, Three, and Four* are the trilogy that will take you further into the larger world where the forces get stronger and the stakes higher. The Hobbit had all the elements though, and the hero of the hobbit was the hero of the whole trilogy. You've begun. Would you like to cross the river into greater commitment? If so, the whole plan follows.

TRACKS

The following six tracks are embedded into the Resource Trail throughout all levels of Kamana. As you progress, you will be taken deeper into each of these subjects.

Hazards & Inspiration
Inspirational stories from native elders and people closely associated with the natural world; assessment of the modern environmental education movement; organization of resources; understanding the "mind's eye" technique for study; self-sufficiency skills in using resources; foundations of taxonomy; hazards of the wild.

Mammals
Natural history, physiology, and strategies of mammals; tracking skills: identification of sign, aging, ecological tracking.

Plants
Taxonomy and identification of plants; research native use of plants in crafts and as food and medicine; overland navigation techniques including aidless navigation.

Ecology
Indicator species (invertebrates, amphibians and reptiles); prediction of animal behavior and plant species location based on knowledge of ecology; interplay of extremes and bird's eye viewing of land features; conservation ecology; the history of the land and the native people's staple resources; natural community dynamics; stewardship.

"Never before have I felt so alive, so excited about each day. The research made me connect with whatever I was studying, the daily visits to my outdoor study area gave me a sense of belonging, the awareness exercises made miracles become normal occurrences. Learning so many new things was exciting and challenging. Since everything I was studying was right outside me door it made my surroundings come alive and interact with me in a totally new way."

—*Marcia Kramer, Kamana Four graduate*

Trees

Taxonomy and identification of trees; trees as they affect aspects of the landscape; research use of trees for survival, food, medicine and in other native lore.

Birds

Taxonomy, physiology and behavior of birds; migration and range maps; basics of understanding the language of birds.

Wrapping the Bundle: Tying the Trails Together (The Final Synthesis of Kamana Skills)

Synthesis of the two trails of the Kamana program: 1) Nature Awareness Trail Field Exercises and Field Inventories and 2) Resource Trail Research. Review of background basics; tracking skills learned from study of mammals; self-sufficiency in plant skills; field ecology; review of tree lore for survival; review of bird language for awareness; overall closure for Kamana path. This assignment is sent after students complete *Kamana Four*.

---

www.WildernessAwareness.org contains:

- Information on the benefits of Student Services
- Current information on course prices, *Kamana Two* servicing fees, mailing addresses, resources, etc.,
- More detailed information on all Kamana levels
- *Songline* (First section of *Kamana Two*)
- Sample exercises from higher Kamana levels.

KAMANA LEVELS

Kamana One: Exploring Natural Mystery
How long it takes to complete: Four to six weeks
Includes: *Kamana One: Exploring Natural Mystery (Introduction, Nature Awareness Trailhead. Resource Trailhead)* Optional Student Services at Kamana.org. Letter and Certificate of Completion sent upon submission of Field Pack
Resources to buy: *Readers Digest: North American Wildlife, Seeing Through Native Eyes* (8 CD's series) with Jon Young.

Kamana Two: Path of the Naturalist
Prerequisite: *None*
Includes: Binder, *Nature Awareness Trail Two, Resource Trail Two*, Field Journal pad.
How long it takes to complete: Average 6-8 Months
Student Services support through Kamana.org:
Student Services are highly recommended for students doing Kamana Two, Three and Four. Students who have support during their journey are much more likely to finish the program. Services include personalized feedback, connection to the Kamana community, multi-media Kamana-based content, video of Jon Young, a certificate upon completion, and more!
Structure: Resource Trail: Field journaling from each of the 6 Resource Trail tracks; Nature Awareness Trail: 3 monthly Field exercises, 12 weekly Naturalist Inventories. Total of 4 Field Packs must be handed in to complete.
Required Resources: Books/Audio: *Giving Thanks: A Native American Good Morning Message* (children's book) by Jake Swamp, *Ingwe* (book) by Ingwe OR *Spirit of the Leopard* (CD) by Ingwe, *Seeing Through Native Eyes* (8 CD series) with Jon Young (if starting Kamana at *Kamana Two*)
Field Guides <u>Peterson's Field Guide to:</u> *Mammals, Reptiles and Amphibians* (your region), *Animal Tracks, Venomous Animals & Poisonous Plants, Wildflowers* (your region) or a good local plant guide; *Sibley Guide to Birds (your region), Birder's Handbook* (Ehrlich, Dobkin, Wheye*); Audubon Guide to Trees* (east or west); *Newcomb's Guide to Wildflowers Golden Guides to: Insects, Pond Life*.

Kamana Three: Deepening the Roots of Nature Awareness
Prerequisite: *Kamana Two*
Includes: Binder, *Resource Trail Three, Nature Awareness Trail Three*, field journal pad.
How long it takes to complete: Average of 7-10 Months
Structure The Resource Trail will now look at your journals from "a broader perspective." Valuable taxonomy skills and family studies will precede more involved journaling. This is the beginning of your ecological view. Nature Awareness Trail: 4 more Field Exercises, advanced routines for weekly inventories (16 more). Total of 5 Field Packs must be handed in to complete.
Required Resources: Required *Botany in a Day* (Tom Elpel); *Skulls & Bones* (Searfross); <u>Peterson's Guides:</u> *Medicinal Plants & Herbs, Edible Plants, Audubon Guide to Insects and Spiders,* a college level Biology textbook.

Kamana Four: The Complete Naturalist
Prerequisite: *Kamana Three*
Includes: Binder, *Resource Trail Four*, *Nature Awareness Trail Four*, field journal pad, *Trails/Wrapping the Bundle* assignment (sent when level completed)
How long it takes to complete: Minimum 6 Months, Average of 8-12 months
Structure: The Resource Trail is now taken from a complete ecological perspective after making master and focus lists. Over half the field journaling in the entire course is done at this level. A tracker in any field will now see how natural communities work together. You're now ready to understand focus and the key to efficient learning in this field of study that can be perceived as infinite and overwhelming. Nature Awareness Trail: 5 more Field Exercises, advanced routines for weekly inventories (24 more). Total of 6 Field Packs must be handed in to complete the level, in addition to *Wrapping the Bundle*, which ties all your experiences from both trails together. *Kamana* certification is granted upon submission of this assignment.
Required Resources: *Stoke's Animal Tracking & Behavior;* Stokes Field Guide to Bird Songs Audio, <u>Peterson's</u>: *Forests* (your region); other resources such as survival and local ethnobotany books.

Note about Required Resources: We try our best to only require books and guides that will be lifelong friends, not books you stick on a shelf and never look at again after you're finished. If you're short on cash you can always find most of them at a public library. Guides you buy for earlier levels will be used throughout the entire program. All resources are for sale at our web site.

All resources are available at www.WildernessAwareness.org.

How long will the *entire* course take? It's up to you.

The time length we give is based on our experience with the student who has a job, a family and maybe even is going to school part time. Some may finish in half that time and some may take long breaks between each level. The important thing is that you are consistently working on the Kamana routines while you are enrolled in a class, whether you finish in half the time we give or the full amount of time. *Kamana One* is designed to give you an idea of what life might be like with Kamana as part of it. It is wise to begin *Kamana Two* after you know you can devote an average of an hour a day toward study if you want to complete it in four months.

Kamana Two Student Services Option

When you purchase *Kamana Two*, you are purchasing all the materials you need to take yourself through the course (minus the required field guide resources). For an additional fee, you can sign up for Student Services on Kamana.org. Services include personalized feedback, connection to the international Kamana community, multi-media Kamana-based content, video of Jon Young, a certificate upon completion, and more!

We recognize *Kamana Two* as being a very important level in Kamana Training. It is in *Kamana Two* that you are introduced to core routines that you will continue to practice throughout the remainder of the Kamana Program. Knowing this, our instructors review your work in *Kamana Two* with the intention of guiding you down the path of least resistance, so to speak.

For expanded information on Student Services including all the important details on the options and tuition fees, please visit Kamana.org.

Kamana Student Services helped me deepen my understanding of place and of the Kamana program itself...I don't think I could have completed it without their positive encouragement...It's just worth it knowing someone is behind you.

–Kamana graduate

The Kamana One Field Pack form and the official Kamana Two order form should be the next two pages. If they are missing, you may download them at www.kamana.org

If a lot of time has gone by since the publishing of this book, we suggest downloading updated forms in case of price, policy or address changes.

Kamana.org

This is the hub for Student Services. Check here for ongoing improvements for the Kamana program.

- Connect with a community of thousands of Kamana students worldwide — or in your backyard!

- Receive personal feedback from Kamana instructors to enhance and guide your journey.

- Receive Kamana video, audio and other resources — not available elsewhere!

- Participate in monthly roundtable phone discussions with the Kamana community…

Sign up for the free Kamana eNewsletter at Kamana.org!

KAMANA
Naturalist Training Program

Kamana One Field Pack

Send in for **FREE**
Certificate of Completion

Please fill this form out <u>completely</u> and include it with your work.

EVERYONE, PLEASE READ:
We realize that some of you may be friends or family members of the original purchaser of this book. You also may have checked it out of the library. In any case, you may send in your completed work (see bottom half of page to see exactly what you need to send in) for a Certificate of Completion and a sample issue of *Foxprint* from Wilderness Awareness School at no charge.

DO NOT SEND ORIGINALS. We encourage you to photocopy your work on recycled paper (double sided) or the blank back side of already used copy paper.

Office use
Init: _____
Filed: _____

Name _____
Address with zip _____
Phone (evening) _____
Phone (day) _____
Email _____

MAIL TO: Wilderness Awareness School •
Please visit www.WildernessAwareness.org or see a recent mailer for current address.

2. Tear off this sheet, fold in half and insert your work in it.

All the above pages have the c icon on it.

(page 242)

☐ Copy of the Tourist Test **reflection (NOT the test)**
☐ Copy of your Final Reflection (pages 217-218)
☐ Copy of ONE Resource Trail journal page of your choice (located at the end of each chapter in Part Three)
☐ Copies **(not originals)** of pages 36, 100, 101, 102

1. Did you include:

Kamana One Field Pack

KAMANA
Naturalist Training Program

Name: _____
Date: _____

KAMANA
NATURALIST TRAINING PROGRAM™

PATH OF THE NATURALIST
KAMANA TWO

CONTINUE THE JOURNEY!

Ready to get serious with the core routines? It's time to begin your monthly Field Exercises, Inventories and Resource Trail journaling work. If you liked working with us this time around, we'd love to have you back. This course will complete the basics for those who want to continue the Kamana path.

When you purchase *Kamana Two* you are purchasing the written materials for the course assembled in a binder, which includes *Nature Awareness Trail Two*, *Resource Trail Two*, and a pad of journal pages.

Student Services with Wilderness Awareness School are available at an added cost through Kamana .org. This servicing includes review of all materials by a trained instructor, , multi-media Kamana-based content (including original video of Jon Young), a forum for connection with the international Kamana community, and a Certificate upon completion. For detailed information on *Kamana Two*, Student Services, tuition fees and more, visit www.WildernessAwareness.org and Kamana.org.

Visit Kamana.org for more information on Student Services.

"Your approach and attitude is unusual, rare and much needed at this time. Your teaching style is very powerful and really makes me want to learn. I have been shown a new way of looking at things, a way which has changed my life. Each lesson is approached with much respect towards the people you learned from, and your passion is reflected in all the material you present. The lessons are clear and accessible. It is a very challenging program and I like the fact that I had to do the work. The material sank in deeper and more profoundly this way—a very practical and applicable format."
Dave Franklin, Kamana graduate

The following may be ordered at www.WildernessAwareness.org, found at a local book store (check used stores) *or* borrowed from a library or a friend:

Required resources:
- *Ingwe*, by Ingwe OR *Spirit of the Leopard* (CD) by Ingwe
- *Giving Thanks*, by Jake Swamp
- Peterson Field Guides to:
    - *Mammals*
    - *Animal Tracks*
    - *Venomous Animals & Poisonous Plants*
    - *Reptiles & Amphibians*
    - *Wildflowers* (your region) or a good local plant guide
- *Sibley Field Guide to Birds* (East or West)
- *Audubon Field Guide to Trees* (East or West)
- *Birder's Handbook*
- *Newcomb's Wildflowers Guide*
- *Golden Guides to: Insects, Pond Life*

Purchasing your resources at www.WildernessAwareness.org supports nature education for kids of all ages.

(If a lot time has passed since purchase of program, check current pricing and school contact information at www.WildernessAwareness.org.)

Name _____

Address with zip _____

Phone (evening) _____ Phone (day) _____

Email _____

Send me:
- ❏ *Kamana Two*, (printed) $135 + **$12 S&H (US Only*) = $147**
- ❏ *Kamana Two*, (digital) **$79.99**

All required resources are available at www.WildernessAwareness.org

WA residents add **8.6%** sales tax.
*Orders outside of the U.S. will be charged extra for shipping if necessary.

Method of payment: Check ❏ Visa ❏ Mastercard ❏ Amex ❏

Name as it appears on the card: _____

Account number: _____

Expiration date: _____ Today's date: _____

Signature _____

AMOUNT ENCLOSED: $ _____

MAKE CHECKS PAYABLE TO & MAIL TO:
Wilderness Awareness School
Please visit www.WildernessAwareness.org or see a recent mailer for current address.

FOX PRINT
www.WildernessAwareness.org

The Voice of Wilderness Awareness School — Sample issue

WILDERNESS AWARENESS SCHOOL

1983–2003 20 Years

KEEP CONNECTED, GET FOXPRINT

Keep connected to our international community of students while receiving educational and inspirational articles on nature education and mentoring. *Foxprint*, our newsletter, delivered three times a year, contains the following:

- Nature Skills
- Mentoring practices
- Student expressions
- Update from the Executive Director
- Featured articles and more!

Learn about nature-mentoring skills

THE ART OF QUESTIONING
By Paul Houghtaling,
Local Programs Director

At Wilderness Awareness School, the process of questioning is one of the most basic – and profound – learning tools that we work with. Whoever it is that is doing the asking, questioning is one of the ways that we can drive our senses to become more deeply involved in what we are experiencing. It can bring us deeply into the moment, present to the wondrous and mysterious things happening around and within us.

In *The Art of Mentoring* program, Wilderness Awareness School founder Jon Young speaks of his experiences as a youth with tracker and author Tom Brown, Jr. He says that one of the most profound ways that Tom kept him continually going back to the forest near his home was through questions. According to Jon, Tom would call him in the evenings and ask him about what he had experienced there. Jon says that when he was 10 years old on his very first outing at this "secret spot," Tom called him that evening to ask if he had

Foxprint Newsletter is delivered three times a year to our donor community. You can receive it for a year by contributing to Wilderness Awareness School. Visit www.WildernessAwareness.org to contribute!

Notes from a Kamana Four Graduate
By John Chilkotowsky

How the Kamana program has supported my vision...

I changed careers because I realized that I was volunteering most of my non-work time with environmental organizations and spending all of my vacation time at Tom Brown's Tracker school. I realized that my vision was to help the younger generations to reconnect to the earth and all of its teachings. I moved to an environmental education center, where my "job" was to teach an appreciation of nature to children. At this time, the Kamana program entered my life.

Around a campfire at a Tracker school class, someone handed me a pamphlet about this program called "Kamana" that Wilderness Awareness School was offering. Kamana. Even its name implied mystery. What was I getting myself into? In my three years on and off with my studies, I needed to face many fears, misunderstandings and doubts about myself, and yet every day at my secret spot was an adventure.

The Kamana program took me from knowing very little about my place and gently opened my awareness up to all of the amazing beings that are always around us. At the beginning, I had the vague feeling that most everything around me was potentially poisonous. I figured that as long as I didn't eat anything and nothing else ate me, I was fine. I learned quickly about the poisonous animals and plants of my area, and this inspired me to move more freely and with greater respect for certain species. As I learned how to move in harmony with nature and to use my senses more deeply, it seemed that everything around me changed - when in reality is was my awareness changing.

How amazing it is to know about a plant on everyone's lawn (if they do not chemically treat it) that is edible, medicinal - can be chewed and put onto nettle stings, bee stings, thorns, etc. and will provide almost instant relief. This same plant can be used in survival situations to create cordage that could be used to suture closed a wound, catch fish for food, or perhaps hold a basket together. Imagine how many other plants are all around us and go unnoticed by most people.

Throughout my journey with Kamana, I had the good fortune of working with youth. I introduced some of my Kamana routines to them, and saw how natural and fun it was for them to become more native to their place. My completion of the Kamana program coincided with my move to Seattle, and beginning work (play) with Wilderness Awareness School. I have been working (playing) with youth and adults using my knowledge gained from Kamana and have been able to respond to other Kamana students through review of their work.

The Kamana program has given me the routines I needed to become a naturalist. It has also given me self-sufficiency in my studies of the natural world and the tools to pass on the information to others.